D1478904

The Grammar of the Real

The
Grammar
of the Real

SELECTED PROSE 1959-1974

JAMES McAULEY

Melbourne
OXFORD UNIVERSITY PRESS
LONDON WELLINGTON NEW YORK

Oxford University Press

OXFORD LONDON GLASGOW NEW YORK
TORONTO MELBOURNE WELLINGTON CAPE TOWN
DELHI BOMBAY CALCUTTA MADRAS KARACHI LAHORE DACCA
KUALA LUMPUR SINGAPORE JAKARTA HONG KONG TOKYO
NAIROBI DAR ES SALAAM LUSAKA ADDIS ABABA
IBADAN ZARIA ACCRA BEIRUT

First published 1975

NATIONAL LIBRARY OF AUSTRALIA CATALOGUING IN
PUBLICATION DATA

McAuley, James Phillip, 1917-
    The grammar of the real.
    Index.
    ISBN 0 19 550480 1.
    ISBN 0 19 550481 x Paperback.

    1. Literature—Addresses, essays, lectures.
    2. German poetry. I. Title.

    809

PRINTED IN AUSTRALIA BY BROWN PRIOR ANDERSON PTY LTD

Preface

IN 1959 James McAuley, who had already established himself as one of our foremost poets, published *The End of Modernity*, a collection (to quote its sub-title) of thirteen 'Essays on Literature, Art and Culture'. In this book he presented his synthesis of beliefs and insights in aesthetics, history, philosophy and religion: a distinctive *Weltanschauung* embracing positive conceptions of the normal state of culture and trenchant criticisms of modern art, poetry and thought.

The present volume is a selection from the essays he has written in the fifteen years since *The End of Modernity*. In many respects it stands in relation to the earlier book as practice does to theory: the same wide range of ideas is here applied to particular writers, concepts and problems.

The four opening essays deal with Australian poets whose work, it seems to an observer, has affinities with McAuley's own poetry, especially in their mastery of the lyric. Those on Shaw Neilson and Judith Wright also call into play McAuley's deep interest in metrics, already demonstrated in *A Primer of English Versification* (1966) and continued in the next essay, 'The dynamics of verse'.

In 'The languages of poetry', which follows, the two great traditional poets, Spenser and Milton, are central to McAuley's argument; this essay thus serves as an introduction to four which focus on them: 'Edmund Spenser and George Eliot' brings *Middlemarch* and *The Faerie Queene* into unexpected but illuminating juxtaposition, 'Politics versus Art' considers the latter in its historical context, 'Milton's difficulties' explains the problems inherent in making an epic out of the story of Genesis, and 'A visit to Bunhill' evokes one of the most memorable scenes in English literary history, the aged, blind, republican, Puritan Milton visited by the younger, royalist, High Church (later Catholic) Dryden, who admired and echoed the older man in his poetry, poles apart as they were in convictions. Dryden is the link to the next essay, which relates Wordsworth and Crabbe to the poetic age that Dryden ushered in.

'Sex in love and literature' explores that series of transitions by which courtly love became romantic love and romantic love became something else—something in which, by modern usage, 'lover' is no longer an exclusively masculine noun—illustrated by the contrast between novels by Tolstoy and Solzhenitsyn. The latter name, of course, brings us close to what McAuley calls, in the next essay ('On being an intellectual') 'the Deuteronomic situation: a choice . . . of life or death, of a blessing or a curse'. The remaining essays, in their various ways, are all concerned with this choice. 'We are men—what are you?' deals with the relations between modern and primitive societies, a question of particular relevance to New Guinea, where McAuley once worked (during his time at the Australian School of Pacific Administration) and where he confronted facts which were to change his whole life, as 'My New Guinea' tells.

The last three essays are about three German writers who each understood the choices available to him: Joseph von Eichendorff, who symbolized what McAuley sees as 'the inner crisis of European literature', Albrecht Haushofer, whose *Moabiter Sonette* were written while he was in gaol for his opposition to Hitler, and Georg Trakl, whose poems (often set in McAuley's beloved Salzburg) are visions of damnation and innocence.

For me—and I am sure that I will not be alone in feeling this— the essays in this volume have a twofold interest. On the one hand, they set up interesting connections between their outwardly disparate subjects: to take one example, Albrecht Haushofer, lying dead in the Berlin gaol clutching the exercise book with the *Moabiter Sonette* in it, represents one way of answering tyranny, while Spenser in *The Faerie Queene* represents another and Solzhenitsyn yet another. But these essays also have the value of shedding light on McAuley's poetry. His accomplished rendering of Rilke in 'Autumn' is paralleled by his versions of Haushofer and Trakl here, and the reader who knows 'New Guinea' (written 'in memory of Archbishop Alain de Boismenu, M.S.C.') for example, must have his understanding of this—and many other poems—deepened by reading 'My New Guinea'. One could multiply instances like these: in both poems and prose we have the fruits of James McAuley's powerful, wide-ranging and courageous mind.

Eight of the essays have not been published before. Six have appeared in *Quadrant*: 'An imprint of Slessor', XVII, 1 (1973) 5-10; 'The languages of poetry', VIII, 2 (1964) 19-26; 'Sex and love in literature', XVI, 4 (1972) 15-23; 'On being an intellectual', IV, 1 (1959-60) 23-31; 'We are men—what are you?', IV, 3 (1960) 73-9; and 'My New Guinea', V, 3 (1961) 15-27. Three have appeared in *Australian Literary Studies*: 'Shaw Neilson's poetry', II (1966) 235-53; 'Some poems of Judith Wright', III (1968) 201-13; and 'The poetry of Rosemary Dobson', VI (1973) 3-10. *Edmund Spenser and George Eliot: a Critical Excursion* was published in 1963 by the University of Tasmania; it was James McAuley's inaugural lecture as Professor of English, delivered in Hobart on 4 April 1963. With the exception of 'The languages of poetry', which now is printed

in a longer form, the essays have had only a few verbal alterations
made to them, and no attempt has been made to delete evidence of
the date of composition, which appears at the end of each essay.
Translations, if not acknowledged, are McAuley's own; so are italics
used in quotations in the essays on Shaw Neilson and Judith Wright
to make metrical points.

The title of the volume is taken from phrases in the second stanza
of McAuley's poem 'Credo':

> The meaning not ours, but found
> In the mind deeply submissive
> To the grammar of existence,
> The syntax of the real . . .

This poem will be found in McAuley's *Collected Poems 1936-70*
(Sydney, 1971, p. 192).

Grahame Johnston

Acknowledgements

For permission to reproduce copyright material by other authors
we are indebted to the following authors and publishers—Rosemary
Dobson: Angus & Robertson, from *Selected Poems*; Albrecht Haushofer: Dr Heinz Haushofer, from *Moabiter Sonette*; Shaw Neilson: Angus & Robertson, from *The Poems of Shaw Neilson*; Kenneth Slessor: Angus & Robertson, from *Poems*; Georg Trakl: Otto
Müller Verlag, Saltzburg, from *Dichtungen und Briefe*.

Contents

Shaw Neilson's poetry

IN the biographical notes which James Devaney encouraged him to produce Shaw Neilson tells how in 1926 he visited Sydney, meeting for the first time A. G. Stephens who had encouraged and promoted his work for over two decades. Stephens introduced him to Mary Gilmore, who arranged that he should meet Brennan and John Le Gay Brereton. He had lunch with Brennan and John Quinn and others, presumably at Paris House in Phillip Street, and was impressed by the fact that French was spoken: 'I believe I was the only person there who did not understand the language'. Even at this distance in time one writhes in embarrassment. Next day, however, he went for a ferry ride with A.G.S. and Brennan and two others, and had a long talk with Brennan on his way home: 'although he had such knowledge and such achievements, he spoke as simply to me as though we had been mates in the bush together'.[1]

What a curious conjunction! The scholar who set himself to be an hermetic artist in the Symbolist school, and the quiet workman who perhaps never heard of Mallarmé or Verlaine (unless at lunch that day), but who, as his editor A. R. Chisholm rightly claims, worked intuitively in a manner that bears some analogy with the work of the Symbolists.[2] With regard to Brennan, my recurring spells of interest in him have brought me fairly steadily to a reluctant lowering of my estimate of his artistic achievement.[3] This has not been so in the case of Shaw Neilson: at each re-reading one is confronted again with the weaknesses and limitations which have to be admitted, but one's perception of a rare true quality is confirmed.

The great drawback with Neilson is an imperfect control of language. Brennan's hapless conglomerate of poetic diction is there to remind us that this would not necessarily have been improved if Neilson had had a more developed literary formation; though one is entitled to guess that Neilson's intuitive gift might have taken him further in purifying and renewing the inheritance of late nineteenth-century poeticism. As it was, Neilson's knowledge and critical sense were very much restricted. From scattered information, chiefly in Devaney's book, it appears that he read Burns, Hood, *The Ancient Mariner*, Scott, some Shelley, Keats, Tennyson (he didn't like *In Memoriam*).[4] He never read Blake. One has to add Ella Wheeler Wilcox, John Greenleaf Whittier, Swinburne, and Charles Kingsley to his background; and shouldn't forget Irish and Scottish

1

folksong, Victorian drawing-room ballads and Stephen Foster, about whom he wrote a poem which could be self-descriptive:

> Who was the man? he was not great or wise,
> He lived in sore distress,
> Always he went with pity in the eyes
> For burnt-out Happiness.
>
> He who was poor had melodies of gold,
> He had the rude man's Art;
> No one can now deny him—he could hold
> The quick roads to the heart.[5]

A poem he wrote in 1925 called 'The Flight of the Weary', which he later nominated as 'about my best', will illustrate the problem he sets us.[6] It is addressed to a crippled seventeen-year-old girl. The third stanza reads:

> In moods of unmeasured magenta
> The sun has apparelled the day:
> The leaves are as words in a fable
> Or tears that come out in a play:
> Oh, you with a year to a sorrow!
> The cynical Summer and Spring
> Shall both be ashamed of their dancing,
> And you shall hear many birds sing.

I think these lines show us what is meant by saying of the poetic diction that it has not been purified. The words irresistibly stir in us unwelcome associations, a sense of second-hand sentimentalities and fancifulness which constitutes an *interference*, so that the genuine sentiment does not come through. I am not objecting to the expression of life-weariness and the desire to escape which the middle-aged poet shares with the crippled girl; I leave that to hardier life-affirmers. But what is one to make of a line like 'In moods of unmeasured magenta'? Neilson attached habitual meanings to colours; in the previous stanza he has already prepared us:

> The lights in the leaves are of scarlet,
> The colour that comes to redeem:

and in the stanza which follows he says:

> Come, let us escape in the scarlet!

But the associations of magenta, a synthetic aniline dye invented in the mid-nineteenth century and named after a minor Italian battle, are not helpful: it reads like a successfully grotesque parody of Swinburne. How could he have thought he was doing well?

There is another detail of this poem that is worthy of remark. A. G. Stephens objected to the lines in stanzas 1 and 4 which express a dislike of the smell of the sea: 'You love not the scent of the sea', and 'Oh, we have been sorry and soiled by / The low-living scent of the sea'. Neilson withstood this objection, because 'I have never liked the sea, and the smell of the sea repels me very much'.[7] This is an unexpected private relation to the sea, which he arbitrarily makes the girl share; but even when the phrases are thus explained they do not develop much significance in the poem. 'You love not the scent of the sea' reads like a loose Swinburnian routine of amplification; and the epithet 'low-living' sets up an irrelevant or nonsensical train of ideas.

Shaw Neilson admitted that no one else seemed to agree with his valuation of this poem. What is disconcerting is to learn that A. G. Stephens cherished as *his* favourite poem 'Heart of Spring' (written in 1902), and made it the title-poem of the collection he published in 1919. It begins:

> O Heart of Spring!
> Spirit of light and love and joyous day
> So soon to faint beneath the fiery Summer:
> Still smiles the Earth, eager for thee alway:
> Welcome art thou, so ever short thy stay,
> Thou bold, thou blithe newcomer!
> Whither, or whither this thy journeying,
> O Heart of Spring!

From this distance, across the shifts of literary fashion, one can hardly see what made A.G.S. prize this exercise in poeticality, and it is a relief to learn that Shaw Neilson was equally surprised: 'I always thought it was a poor thing', and 'I never cared for it much'.[8]

There is a natural tendency to compare Shaw Neilson with other lonely, surprising, self-taught poets. Doubtless a comparison with W. H. Davies is closest: both poets suffered from uncertainty of taste and control; both achieved a few delicate lyrics and some poems of human pity and protest; Davies is stronger in everything—*except* that strange 'enchantment' whose light touches many of Neilson's poems, even flawed and wayward ones.[9] It is with Clare and Blake, however, that I should like to pursue briefly a comparison, because the attempt to discriminate between accidental and essential similarities can bring out some interesting features.

The likeness to John Clare lies chiefly in the personal circumstances.[10] Both poets had very little schooling. Clare later acquired a not inconsiderable general culture by his own efforts. Neilson's reading appears to have remained meagre, and later his bad eyesight restricted him. Both experienced in themselves and their families the grinding harshness of the lot of the rural labourer and the struggling smallholder. Neilson's account, as given in Devaney's book, of the vicissitudes of his childhood, youth and manhood pulls one back almost unbearably to the rock and clay of the basic Australian experience of so many families in previous generations. There was, for example, the new start the family made at Eureka in 1902, when Shaw Neilson was thirty. His sister Maggie was away working, but contracted tuberculosis and had to be brought home. They had no money, no seed-wheat, no land cleared for crops, and lived on rabbits. They built a little hut for Maggie, and John slept nearby: 'Often at midnight she would ring the bell for me to come over and have a talk with her. It was very lonely for her when she was lying awake on the long winter nights, and at times the cough would be troublesome'.[11] Maggie, like her father, remained indomitably cheerful to the end. Shaw Neilson was not a self-pitying or complaining sort of man, but there were times when the hardship and worry got him down. John Clare, in the midst of want and anxiety and frustrated hopes, became mentally ill and spent the later years of his life in hopeless insanity. Shaw Neilson did not collapse in this way, but there appear to have been times of acute and prolonged depression amounting to mental illness.[12]

In their work, the differences between the two poets are more important than the resemblances. Both harked back to childhood and the natural scenes that impressed their sensibility, making these an image of man's lost Eden innocence. But Clare's strength lay in the same faculty that made him also a very competent field naturalist, the loving record of precise detail conveyed, in the best poems, in the fresh countryman's language of his environment. Neilson's perceptions were not the substance of his poetry to the same extent, and he did not use a local popular vocabulary to refresh his diction. A curious similarity amid difference may be noted. Though Clare was married, and Neilson remained single, both poets directed part of their poetry towards a lost love. In both cases, the more directly and personally the poem seems to relate to this lost love the poorer the poem becomes. Neilson's love poetry succeeds only when love becomes an almost impersonal thing.

The reasons that prompt people to compare Shaw Neilson with Blake are the 'visionary' quality that one senses in his work, the lyrical perfection of the best poems, and also the fact that both poets were outside the educated literary circle of their time, though they might be haphazardly noticed and 'taken up'. The differences in temperament, in range, and poetic achievement are obvious; but there are one or two comparisons which I should like to pursue.

In the first place, both poets' work and attitude are deeply affected by a decidedly negative reaction to the religion of their childhood. Blake rebelled furiously against Nobodaddy, the Jehovah-figure which seemed to preside over conventional piety. Neilson's mother inculcated a rigid and gloomy kind of Calvinism which made God a forbidding and very fearsome presence, blocking for the rest of his life, it seems, any possibility of orthodox religious commitment; though, like Blake, Neilson's naturally religious temperament found its own path to the conception of a God of mercy, love, and joy. The poem he dedicated to Mary Gilmore, 'The Gentle Water Bird', speaks more directly than most. He speaks of the fear that hung over his childhood, even in his play:

> God was above me, always frowning through,
> And God was terrible and thunder-blue.[13]

Even the flowers and the rainbow seemed unable to rest simply in their own beauty, but 'trembled because of God's ungracious scheme'. But then he recounts how in contemplation of the 'blue crane' (the white-faced heron) he reached a different feeling about the nature of God.[14] As Chisholm has pointed out, the cranes he knew as a child in the swamps at Minimay came to be for him intermediaries between earth and heaven.[15] In 'The Crane is my Neighbour' the same function is implied:

> The bird is a noble, he turns to the sky for a theme,
> And the ripples are thoughts coming out to the edge of a dream.

The bird lives within a 'dream', a spiritual realm, and the poet on the outside sees the ripples as communications coming towards him from that realm of the unsayable. But the bird is not a preacher, nor a propagandist, nor a maker of demands:

> He bleats no instruction, he is not an arrogant drummer;
> His gown is simplicity—blue as the smoke of the summer.[16]

The word 'drummer' may not at first seem apt to the reserved but unmistakable implication that the bird is a better representative of heaven than a parson in a black preacher's gown; but we may recall that Neilson's sister Maggie shared her mother's religious enthusiasm, and both for a time joined the Salvation Army. Perhaps this particular association joined with the colloquial phrase about having something 'drummed into' one, may validate the term, as something more than a rhyme-word pressed into service.

The notion of the birds as having a special nearness to God persists in a different poem, 'The Poor Can Feed the Birds', which also sets false institutional religion against the true religion.[17] While the rich misunderstand and insult God in their churches, the poor enter into the right relation with God because 'they feed the birds for Him'. The poem is of mixed value artistically. The stanzas relating to the rich men's churches and their God come as near as Neilson's soft inward voice can come to a brassy rhetoric. But the stanzas con-

cerning the poor have some of Neilson's characteristic moments of
feeling and vision:

> Shyly they come from the unpainted lane;
> Coats have they made of old unhappiness
> That keeps in every pain.

> But 'tis the poor who make the loving words.
> Slowly they stoop; it is a sacrament:
> The poor can feed the birds.

> Old, it is old, this scattering of the bread,
> Deep as forgiveness, or the tears that go
> Out somewhere to the dead.

> The feast of love, the love that is the cure
> For all indignities—it reigns, it calls,
> It chains us to the pure.

> Still will the poor go out with loving words;
> In the long need, the need for happiness
> The poor can feed the birds.

The language defines with sensitive reticence what the poet wants
to say. An analogy is discreetly suggested, but not explicitly pressed,
between the feeding of the birds and Christ's feeding of the multi-
tude, as well as his giving of the eucharistic bread. The continuing
religious implication is kept at a distance from any doctrinal formu-
lation by the indefiniteness of phrasings like 'the tears that go/Out
somewhere to the dead', and the way that the eucharistic phrase 'the
feast of love' is further developed in the phrases that follow. Neilson
is not being merely evasive or vague, but rather concerned to render
precisely a state of mind which has a religious orientation while not
being able to make much positive affirmation. Nevertheless, I do not
think one can quite explain away some unsatisfactory features.
'Deep . . . as tears' is already questionable; and 'It chains us to the
pure' has an odd awkward ambiguity of meaning and an unclear
range of associations. It is at such points that one is uncertain—unwilling to censure the text in case a more attentive and delicately
perceptive reading may, after all, justify it; yet inclined to think that
here is an example of weakness in diction arising from a certain
clumsiness and lack of self-clarification in the poet. On the other
hand one must acknowledge in this poem, not only the sensitively
deflected use of the language of sacramental religion, but also the
human pathos which is one of Neilson's strongest and most authentic 'notes': which is evident in a line like:

> In the long need, the need for happiness . . .

It is in the context of the other bird poems that one can feel sure
that Chisholm has not gone astray in making much of the lyric

'The Smoker Parrot'.[18] (This is the Regent Parrot, *Polytelis anthope-plus*, which is yellow on the breast and parts of the wing, greenish above, with a touch of pink on the wing, and wing-quills and tail feathers an iridescent black.) Chisholm sees the bird as 'a symbol of completeness', as if it made present with unusual plenitude and richness an intimation of a higher reality.

> He has the full moon on his breast,
> The moonbeams are about his wing;
> He has the colours of a king.
> I see him floating unto rest
> When all eyes wearily go west,
> And the warm winds are quieting.
> The moonbeams are about his wing:
> He has the full moon on his breast.

It is true that, if one abstracted this lyric from the rest of Neilson's work, one might be more hesitant in accepting it as representing a moment of 'vision'—though I think the text gives enough indications to support the view that there is an intrinsic symbolism, and the peculiar movement of the poem gives it a stilled intensity.

Before leaving this excursus on the bird poems, I should like to mention two others. Firstly the pleasant poem about the plover, 'The Little Militant', which has a Frostian glint in the line:

> His doubt in mankind still remained unshaken.

Secondly, the poem 'The Whistling Jack', in which the butcher-bird also becomes the bearer of a heavenly message, this time in rebuke of a mankind that is the most cruel and destructive of all animals, and yet is sentimentally shocked by the butcher-bird's killing of a tiny chick.[19]

In pursuing the line of enquiry opened up by my initial comparison between Blake's rejection of institutional religion and Neilson's, I have not tried to keep Blake too closely in view. I should like now to return to make a second point, which is that both of these poets who loved children and celebrated childhood in their poetry were childless. Apart from the fact that this cut them off from the full range of experience with children, there is a consequence of perhaps deeper importance. Blake had the responsibility of a household only in a minimal way. He had to support his wife Catherine, who was selflessly loyal to Blake's conception of his artistic and intellectual vocation; but he did not experience the much more complete involvement in the mundanities, and the claims and counterclaims of competing needs and responsibilities, which parenthood would have brought—as the unfortunate John Clare knew. There are times when I feel that one of the final reservations one must have about Blake is that his poems of 'experience' and his visionary construc-

B

tions are *too* imaginatively free—free of sufficiently testing involvement. This is not the place to develop this further in regard to Blake, but what of Neilson?

First, it must be pointed out that, though Neilson remained unmarried (whether through temperament or poverty is not clear, though I am inclined to think the former) he remained close to his own family household, sharing its vicissitudes and burdens for a great deal of his early manhood, and never losing touch for long. Still, the pattern of his life did become that of a casual and drifting day-labourer, never stopping in one job for long, and not bearing the primary responsibility for maintaining a household and shaping other lives.

In the case of Neilson, one can observe that this may mean a certain limitation in experience without wishing to press the point. Neilson advances no claims to omnicompetence; he is the least likely person to insist on his view of things being particularly right: we have no need to defend ourselves against a man whose song was always delicate and who sang no loud hymn—as we have sometimes to defend ourselves against Blake, who can drum arrogantly enough at times and solve out of hand all the problems of marriage, government, religion and science.

Neilson's songs of experience are not often complaints about his own difficulties. They are characteristically the compassionate observations of an onlooker. This poetry of human pathos is the side of Neilson which tends to be obscured by too much insistence on his refined visionary lyricism. It is close to the ballad style; it is not fully protected from sentimentality of phrase or idea—though more of phrase, because Neilson is a realist in his perceptions of people, and oversimplifies or resorts to clichés mainly through clumsiness when his inspiration flags. A poem like 'In the Street' is not a success, yet it could perhaps have been so—and it certainly illustrates the characteristic position of the poet as the compassionate bystander. 'The Moon was Seven Days Down' is the poet's own choice amongst his ballads,[20] though 'The Ballad of Remembrance' has strong claims, especially because of the well-managed tension created by the teller's attempt to defend the English against his interlocutor's story of his convict father.[21] 'The Soldier is Home' belongs to the same idiom: it is an early poem, written after the Boer War, and the protest of passionate pity comes through:

Now shall he sit in the dark, his world shall be fearfully small—
   He shall sit with old people, and pray and praise God for fine weather:
Only at times shall he move for a glimpse away over the wall,
    Where the men and the women who make up the world are striving
     together!
    Oh! yes, the soldier is home!

Simple, salt tears, full often will redden his eyes;
  No one shall hear what he hears, or see what he sees;
He shall be mocked by a flower, and the flush of the skies!
  He shall behold the kissing of sweethearts—close by him,
    here, under the trees—
      Oh! yes, the soldier is home![22]

I know by experiment that these poems communicate quite powerfully when transferred from the page to their natural medium, the
speaking voice. But the poem that stays in my mind, amongst these
poems of pathos that have the idiom of popular recitations, is 'Half
a Life Back', which begins:

Half a life back now the faces careworn or sunny,
  Stare as we knew them, patient with heavy goodbyes;
Yet they give still the good warmth and the taste of the honey:
  Neighbour! oh, neighbour! the light has gone out of their eyes.[23]

The phrasing of the poem is awkward and a little arbitrary and un-
focussed in places, but the essential structure is good, with its retrospect from the mid-point of life to the faces of the past, caught in a
stillness as in old photographs, and its lateral appeal to the 'neighbour' who shares the experience of that complex loss which is so
simply stated: 'the light has gone out of their eyes'.

I have stressed the effectiveness of these poems of compassion
because Neilson has been a little too much viewed only in a few
moments of rare lyrical delicacy. Among the poems of experience
there is another group which should also be noted. These are poems
on the theme of death, the best of which are truly impressive, and
provide also interesting examples of Neilson's fingering of verse.
For example, 'The Old Man in the Autumn' has as its metrical base
an amphibrachic dimeter, with free substitutions:

The calm is unceasing
The soul would delay; . . .[24]

Some of the lines could be regarded as deserting the dimeter framework to become a trimeter, but what Neilson seems to be doing is to
keep the dimeter framework and trust his ear to take the liberty of
hypermetrical syllables; for example in the lines

He the Únseen | in Áutumn |

and

Oh, the Únseen | —I líke not |

(My metrical reading requires the *first* syllable of 'Unseen' to bear
the main stress and the metrical accent). It also provides a delicate

suspension of the first word in this line, which bears a fair amount
of stress but not a metrical accent:

$$\overset{/}{}\quad\overset{/}{}$$
Steps not far | away |

Even in the second-last stanza of the poem, I think it possible that
we are to read the first and third lines as framed on the dimeter
measure, though with extreme liberty of hypermetrical feet:

$$\overset{/}{}$$
He offered wisdom; | already |
I am | too wise, |
$$\overset{/}{}$$
With all my years | counted up |
At the back | of my eyes. |

If one were dealing with this stanza in isolation one would, of course,
assume that the lines in question were trimeters:

He of|fered wis|dom; already |

and

With all | my years | counted up |

I have suggested for consideration a 'queer' rather than the conventional metrical view of the lines, because I am trying to feel my
way back to the way Neilson worked, and because pace and disposition of stress and pause in reading will tend to be affected by the
view one adopts.

Two other striking poems, which form a pair, are 'Say Summer
Shall Not Die' and 'Tell Summer That I Died'.[25] In both the rhetorical strategy is to use an obviously false statement or impossible
demand (contained in the title phrases) to force our minds to a
translatio, an intuitive leap; and one is reminded of Neilson's comment generally on the lyrical mode: 'Some people seem to think
that it should be as definite as an ironmonger's catalogue, and as
dogmatic as a Calvinistic sermon'.[26] In the first poem the meaning
is not merely the perennial recurrence of summer, as the first stanza
suggests; 'summer' has become a climate of the spirit, a plenitude
which can be maintained even though we decay, so long as we defy
the negative power that would inhibit love and daring. The second
poem shows us the old man in the body's winter who still keeps the
'fire within': the affirmation now is that *he* will die, but that 'summer' remains always available as the proper climate of the living.
This poem has an affinity with 'The Fire Unquenched' which con-
trasts the death of individuals with the eternal renewal of love:

> But Love it resteth not nor ever will:
> It hath no end, and who shall call it sire
> From out whose womb came Love that is a fire?[27]

One of Neilson's very finest lyrics, 'The Hour of the Parting', may be considered along with the poems on the theme of death.[28] The poem develops the notion that to part is to die a little:

> Parting is of the cold
> That stills the loving breath,
> Dimly we taste the old
> The pitiless meal of Death.

'Dimly' because parting is an obscure foretaste of death, a kind of sacramental anticipation and participation. The quiet but distinct rhetoric of these lines is effective, and the verse-movement is sensitive. This is one of the few poems in which the phrasing holds up all the way. 'Shall we *assault* the pain?' is unusual, but justifies itself: to assault being to advance resolutely upon, to crush the pain against one's breast by coming to the precise moment of parting. In the second stanza the imagery of the sea voyage functions also in suggestion of a mental state:

> There is a *gulf* behind
> Dull voice and fallen lip,
> The *blue smoke* of the mind,
> The *gray light on the ship.*

From poems of experience we move to poems of innocence, including celebrations of the land of childhood, of which the best is 'The Poor, Poor Country'. Sad to record, A. G. Stephens rejected this poem[29]—'too long, flat and slow. The Spring surge has left your brain'—and did not like the movement of the refrain line, which seems to me one of the particular beauties of the poem: it is an iambic hexameter line, delicately poised and subtly varied, with a distinctive floating terminal cadence: no | pauper | was I |. The other lines making up the quatrains are 'fourteeners' with the metrical caesura usual to this kind of verse. But the first line of the poem is an exception, being an hexameter:

> Oh 'twas | a poor | country, | in Au|tumn it | was bare |

unless it can be brought, with some difficulty, to a heptameter thus:

> Oh 'twas | a po|or coun|try, in | Autumn | it was | bare |

'Poor' seems to have disyllabic value in some other places, for example in stanza 3:

> And in | that po|or coun|try no | pauper | was I |

In stanza 2 there is another line which one would normally treat as an hexameter:

> 'Twas on | the brown | water, | in the | green leaves | it hung |

though I wonder whether lengthening of both the relevant vowel-sounds did not make the poet hear it as a heptameter:

'Twas on | the bro|wn wa|ter, in | the gre|en leaves | it hung |.

We may note also in stanza 3 a line that swings ambiguously between a hexameter, which makes good rhythm:

/ /
I wa|ded out to | the swan's nest | —at night | I heard | them sing, |

and a heptameter, which satisfies the prevailing pattern:

I wa|ded out | to the | swan's nest | . . .

Once more the interest in such fine points lies in trying to feel one's way back to Neilson's intuitive metrical sense; it is to be noted that slightly different performances of the line tend to follow the metrical view we take—and if one does not think slight differences (which we feel but do not necessarily analyse metrically) of vital importance one should give up reading song-lyrics.

With the exception of a jingling lapse in stanza 4 ('I saw in sleep the Bunyip creep') the language of this poem is solid, the phrasing sensitive, and both visually and phonically interesting:

I saw the black duck in the reeds, and the spoonbill on the sky, . . .

My riches all went into dreams that never yet came home,
They touched upon the wild cherries and the slabs of honeycomb, . . .

The blue cranes were my nearest friends, and I mourned to see them go:

I watched their wings so long until I only saw the sky, . . .

Nearly everywhere in Neilson there is a hint, a possibility, an evanescent presence of fine poetry; but often the gleam is wasted in a poem that has no sustaining sureness or enough self-critical purgation. 'The Lover Sings' (written by 1906) is an example: the true poem is unrealized behind the period verbalizing that Neilson helplessly falls into: yet the clear-toned opening promises something:

It is not dark; it is not day;
The earth lies quivering to the dew:
Shall we not love her? All men may.

It flickers again for a moment:

Wrapt in a fire he leaps, he flies . . .

and beautifully emerges once more towards the end:

Deep is the dark, it drinks the day:

but the poem has not caught up with its promise.[30]

Even in the much admired 'The Orange Tree', I am left partly uneasy, for all the reassuring and sensitive explication that A. R. Chisholm gives in his introduction.[31] Strangely enough, it is not the girl's sense of the unsayable which causes difficulty here: the poem's great merit is to suggest this convincingly. It is rather the wide indefinite circlings of the girl's questioner that provoke puzzlement and doubt. Chisholm's reading of some of the hermetic lines is possible and helpful, but does not impose itself as inevitable: when one returns from the exegesis to the bare text, doubt sets in whether we can really know the precise intention of:

> Does the compulsion of the dew
> Make him unknowable but keen
> Asking with beauty of the blue?

and still worse, whether any explanation would rescue the tone and quality of the words. Some of the language comes from the late nineteenth-century stock of poeticism:

> In a *mad escapade* of spring
> *Ere* he could make a fond adieu . . .

and works at a level of what looks like sentimental cliché:

> Is it a fluttering heart that gave
> Too willingly and was reviled? . . .

even descending to the perfunctory manufacture of phrases meant to stuff out the stanza with something emotionally impressive, though of very doubtful value and relevance:

> Is it the stammering at the grave,
> The last word of a little child?

It may be that I have failed to see this side of the poem aright; with such lyrics the right attunement of our sensibilities is all-important. But we expect the words to guide and control that attunement, and this is what does not happen convincingly on the questioner's side of 'The Orange Tree', in spite of the poem's beauty and fascination.

The delicate and visionary lyrics are woven from strands of childhood, youth, spring, and young love—love as an almost impersonal enchantment and a cosmic spirit—with a hint of heaven, and a recurring under-theme of death. They can dip into evocations of romance and sensuous pleasure:

> When schoolboys build great navies in the skies
> and a rebellion burns the butterflies:[32]

and:

> Night—and the silence honey-wet:
> The moon came to the full:
> It was a time for gentle thought
> and the gathering of wool.[33]

But their main aim is something beyond the margins of sense. 'Song

be Delicate' is the supreme example of Neilson's allusive and elusive
art, which binds all the themes together, and controls our response
with sureness, in an exemplification of the *ars poetica* it states:

> Let your song be delicate.
> The skies declare
> No war—the eyes of lovers
> Wake everywhere.

The versification is masterly.[34] The initial refrain line is free-floating
in metrical ambiguity. I am inclined to scan it as a trochaic trimeter
with an extra last syllable; but it could be resolved as a trochaic
tetrameter, or as an iambic trimeter with an extra first syllable. The
indeterminacy of its metrical base does not matter—the line recurs
unchanged except for the alteration of 'song' and 'voice'; and I
think this privileged indeterminacy is *felt* as a subtle pleasure. Then
in the first stanza the iambic metre of the remaining three lines is
not declared flatly with end-stopped lines, but passes immediately
and with poised serenity into enjambment without loss of form. In
each quatrain the trimeter-dimeter alternation remains basic, with
sensitive substitutions:

> Is love | little love | crying |

In the second-last stanza the prevailing iambic pattern seems to
indicate the best logical reading:

> All their | day's love | is sunken |

In the last stanza the irregularly lengthened third line stands out in
the delicate rhetorical structure, and prompts me once again to
speculate on Neilson's metrical sense. Did he regard himself as ex-
tending this line to a tetrameter, as the ordinary conventions of
scansion would assume:

> Death is | abroad | ... Oh, the | black season |

or did he (as I suspect) feel the line to be still within the trimeter
frame, with an extraordinary licence of hypermetrical syllables in
the last foot, running together towards the one peak of stress in
'season'?—

> Death is | abroad | ... Oh, the black season |

Once more, one's performance of the line will tend—not inevitably,
but naturally enough—to differ, in pace and disposition of stress and
pause, according as one accepts the normal scansion or admits a
'queer' scansion as possibly nearer to Neilson's feeling for the line.

Regretfully I cannot wholly share the high estimation generally accorded 'Love's Coming', where, to my sense, the verbal control of our responses wavers at times, and a hint of cliché and sentimentality appears. I mention it as providing another instance of Neilson's elusive metrical practice.[35] Here the special effect of the versification arises from the continuous maintenance of metrical ambiguity. Most of the lines submit well enough to being scanned as trimeters; as lines 2 and 3 of stanza 2 seem positively to require:

> Quiet|ly as | lovers |
>   Creep at | the mid|dle moon |
> Softly | as play|ers tremble |
> In the | tears of | a tune. |

But already in the first and more clearly in the fourth of these lines one can see a dimeter pattern which is ready to assert itself:

> In the tears | of a tune. |

That this dimeter alternative is really the prevailing pattern seems clear from the fact that a few of the lines submit to being trimeters only if one allows monosyllabic feet, not a normal provision in English metre or in Neilson's work:

> Love | came so | lightly |

and

> Came the | shy | pilgrim |

while a dimeter reading comes readily:

> Love came | so lightly |

and

> Came the | shy pilgrim |

But metrical ambiguity persists in the poem. I find that I read it mainly in the dimeter pattern, shifting towards trimeter when that is more natural, and experiencing some lines as evenly balanced between the two metrical hypotheses: for example, with the effect of equalizing the stress on the first three syllables of the second of these lines:

> Quietly as lilies
>   *Their faint vows* declare . . .

Such ambiguities readily arise with short metres, though it is rare for them to be so pervasive as here: only one line ('Softly as players tremble') strongly resists a dimeter interpretation; the rest swing delicately from two main points of accentual attachment, even if a third metrical accent can also be supposed in all and naturally preferred in some. Again one is left with admiration for Neilson's intuitively fine ear; and with an unresolved speculation, which we may not be able to conclude, about the way Neilson regarded some of his metrical effects.

Devaney records Neilson as saying: 'anything of Botticelli's I see fills me with emotion. Prints of other great pictures seem to leave me cold'.[36] It is an interesting stray comment. The affinity is one that one might have guessed. And the implication of a highly selective and specialized temperament is worth pondering. Neilson seems a curiously passive onlooker on life: with this one faculty, that over a narrow band he could receive and transmit impulses of subtle feeling and longing, or of a grave pity—not in any particular way as *his* experiences, but as 'communications' for which he was the imperfect vehicle.

A poem which has not been much noticed, called 'You Cannot Go Down to the Spring', will serve as a final example.[37] I had passed over it many times before its merits, which now seem to me very great, caught my attention. The strong, possibly too automatic, s-alliteration in the first line, the lack of overt connections in its paratactic construction, the oblique phrasing, may all raise the doubt, never far from us with Neilson's poetry, whether this is a success or a near-miss. I can only say that repeated readings have convinced me of its rightness:

> The song will deceive you, the scent will incite you to sing;
> You clutch but you cannot discover: you cannot go down to the Spring.
>
> The day will be painted with summer, the heat and the gold
> Will give you no key to the blossom: the music is old.
>
> It is at the edge of a promise, a far-away thing;
> The green is the nest of all riddles: you cannot go down to the Spring.
>
> The truth is too close to the sorrow; the song you would sing,
> It cannot go into the fever: you cannot go down to the Spring.

A paraphrase must seem intolerably clumsy. It is primarily the poet himself who is being addressed. There is a mystery of being which the Spring hides but suggests. The poet can receive what is evident to the senses: the scent, the colour, the light, the sounds: but he cannot penetrate beyond them to the meaning, the promise, the intrinsic fever. The approach to that inwardness is pain: 'the truth is too close to the sorrow'. And, though the poet tries to render that perennial 'music', his song will fail him: 'you clutch but you cannot discover'. The new life and growth remain 'the nest of all riddles'. Romantic and symbolist poetry has never gone further while remaining true to itself.

1966

NOTES

1 James Devaney, *Shaw Neilson* (Sydney, 1944), pp. 134-5.
2 A. R. Chisholm, *The Poems of Shaw Neilson* (Sydney, 1965), pp. 10-22.
3 See my *Christopher Brennan* (rev. ed., Melbourne, 1973), especially pp. 41-51.
4 Devaney, pp. 5, 9, 10, 157, 185.
5 Chisholm, p. 175.
6 Devaney, pp. 12, 47, 198. For 'The Flight of the Weary', see Chisholm, pp. 105-6.
7 Devaney, pp. 198, 47.
8 Devaney, pp. 89, 198.
9 T. Inglis Moore makes this comparison in *Six Australian Poets* (Melbourne, 1942), p. 64.
10 Douglas Stewart has commented on this in *The Flesh and the Spirit* (Sydney, 1948), pp. 174-7.
11 Devaney, p. 11.
12 The references to these periods in Devaney, pp. 75, 83, 91-2, suggest that the disturbance should not be underrated.
13 Chisholm, p. 67.
14 The bird is identified as a 'blue crane' in the comment on the poem recorded in Devaney, pp. 198-9, where Neilson insists that it was in fact the contemplation of the bird, which did not seem to be frightened by God, that gave him his 'first idea of right religion'.
15 Chisholm, pp. 33-9.
16 Chisholm, p. 66.
17 Chisholm, pp. 264-5.
18 Chisholm, pp. 59-60; for the poem, p. 265.
19 Chisholm, pp. 241, 194-6.
20 Chisholm, pp. 74-6; Devaney, p. 198.
21 Chisholm, pp. 101-4.
22 Chisholm, pp. 170-1; Devaney, p. 203.
23 Chisholm, p. 115.
24 Chisholm, p. 248.
25 Chisholm, pp. 262-3.
26 Devaney, p. 176.
27 Chisholm, pp. 250-1.
28 Chisholm, p. 72.
29 Devaney, pp. 43, 48-9, 201; for the poem, Chisholm, pp. 77-8.
30 Chisholm, pp. 73-4.
31 Chisholm, pp. 62-3, 22-5.
32 'The Sweetening of the Year', Chisholm, p. 178.
33 'The Eleventh Moon', Chisholm, pp. 96-7.
34 Cf. the analysis by T. Inglis Moore, pp. 76-8, which is sensitive but inclined to confuse metre with stress-values. For the poem, Chisholm, p. 65.
35 Chisholm, p. 64. Cf. Inglis Moore, p. 78.
36 Devaney, p. 110.
37 Chisholm, p. 234.

An imprint of Slessor

I MADE an occasion to meet Slessor for the first time in 1956 when I began to edit *Quadrant* and he had taken over the editorship of *Southerly*. He asked me to lunch. We talked about our preferences among Australian poets. I said that Brennan had meant much to me because he seemed the only poet in the Australian tradition deeply involved in the symbolist tradition, though Shaw Neilson later began to mean more as a lyric poet, and also a symbolist in a native way. He said it was McCrae who had been such a starting-point for him—and of course this comes out very clearly in the series of lectures on Australian poetry he gave in 1954 at Sydney University and in the poem he wrote in tribute.[1] I confessed that I could not get on with McCrae's work at all. Later on, Hal Porter joined us, and Slessor, who was publishing as much of Porter's work as he could get, said to me jokingly: 'You lay off this man, he's mine'. And one can see that, in spite of the obvious differences, Slessor would respond very keenly to Porter's imagist virtuosity.

We met again once or twice before I left Sydney. One occasion was as guests of the Savage Club. I knew we were expected to sing for our supper. I felt I had no poem suitable for the occasion, and in desperation sat in a milk-bar and wrote 'To a Young Lady wearing a Picture-Map Dress' which I later put in *Quadrant*.[2] Slessor chose to read 'Vesper-Song of the Reverend Samuel Marsden', a rather grim piece of entertainment.[3] Slessor was not a particularly good reader, but I remember what effective work his mouth made of the phrase 'my vellum of puffed veal'. For a moment one had external witness of that quick inner ear for curious phonetic textures.

It was late in the 1960s that I again began to meet Slessor. It was his presence on the National Literature Board of Review that encouraged me to bear the discomfort of the ungrateful office of advising Ministers of Customs on literary censorship. Slessor was meticulous in his careful discharge of his duty: more legalistic in approach than most of us, in that he related his opinions more closely to the wording of the regulation; but always temperate and sensible. We managed to get in a lot of talk around the meetings, and Slessor continued to show his up-to-date knowledge and generous interest in the work of other Australian poets.

On an occasion when the Board had a meeting in Hobart, he came down with his son Paul to stay for a day or two. I had felt increasing affection and regard for him and had begun to wish we had got to know one another much better. I knew that he might not have much time left. There was a pleasure and pathos in having him with us. We took him to the eminence of St John's Park, stood by the monument to Matthew Forster, one time Comptroller-General of Convicts, and looked back towards the entrance to our own street, where Blackburn's fine Congregational church stands. That view is now indelibly associated with his presence.

On the night I heard of his death I was returning from South Australia, and staying overnight at the motel at Tullamarine. Adelaide that day had been disturbed by street demonstrators deliberately pulling on a clash with the police. Public reasons, exemplified by this small ugly farce, combined with some private ones to leave me depressed; and now I thought of the sadness and lostness that had seemed to lie beneath Slessor's courtesy and good-humour and pleasure in things. That night I wrote a dark-toned poem called 'Winter Drive' which has all these elements in solution within it. In a way, it is my elegy for Slessor. By an irony, when I sent it to *Poetry* (Chicago) the editor put it, without my consent, into an issue of political protest poems, turning me into an involuntary member of a literary demonstration of a sort that Slessor would have had as much distaste for as myself.[4]

Slessor's poetry matters far more than his prose, but once one knows the fairly small body of his poetic work it is interesting to look at the prose and see connections. The selected prose pieces in *Bread and Wine* (1970) give representative variety: reminiscences of Sydney in the 'twenties and 'thirties; Slessor's personal survey of Australian poetry and some explanatory comments on his own poems; and some of his war despatches from the Middle East.[5] To these must be added at least the text of an address on 'Modern English Poetry' given to the Australian English Association and the text of an A.B.C. broadcast, 'Writing Poetry: The Why and the How', made in 1947.[6]

In the non-literary prose we pick up small details that reappear in the poetry. For example: the green-scaled copper of the poem 'Nuremberg' is cognate with Slessor's pleasure in

> the copper spire of St James's Church in King Street . . . its lovely scales of verdigris giving the copper a green like tarnished snow, an old, dim, decayed, peeling almond-green . . . (p. 9)

In this instance, the latent rendering of visual detail is taken further in the prose; and one sees how the poet had to draw on local impressions as well as books and pictures to bring his exotic creations into being. In the same piece, the line 'And Time flows past them

like a hundred yachts' (in 'Out of Time') is illuminated by a description of the Harbour:

> Flights and volleys of yachts drift over it continuously, scattered like the
> fragments of a white flower, yet forming in the end into the helter-
> skelter pattern of a race. (p. 6)

In another piece, Moorebank, which is mentioned in 'Five Bells', is
revealed as the site of Harley Matthews' vineyard, by George's
River outside Liverpool, which 'will be remembered always by the
scores of writers, artists, eccentrics and spare-time philosophers who
were lucky enough to have drunk the good red Matthews wine there'
(p. 35).

In the literary pieces, a number of interesting features appear.
Max Harris is right in saying that Slessor is not an 'intellectual' poet
but 'emotional and evocative'; but that does not mean that Slessor
does not want intelligence to be used in poetry.[7] He dislikes the idea
that poetry can be produced 'by a kind of spontaneous and entirely
uncerebral combustion' (p. 95). In his criticism of James Lionel
Michael (pp. 62-3), and still more of Kendall (pp. 84-7), Slessor
amusingly and unsparingly shows his conviction that words must
not be arbitrarily chosen and loosely used for the convenience of
rhyme, and that they must submit to strict tests for meaning. Implicitly Slessor offers his own work—even when it presents some
difficulties in theme and phrasing—to the test of accuracy and in-
telligibility. If we find lapses from this standard, as we do here and
there, then they are lapses the poet would himself be willing to
acknowledge.

The kind of accuracy Slessor sought was especially a true presentation of 'the image of actual experience'. This phrase comes from
his discussion of Norman Lindsay's influence. Slessor does not en-
dorse all Lindsay's views, but he plainly is at one with Lindsay
when he says:

> Lindsay's doctrine insists on the concrete image, and it is not without
> significance that most of the Australian poets whom he may be considered
> to have influenced show the same abhorrence of abstraction. (p. 124)

Insistence on the concrete image can be combined with various intentions and produce many different poetic results. It does not
necessarily lead in the direction of Slessor's early work. That work
owed a great deal to the influence of Hugh McCrae, and it is interesting to see how much of his praise of McCrae casts a reflection
on to his own work. Of McCrae's 'Joan of Arc' he says:

> Indeed, in its glowing dyes, its romantic gusto and its minutely finished
> detail, it has some of the effect of a fourteenth-century illuminated parch-
> ment . . .And it seems that Hugh McCrae grows so intent on illuminating

the tiny details of his manuscript, the tips of the angels' wings, the lips
of the cherubs, the fire from the dragons' nostrils, that he forgets the
larger chronicle which it was his purpose to inscribe. (p. 107)

Slessor speaks also of 'the clusters of exciting and almost physically
palpable images' (pp. 107-8).

Most of Slessor's critics have acknowledged, with more or less
reservation as to its value, the virtuosity of that side of Slessor's
poetry that lies nearest to McCrae. It belongs to a mode of poetry
bounded on one side by 'nineties dandyism and on the other by the
artifice of Edith and Sacheverell Sitwell. Slessor defends McCrae
from the critical complaint that McCrae's mannered exoticism is
remote from reality:

> Is it extraordinary that the poet's world should seem as actual to him as
> any other world? Surely the world of Hyperion seemed more real to
> Keats than the England of the nineteenth century. (p. 103)

Surely not; Keats was not only aware of the fragility and evanescence
of the worlds which fancy could momentarily create, but also increasingly troubled about their relation to reality. There are problems involved in the creation of artificial paradises which do not
seem to have bothered McCrae and which Slessor does not here
consider. Again, Slessor defends McCrae against the complaint that
his landscape is not Australian by saying that 'neither is it English,
American or Chinese':

> The country of his poems is the mapless country of the mind . . . (p. 103)

This is so for McCrae's poetry, whether it is set in France or in
Australia or elsewhere; and so it is for Slessor's early work, whatever
the supposed scene and period. But the problems are not solved
simply by asserting the poet's liberty to inhabit Faery or Cockayne or
Bohemia or Cuckooz Contrey. These mapless countries of the mind
may in varying degrees serve as means of play, or of refuge, or of
holding a mirror—even though a transmogrifying one—seriously up
to reality. In Slessor's case, though I respond happily enough to
some of his virtuoso *bravura*, I think it produces more valuable
results when some significant relation with *our* reality is discern-
ible. The improvement in Slessor's poetry involved a strengthening
of its relation to experience, though inevitably within Slessor's
limits. What those limits were has been acutely seen by Max Harris,
whose study, for all its slapdash and infelicities, is humane, sympathetic, forthright, and perceptive. I want to examine four poems
as moments in the poet's growth.

Slessor has himself acknowledged three periods in his writing.[8]
'Winter Dawn' belongs to the early period. The imagistic virtuosity
is applied to an early morning in Sydney. Already some of the ma-

terials of 'Five Bells' are present. The poet is the observer looking out through the window-pane, seeing the Harbour and the city and suburbs. Phenomena of air and water and earth become interchangeable, and also of heat and cold:

> At five I wake, rise, rub on the smoking pane
> A port to see—water breathing in the air,
> Boughs broken. The sun comes up in a golden stain,
> Floats like a glassy sea-fruit. There is mist everywhere,
> White and humid, the Harbour is like plated stone,
> Dull flakes of ice. One light drips out alone,
> One bead of winter-red, smouldering in the steam,
> Quietly over the roof-tops—another window
> Touched with a crystal fire in the sun's gullies,
> One lonely star of the morning, where no stars gleam.

By the second stanza an attitude begins to be defined to the urban human world. The sun bestows a gilding and diamond glitter on the scene; but these are 'dead suburbs', dormitory suburbs where men sleep in their houses as the dead sleep in the cemeteries to which Slessor will refer in 'Five Bells'. Men sleep like mummies in stone coffins awaiting resurrection. The poet's vision rejects and destroys the city, reducing it to:

> a shell of bricks and paper,
> Empty, without purpose, a thing not comprehended,
> A broken tomb, where ghosts unknown sleep.

The immediate actual world has become senseless, unreal, a realm in which men sleep the sleep of spiritual death. Where then shall the poet look for life and true awakening? The last stanza says:

> And the least crystal weed, shaken with frost,
> The furred herbs of silver, the daisies round-eyed and tart,
> Painted in antic china, the smallest night-flower tossed
> Like a bright penny on the lawn, stirs more my heart,
> Strikes deeper this morning air, than mortal towers
> Dried to a common blindness, fainter than flowers,
> Fordone, extinguished, as the vapours break,
> And dead in the dawn. O Sun that kills with life,
> And brings to breath all silent things—O Dawn,
> Waken me with old earth, keep me awake!

The 'mortal towers' are the city buildings, losing their brightness as the glitter and shine of wetness dries off roofs and windows. Man's world is deadened in daylight, even while it springs into activity. From it the poet turns to the natural world, where the sun can bring silent things to genuine life. He wants to share in earth's wakening. It is a romantic-Wordsworthian turn of sentiment, a conditioned literary response. It is all the more unconvincing—but beautifully unconvincing—because the poet changes the scanty natural things that peep up in the dead city into artificial things: the frosted weeds are crystal, the frost-furred herbs are silver ornaments, the daisies look like flowers painted on china, the smallest night-flower (any fallen blossom?) is like a bright penny. It is not really naturalness that here engages the poet's feelings.

We hear little in subsequent poems of nature as a spiritual resource, though nature continues to provide the poet's sensibility with important materials.

It is in his second period that Slessor wrote the suite of poems called 'The Old Play' which includes the following lyric:

> A bird sang in the jaws of night,
> Like a star lost in space—
> O, dauntless molecule to smite
> With joy that giant face!

> I heard you mock the lonely air,
> The bitter dark, with song,
> Waking again the old Despair,
> That had been dead so long.

> That had been covered up with clay
> And never talked about,
> So none with bony claws could say
> They'd dig my coffin out.

> But you, with music clear and brave,
> Have shamed the buried thing;
> It rises dripping from the grave
> And tries in vain to sing.

> O, could the bleeding mouth reply,
> The broken flesh but moan,
> The tongues of skeletons would cry,
> And Death push back his stone!

There is a terrible pressure behind this poem, which communicates a sense of desperation but threatens loss of control. The bird is live spirit, which can sing, rejoice, awaken. It is no manifestation of kindly Nature, however: quite the contrary, it is beauty, courage, hope, menaced by the universe, by the dark destroying ultimate reality. In the human listener, the bird's song wakes what had seemed dead and buried. It is called 'the old Despair', but it is really the poet's self ('They'd dig my coffin out'). This bleeding broken corpse tries to respond to the bird's 'music clear and brave': if only it could, a miracle might happen, and death-in-life might

c

cease to be the truth of our experience. 'Death' in the last line I take to be practically identical with 'Despair' and 'the buried thing'—all referring to the entombed self.

Later still comes the eerily desolate lyric 'Cock-Crow' which enacts a situation even closer to the theme of 'Five Bells', though in relation to one deeply loved:

> The cock's far cry
> From lonely yards
> Burdens the night
> With boastful birds
> That mop their wings
> To make response—
> A mess of songs
> And broken sense.
>
> So, when I slept,
> I heard your call
> (If lips long dead
> Could answer still)
> And snapped-off thoughts
> Broke into clamour,
> Like the night's throats
> Heard by a dreamer.

In 'Writing Poetry: the Why and the How' Slessor commented on technical aspects of this poem, the use of 'half-rhymes with an interlocking system of repeated vowel sounds and consonant sounds' to express 'the sense of remoteness and great distance which comes sometimes in a dream'.

The first stanza states an external reality: the cock crows in the night and all around there comes the distant confused response from other birds. This event enters the mind of the sleeper and is transformed into something else: the dead one calls, and the dreamer's broken-off hopes struggle futilely to respond and make contact. The poem is unfortunately flawed by some dislocation: if the 'lips long dead' are those of the dead one whose call corresponds to the cock's far cry, then they should not be *answering* but *initiating*; and the likening of the dreamer's response to 'the night's throats *heard by a dreamer*' is also slightly confusing. Even with these minor flaws it is a moving poem, and employs Slessor's skill with words in the service of a real experience of loss and incommunicability.

Though 'Five Bells' is only precariously an artistic unity and has unfortunate faults in phrasing, I am sure that it deserves the special position it has been given in Slessor's work.[9] It does represent a summation, a last encounter. It is deeply serious, but I do not think it really fulfils the role Max Harris assigns to it:

> With 'Five Bells' there is a new, quasi-religious development. Slessor is now, as a poet, as a repository of human memory, *responsible* for the dead. In the absence of any god or eternal life, the poet is the humble vessel affording human life such perpetuation as is possible. Slessor's thought about memory, metaphysically as elementary as it is, has given him a sense of total human responsibility, personal responsibility, the responsibility of the priest, and, along with it, a high conviction about the worth of life itself . . . Throughout, by an unforced incremental process, the living image of the dead Joe is built up. He is not subsidiary to the poet's experience of this long memory-recall . . . Slessor has kept perfect faith with his principle of living out other men's lives in his poetry.[10]

As I read it, the poem consists of negatives within negatives, failure within failure, and its strength is its trueness to the experience. The 'argument' involves two lives, the poet's and Joe's, and it is with the poet's attitude to life that it begins. He has abandoned interest in the fidget of actuality: *his* Time is the still depth of the past, of memory. It is true that at the commencement the poet seems confident that memory can bring the dead to life, taking as an example the sudden thought of Joe who was drowned in the Harbour long ago.

But the resuscitation does not work. Joe is 'gone even from the meaning of a name': all that comes up from the depths of memory is odd pointless bits and scraps, not a person. The 'profitless lodgings' that he brings up are specified in an inconsequential mutter:

> . . . unimportant things you might have done,
> Or once I thought you did; but you forgot,
> And all have now forgotten—looks and words
> And slops of beer;

and so on. Joe as a Bohemian in Sydney does not come to life; there is only a debris of stray trivialities. Joe has died a double death: one may *imagine* him as a being beyond our space and time, trying to communicate, but in fact he is non-existent; and when memory tries to bring him back in its own medium it retrieves only a few shreds of pointless detail.

The one coherent and, in a sense, meaningful recollection of Joe that memory brings is the outline of a process: Joe's life was a process of regression and defeat. Joe in Sydney had at first some kind of energy, however whirling and arbitrary and trivial; Joe in Melbourne seemed to be settling into mere conformity, from which the poet's recollection can gather even less of significant detail; Joe back in Sydney was (as the poet now is) in retreat from present actuality and looking back into the past. So another negative is added.

Not only is Joe now nothing in reality, and virtually non-existent in the alternative mode of memory: the sole coherent thought of him is of a running-down process which seemed to lack point or purpose. And this individual failure of Joe to achieve meaning corresponds to the lack of any apparent purpose or meaning to be found in life and the world in general. Perhaps if there were a cosmic purpose there could have been some point to Joe's life, and perhaps then there could have been something still left of Joe that one could communicate with . . . the thought is not fully articulated:

> If I could find an answer, could only find
> Your meaning, or could say why you were here
> Who now are gone, what purpose gave you breath
> Or seized it back, might I not hear your voice?

But, as it is, corresponding to the name 'Joe Lynch' there is now virtually nothing; only some vanishing shreds of memory that have no meaning. And thus the poet, who finds the present valueless and conceives no eternity outside time, also finds that what he elected as 'his Time', the past in memory, also yields no life or consolation or hope.

The concluding passage is a symbolist cadence. The surface actuality has a glitter of beauty, but it is cold and desolate, and wearyingly repetitive, and underneath and above there is utter dark. Nothing has been found in this brief instance of search: there was nothing to be found. The five bells, ringing out of the emptiness of time, prevail.

1972

NOTES

1 For the lectures, see 'Australian Poetry and Norman Lindsay' and 'Australian Poetry and Hugh McCrae', *Southerly* XVI (1955) 62-72 and XVII (1956) 128-37, reprinted in A. K. Thomson (ed.), *Critical Essays on Kenneth Slessor* (Brisbane, 1968), pp. 157-71, 172-83.

2 *Quadrant* II, 1 (1957) , 8.

3 *Poems* (1957), p. 97.

4 *Poetry* (Chicago) CXX (1972), p. 334.

5 References in the text in parentheses are to pages of *Bread and Wine*.

6 'Modern English Poetry', first printed in the Sydney University *Union Recorder* (1 October 1931), has been reprinted as Australian English Association Offprint no. 9 (October 1931); in Thomson, pp. 139-46; and in *Southerly* XXXI (1971) 272-80. 'Writing Poetry: The Why and the How', first printed in *Southerly* X (1948) 166-71, has been reprinted in Max Harris, *Kenneth Slessor* (Melbourne, 1963), pp. 43-7, and in Thomson, pp. 152-6.

7 Harris, p. 19.

8 See Clement Semmler, *Kenneth Slessor* (London, 1966) , pp. 13ff.

9 The most important fault seems to me to occur in the lines:

> Staked bone by bone, in quiet astonishment
> At cargoes they had never thought to bear.

'Staked' does not have a clear application. But the real problem is in the phrase 'they had never thought to bear'. The passage ought to be rhetorically presenting the dead as astonished at the lack of correspondence between the pious promises of resurrection and heaven inscribed on their tombstones and the actual nothingness of death. But why wouldn't they have expected to bear such inscriptions? I have found that, when pressed, readers of these lines mostly take refuge in one or other of two interpretations, equally inappropriate: (a) the dead are astonished to find themselves described as loving husband, beloved father etc., (b) the dead never thought to bear the tombstones because men never quite believe they too will die.

10 Harris, pp. 27-9.

Some poems of Judith Wright

I WANT to consider first of all some of the very good poems in Judith Wright's first two volumes. A few of these stand out in an order of excellence of their own, though surrounded by others of considerable interest.

In *The Moving Image* (1946) the poem 'Bullocky' has proved most durable in general liking and critical estimation. It is an evocation of the pioneer past of the Hunter River district. In the first stanza the word 'widdershins' catches the mind with its unexpected rightness:

> Beside his heavy-shouldered team,
> thirsty with drought and chilled with rain,
> he weathered all the striding years
> till they ran widdershins in his brain:

'widdershins', meaning in the opposite direction or backwards, defines the movement of the rest of the poem, which is a backwards look into time. The bullocky is seen as leading the entry of a new people into a new Promised Land. The identification of the bullocky with Moses is imputed in stanzas 3 and 4 to the bullocky himself, more perhaps for dramatic emphasis than as a probability. The result is a double-image effect. We see the bullocky, but we see also a symbolic fiction superimposed on or coalescing with the natural scene:

> All the long straining journey grew
> a mad apocalyptic dream,
> and he old Moses, and the slaves
> his suffering and stubborn team.

> Then in his evening camp beneath
> the half-light pillars of the trees
> he filled the steepled cone of night
> with shouted prayers and prophecies.

The latter stanza presents the bullocky at his camp-fire, but the scene is also wrought to a cathedral-image: the trees are pillars, the fire-light scoops out a steepled cone in the dark. There is thus the simultaneous presentation of type and anti-type: a meaningful symbolic pattern is adduced from the past, together with the new reality which fulfils the pattern in an unexpected way. The effect in the above stanzas is mainly a visual one: it is not just a stir of allusions in the words, for a definite picture is created.

In the next stanza the double-image effect is produced in sound:

> While past the camp fire's crimson ring
> the star-struck darkness cupped him round,
> and centuries of cattlebells
> rang with their sweet uneasy sound.

A delicate play of meanings and associations occurs on the word 'centuries', meaning hundreds, as well as ages of time. The bells are actual in the bullocky's time, but they also ring out of a deep and mysterious past (a 'star-struck darkness'), because the patterns of the past are being re-enacted. It seems right to allow the cathedral image of the previous stanza to influence the reading, so that the suggestion of sanctuary bells is not excluded, though not unduly stressed. Perhaps there is also, in the use of the word 'centuries', a faint sidelong reminiscence of Traherne's use of the word in *Centuries of Meditations*. The word 'uneasy' in the last line is superbly right, combining as it does an accurate physical impression with a vague fleeting suggestion of uncertainty. It is surely permissible to explicate these subtle subordinate filaments of meaning or association, so long as it is understood that by bringing them to the surface in sharp focus we tend to distort their proper effect: the reader must restore the disturbed balance when he turns from the interpreter's laborious clumsiness back to the text—with perception nevertheless sharpened, one hopes.

In the last stanza of 'Bullocky' the double-image effect reaches its climax and justification. The bullocky lies buried in the soil as Moses was buried in the Promised Land.[1] The root of the vine—the reference is to the vineyards of the Hunter River district—reaches down to grasp the bone:

> O vine, grow close upon that bone
> and hold it with your rooted hand.
> The prophet Moses feeds the grape,
> And fruitful is the Promised Land.

Again the effect is sharply visual: the root becomes at the same time a hand reaching down to *take hold* of the past. The meaning is that the fruitfulness of the land is rooted in the lives and work of the pioneers, and it must hold close to its origins, its tradition, and be nourished by it.

The typology used in the poem, comparing the new settlement to the entry into the Promised Land, has been a natural and recurring one in colonial literatures. Sometimes it has been required to carry the burden of Utopian hallucinations, sinking down to clichés of political rhetoric. But Judith Wright does not embarrass us with the crackpot portentousness that O'Dowd would have put into such an analogy.[2] Equally, she did not feel compelled to make the analogy work with that evasive irony which is a disfiguring tic in modern poetry. There is an obvious tension between the hallowed grandeur of Moses and the raw actuality of the bullocky: but the poem accepts this and overcomes it. The bullocky's role is ennobled without being falsified.

The poem's quiet assurance in what it is saying is reflected in its simple firm structure. The iambic tetrameter quatrains, rhyming only in the second and fourth lines, regularly divide, according to their grammatical articulation, into matching halves: two lines plus two lines. Each of these halves tends, moreover, to form a single long line, an octameter with a crease in the middle:

> Then in his evening camp beneath the half-light pillars of the trees
> He filled the steepled cone of night with shouted prayers and prophecies.

Within this metrical framework the poem moves by successive statements, not by argument. The statements are for the most part grammatically co-ordinate, linked by 'and' or an equivalent.[3] There is also a good deal of parallelism, though not too rigidly enforced:

> Grass is across the wagon-tracks,
> and plough strikes bone across the grass,
> and vineyards cover all the slopes
> where the dead teams were used to pass.

Particularly in the later part of the poem, the effect of this organization is responsorial: the second half of the stanza 'answering' the first as in the Ambrosian hymns. There is thus a fundamental constitutive dualism governing the poem in every aspect.[4]

In Judith Wright's second volume, *Woman to Man* (1949), the title-poem is by common consent the summit of her achievement. I hope that a close and rather technical examination of the poem will illuminate its peculiar rightness.

The grammatical structure of 'Woman to Man' is the main engine of its expressive power. Phrase is laid by phrase, clause by clause in a continued insistent parallelism. The successive parallel statements are not linked by co-ordinating conjunctions. To use a technical term, the poem proceeds by parataxis. This simplest of all forms of grammatical articulation is the mode of a great deal of poetry. A complex grammar with subordination of clauses as well as varied co-ordination is natural when the logic is argumentative; but poetry often moves simply by successive strokes, whose relationships the mind supplies without the need of connective words. The first stanza moves by appositions: the second and fourth lines amplifying the first, and the last line amplifying the third:

> The eyeless labourer in the night;
> The selfless, shapeless seed I hold,
> builds for its resurrection day—
> silent and swift and deep from sight
> foresees the unimagined light.

In the second and third stanzas the parallel clauses and phrases unfold paratactically, except for the third line of stanza 2 which twists the paradox tighter:

> *yet* you and I have known it well.

This rhetorical parallelism is not static, but dynamic and cumulative, moving forward with increasing urgency to the climax in the last stanza, when meditation on the mystery of conception and gestation changes into an anticipation of the moment of birth:

> This is the maker and the made;
> this is the question and reply;
> the blind head butting at the dark,
> the blaze of light along the blade.
> Oh hold me, for I am afraid.

'The blaze of light' symbolizes the first flash of light and consciousness, but first of all refers literally to the knife cutting the cord. The sudden change of feeling and direction in the last line is very effective, as the woman turns from absorption in the inner mystery to utter a direct personal cry to the man.[5]

It is a sign of complete inspiration when the phonic texture of the poem supports the meaning, giving a true registration of feeling and a sense of woven unity. For example, in the first stanza the sound announced in 'eye' recurs significantly, and together with other details creates an incantatory effect, drawing us into the woman's absorption in the mystery. One need hardly point out in the last stanza the reinforcement of the meaning by the heavy insistent alliteration and the management of stress.

Another sign of mastery is the expressive use of 'word-build'— the size, shape, and stress-profile of individual words.[6] Thus in the first two lines there are four emphatic two-syllabled words with the same 'trochaic' profile, set *across* the iambic metrical frame, not coinciding with it:

> The *eyeless labourer*[7] in the night,
> the *selfless shapeless* seed I hold

This has its own absorbed insistency, but it also enables the big word 'resurrection' in the third line to emerge more noticeably:

> builds for its resurrection day.

In stanza 2, monosyllables notably predominate, tending to slow the lines and increase the effect of deliberation. Stanza 3 continues in the first two lines with monosyllables, and thus ensures that the peaked structure of line 3 stands out:

> the *precise crystals* of our eyes.

(The metrical pattern again cuts across the word-build.) Similarly in this stanza the monosyllables of line 4 enable the important epithets in the last line to emerge with full effect:

> the *intricate* and *folded* rose.

Judith Wright seems to me to have been at this period of her work a poet who worked intuitively, almost gropingly, towards the expression of a particular sense of the mystery of organic life and process and of human passion. 'Woman to Man' brings these two things into a single focus. When her intuition succeeds, the formal elements of the poetry follow suit: image, grammar, phonic texture, versification come together and co-operate. The phrasing in 'Woman to Man' puts some strain on our understanding, but I think it justifies itself. All the references to the unborn child develop one of two ideas. (1) The child is the product of two persons who have become one; by a metaphorical leap, the child *is* these two: the man's strength of body, the passionate tension of the woman's breast, the clarity of the eyes of both, constitute the being of this 'third who lay in our embrace'. (2) The child is not just the effect or result of their union: it is also its 'final cause', teleologically speaking: that is, it is the end to which their love is ordered, the end which also determines the process, unconscious but unerring, of growth in the womb.

I should like to consider two other poems in Judith Wright's second volume, which also seem to me to exhibit the coherence of her art at its best. 'The Bull' combines a splendid celebration of organic life—in particular of fulfilled sexuality—with a kind of lament and fear. The first stanza presents an image of sensuous magnificence, to which everything contributes:

> In the olive darkness of the sally-trees
> silently moved the air from night to day.
> The summer-grass was thick with honey-daisies
> where he, a curled god, a red Jupiter,
> heavy with power among his women lay.

Among the expressive felicities of this texture I hope it will not seem too fanciful to draw attention to the word 'olive' in the first line. Its consonants are picked up again in 'si*l*ently mo*v*ed'; the 'l' sound is then carried forward into 'cur*l*ed god', while the 'v' sound is carried forward into 'hea*v*y with power'—prominent and highly expressive words which make these linkages of sound effective. This may be conscious artifice on the poet's part, or intuitive rightness: the distinction is rather unreal. In regard to meaning, 'olive' begins as a colour-descriptive word, but its latent possibilities of suggestion are, it seems to me, stirred retroactively by the image of the curled god, the red Jupiter. The latent suggestions are of ripeness, fullness, oil, anointment, an athletic body gleaming. Again one must admit that explicit analysis tends to distort the text by its thick-fingered laboriousness; but the problem is to make the text account for a complex significance and a sensuous effect which are certainly there.

The poem goes on to show us this sovereign power suddenly lose its godlike authority. It is introduced by the obvious but delightful ingenuity of expressive sound-play in the lines:

> But summer's bubble-sound of sweet creek-water
> dwindles and is silent . . .

where the kinaesthetic element in the use of sounds may also be noted. The bull is driven by dogs, humiliated, unable to cope with these harrying forces of the outer world. I will not stop to comment on the management of sound-quality and rhythm and word-build in these lines; but I want to draw attention to the grammatical and rhetorical structure. Again parataxis prevails, though some of the clauses have a simple co-ordination. Again the rhetoric relies heavily on parallelism in phrase and clause. Monotony is avoided in several ways. For example, one of the statements is cast in the form of a command, and two in the form of a question. Moreover the parallelism does not always coincide with the line-structure:

> What enemy steals his strength—what rival steals
> his mastered cows?

In such a poem we may ask what is the full meaning, of which the presented subject is the overt surface. Poetry always has human reference. If it deals with the non-human, it does so with some implicit or explicit reference to human concerns. It is noteworthy that the bull is anthropomorphized: he lies heavy with power 'among his women', and the image of the 'curled god, a red Jupiter' is anthropomorphic. Here, too, there is a visual double-image effect: we see the bull in the field, at the same time as we see him as a god. The total result is a rich emblem of human instinctual potency and fulfilment.

Again we may note that the poem does not move dialectically or argumentatively, as if proving a thesis. And there is no prepared *irony* of the routine contemporary kind. The second part, when the bull is discomfited and humiliated, does not react destructively on the values affirmed in the first part. The poem does *not* say: *although* the bull seems a god he is only a creature that can be ignominiously reduced to servitude. The paratactic structure preserves the correct relationship: both of the moments of the bull are true and valid, and we must comprehend both in our grasp of reality.

The other poem in the second volume which I want to commend is perhaps a slighter one. 'The Old Prison' does not exhibit the brooding sensual power, the concentrated vehemence of 'Woman to Man' or 'The Bull'; but it has its own intensity and lyrical expressiveness, and again the various factors combine to form a coherent rightness. I should like to point out especially the intonation: that is, the effect of tune created by the varying pitch of the vowels, especially in the first two stanzas. This is a factor of variable importance in poetry, but here it is of the essence:

> The rows of cells are unroofed,
> a flute for the wind's mouth,
> who comes with a breath of ice
> from the blue caves of the south.

> O dark and fierce day:
> the wind like an angry bee
> hunts for the black honey
> in the pits of the hollow sea.

These stanzas give the images which control the poem. The unroofed prison cells suggest a broken deserted hive: but with an inner contrast in the comparison; for this hive was never fruitful, it is sterile, stored with bitterness not sweetness. The other image is that of a flute with holes, through which the wind blows; and again there is a contrast, for this is a stone flute, its music is bitter and desolating, a cry of despair and isolation.

Once more we may note that the grammatical structure of the poem is mainly paratactic, though there is some simple co-ordination by 'and'. Again monotony is avoided by rhetorical means: one statement is turned into a question, another into a O-exclamation. The parallelism and responsorial effect have a cumulative power in the later part:

> Who built and laboured here?
> The wind and the sea say
> —Their cold nest is broken
> and they are blown away.

> They did not breed nor love.
> Each in his cell alone
> cried as the wind now cries
> through this flute of stone.

The stanzas do not all, as they do in 'Bullocky', break into two matching halves: there is some local asymmetry within the general dualistic balance of the whole.

Many of the poems in the first two volumes seem to me interesting and valuable, but not to attain the order of excellence of those I have been commenting on. If I have succeeded in showing how the very best poems work, I may provide some clues about what happens in poems of a perceptibly lower order of achievement, admirable as some of these may be in their own way.

The well-liked poem 'South of My Days' in the first volume seems to me to be of a second order of achievement. The poet is in Queensland, thinking back to New England, and summoning up the New England past as 'Bullocky' did in a different way:

> South of my day's circle, part of my blood's country,
> rises that tableland, high delicate outline
> of bony slopes wincing under the winter . . .

The poem starts with a well-cadenced memorable rhythm. The phrases are striking, though already with a hint of manufacture and proliferation. Gradually the versification spreads out into that treacherous loopy laxity which has been the snare of many Australian poets since Douglas Stewart showed the way. The line hovers and oscillates uneasily between accentual verse and traditional iambic metre; it prefers the loosening effect of feminine endings— twenty-six out of forty here—free from the stiffening of rhyme. This kind of verse needs to be constantly galvanized by special devices. The poem rather advertises its free access to colloquial speech.

> Or mustering up in the Bogongs in the autumn
> when the blizzards came early. Brought them down; we brought them
> down, what aren't there yet. Or driving for Cobb's on the run
> up from Tamworth—Thunderbolt at the top of Hungry Hill,
> and I give him a wink. I wouldn't wait long, Fred,
> not if I was you: the troopers are just behind,
> coming for that job at the Hillgrove. He went like a luny,
> him on his big black horse.

The colloquial phrasing is accommodated, not in strict counterpoint to a metrical pattern, but rather by bending and relaxing the metrical framework.

In its method the poem belongs to the idiom of the 'forties in Australia. The formula, which is still in use, was fresher then. Again

we may note the paratactic structure, with occasional simple co-
ordination ('and', 'or'). Again there is habitual use of rhetorical
parallelism. But now the effect of these forms of organization is not
cumulative, but simply one thing after another, strung along a
thematic thread. This poem lacks the dynamic development of
'Woman to Man'. Its organization is not much above the level of
the shuffled pack of cards to which the old-timer's reminiscences are
compared. The theme—the poet's feeling for the New England past—
is merely an outline, a hold-all for an assortment of impressions.
The poem has to live by the varied momentary attractiveness of its
component pieces. The poet is also not fully absorbed in the theme:
there remains a touch of self-consciousness, the matey hearty knowingness of the Australian littérateur showing his easy familiarity
with outbackery—the very thing that Judith Wright is blessedly free
from for the most part.

Another poem that provokes analysis is the attempt in 'Woman to
Child' to repeat the success of 'Woman to Man'. It is akin in theme,
similar in method, so that the difference is instructive. Though by
no means a mere failure, it does not reach the height of the other
poem, and does not, to my apprehension, have the same coherence.
As one tries to analyze it, one can see that instead of all factors
coming together co-operatively, there is a continuous incipient dis-
organization. For example in stanzas 1 and 2 the child is apparently
already born and is being spoken to. In stanza 3 the child being
spoken to seems to be back in the womb, not yet born. In stanza 4
the child is again already born.

But even in the opening lines there is a disturbance of the time
perspective:

> You who were darkness warmed my flesh
> where out of darkness rose the seed.

The child is already an embryo in the first line when the seed 'rises'
out of the darkness in the second line. Such an objection may seem
ridiculously captious in an individual instance; but these im-
precisions and dislocations have a cumulative effect. One becomes
aware also in the above lines that the poet is under strain to produce phrasing adequate to the sense of mystery intended. The
repetition of 'darkness' is a perfunctory expedient rather than a
real find. In the rest of the stanza a new symbol is taken up, the child
as microcosm. This does not spring out of the first two lines but is
a fresh start, and the two parts of the stanza thus created are not
successfully integrated. It is significant that the sounds clash: the
rhyme-words 'me' and 'see' chime dissonantly against 'seed', and the
off-rhyme 'seed' and 'blood' seems not to accord with the tonality of
the poem.

In stanza 2, the microcosm idea is amplified by parallel clauses which do not quite do their work. There is a faint Shakespearean echo in the platitudinous 'multitudinous' stars—the connection with 'multitudinous seas' prompting the oceanic images which follow. The third line fills out the stanza by adding a phrase alliterated to give it life, but lacking in precision:

> There *swam* the *sliding* continents.

Motion in respect of what? Surely this is not an early reference to the hypothesis of continental drift? Are the continents 'sliding' through air but also 'swimming' because surrounded by water? In the next two lines the segmented phrasing is not rhythmically strong, and the last line leaves us suspended between three possible meanings:

> and love that knew not its beloved.

I presume that this means that the unborn child did not know whom it would love in the future. But this idea is blurred by other possible interpretations: that the child did not yet know its mother; or that the mother held within herself love for the child she did not yet know. An unresolved triplicity of possible meaning could, of course, be the precise intention of the poet; but there is nothing to suggest that this is so.

By the third stanza the poet has sunk into deeper difficulty. An O-exclamation tries to give the poem a new impulse, producing an infelicitous tricycle of sound, O-o-o, in the first line. The difficulty of seeing the syntax of this stanza, or grasping it when it is read aloud, reveals that something is wrong.

> O node and focus of the world;
> I hold you deep within that well
> you shall escape and not escape—
> that mirrors still your sleeping shape;
> that nurtures still your crescent cell.

The child—now an embryo awaiting birth—is 'node and focus of the world' and this 'node and focus' is in a well. The well 'mirrors' (reflects in water? conforms in shape to?) the child's 'sleeping shape'. One has to scratch up tentative meanings, which prove unsatisfactory. Evidently the poet was worried about this intractable stanza, because in the 1963 selection entitled *Five Senses* she attempted a re-punctuation, which created the appearance of new logical connections, but without clarifying the sense or making it move more naturally:

> O node and focus of the world—
> I hold you deep within that well
> you shall escape and not escape—

> that mirrors still your sleeping shape,
> that nurtures still your crescent cell.

Is it now the world that 'mirrors' the sleeping shape and nurtures the crescent cell, as a macro-womb? The poet abandoned this unprofitable 1963 revision in the 1965 Australian Poets selection, which goes back to the original version.

In the last stanza, a partial recovery gets under way, but even here the parataxis and parallelism suddenly get out of hand and set up a thumping burlesque rhythm with an inappropriate House-that-Jack-Built effect:

> I am the earth, I am the root,
> I am the stem that fed the fruit . . .

I have been pulling rather gracelessly at the fabric of this poem because I think it shows how some failure, however slight, in the poet's intuitive grasp of the theme has spreading ill-effects which ingenuity cannot fully overcome. Meanings, images, syntax, phonic texture, versification do not grow perfectly together; there are hairline cracks, and bits of patchwork. Nevertheless, we do respond to the imaginative riches of the poem: the possibilities of the theme, the images, the symbolism, *are* actualized to a considerable extent, whether or not I am right in the foregoing analysis of certain defects.

At a certain point in the career of most poets the first *élan* ceases. There is a time of re-assessment: a need to deepen or widen one's range, a change in values or emphasis. The passage from one state to another is often through darkness and bafflement. Sometimes the poetic solution lies precisely in including this experience of defeat within a new victory. This seems to me to happen in some of the fine later poems of Judith Wright, such as 'Phaius Orchid' and 'The Forest', where it is not only a metaphysical search that is expressed but also the sense of being foiled in that search. The best of Judith Wright's later poetry is not an attempt to reproduce the 'primitive' intensity of the earlier successes but represents the emergence of a more critical awareness, and a fuller conscious control. 'For My Daughter' is a return to the subject-matter of 'Woman to Child'; it is better articulated, though not as sensuously rich. 'Sports Field' develops an extended allegory, which is not a mode used earlier. It has a poignancy which is a gift of the experienced heart. In *The Other Half* (1966), 'Portrait' and 'Naked Girl and Mirror' and 'A Document' stand for a continuing conquest of personal experience— I must admit that I shy away from some other poems which go on about poetry and being a poet. A close formal analysis of the best of the later work would certainly reveal some continuity with the earlier work, but also some difference in spirit, reflected in change and development in method and organization.

1968

NOTES

1 But this is not strictly accurate: Moses was not permitted to enter the Promised Land. He died in sight of it, and was buried in the land of Moab, 'but no man knows the place of his burial to this day' (Deut. xxxiv. 6).

2 Her comments on O'Dowd's 'demagogic rationalism' in chapter 5 of *Preoccupations in Australian Poetry* (Melbourne, 1965) indicate how little sympathy she has with this strain.

3 In stanza 5, the statement introduced by 'while' is made an independent sentence, 'while' losing its normal subordinating function and being a mere coordinator, by a natural licence of usage.

4 The stanzas also fall naturally into couples, with the exception of stanza 3, which stands on its own. It is devoted to making explicit the analogy underlying the rest of the poem. The additional (superfluous ?) character of this stanza, with its slightly officious explanation by slightly strained phrasing ('mad apocalyptic dream' is questionable, and the inversion of 'slaves' and 'team' just a little awkward), seems evident. If I seem to be peering at the structure with niggling pedantry, my excuse is that I want to show how, when Judith Wright is at the height of her inspiration, there is an extraordinary intuitive coherence.

5 The word 'oh' here is so spelt because it is a natural speech usage, not a poetical-rhetorical booster. For this second use, of more dubious value, the poet usually reserves the spelling 'O', as in the last stanza of 'Bullocky', and often elsewhere. In 'South of My Days' both forms are used, 'O' for a literary, 'oh' for a colloquial, purpose. It must be admitted that several poets at this time, including myself, were a little too much given to manufacturing O-antiphons!

6 For the term 'word-build' and the special use of terms like 'trochaic' and 'iambic' in application to the stress-profile of words, rather than to their place in metrical patterns, see pages 54-5.

7 I hope I am right in reading 'labourer' as 'lab'rer' as in the common pronunciation. My point is not much weakened if a trisyllabic reading is preferred.

D

'This Fabled Grace'

THE POETRY OF ROSEMARY DOBSON

IN some poetry the sense of the fineness of artistic organization is a particularly important part of what is conveyed. Among Australian poets Rosemary Dobson's work has always attracted me by this aesthetic quality. I have found more enjoyment in reading and re-reading it than in reading most of my Australian contemporaries. This is true, I know, for quite a number of people besides myself. But wide appreciation of her work has not resulted in many critical essays about her. It is not easy in fact to write about her work. It speaks for itself: not only in what it explicitly says, but also in what it elusively suggests. Nevertheless, I am determined to try to act as an interpreter, to quicken further appreciation. But this is not a comprehensive treatment, merely a response to certain aspects.

In the volume called *The Ship of Ice* (1948) there is a poem called 'Still Life', written when her talent was reaching its first maturity.

> Tall glass, round loaf and tumbled cloth
> And leaning flask of smoky brown,
> The guttered candle and the cask;
> And Time and Silence flowing down,
>
> Welling against the canvas, held
> By stroke and feather-touch of paint
> As one might build a weir to hold
> Some spreading pool in sweet restraint.
>
> Whose was the hand that held the brush?
> And who the guest who came to break
> The loaf which I, three hundred years
> Belated, still reach out to take?
>
> I, who now pour the wine and tilt
> The glass, would wish that well you fare,
> Good sir, who set out food and drink
> That all who see might take and share.

Perfect, except in the eighth line where the vague gesturing use of the word 'some' has been picked up from the bad habit of certain poets, and the word 'sweet' has got a bit tired from the amount of work other poets have made it do.

The poem begins with three lines of pure visual representation, but continues throughout to keep us aware of the physical presence of the picture. Things or impressions are placed with effortless rightness within the logical-grammatical space framed by the verse: there is room enough around them but not too much. The first line presents three objects, the second one, the third two. One might think there is nothing in this: after all, if one is naming objects they have to occur in some order and phrasing. But one has only to look at the work of someone who lacks an instinctive sense of how to dispose things in verbal space to see that a special faculty is involved.

The size and structure of words are also used with instinctive rightness.[1] Throughout the first eight lines there is a series of 'trochaic'-sloping two-syllabled words that refer to some sort of process and create an impression of held movement: 'tumbled', 'leaning', 'guttered', 'flowing', 'welling', 'spreading'. All the other two-syllabled words are of the same 'trochaic' build ('smoky', 'candle', 'Silence', 'canvas', 'feather') so that when the 'iambic'-formed word 'restraint' comes at the end, it comes with appropriate and distinct effect. Again we might think there is nothing in this: of course most words are of one or two syllables, and two-syllabled words are more commonly 'trochaic' in build than 'iambic'. But the fact remains that there are poets for whom words come particularly right because they have a working sense of the expressive value of varying 'word-build', even when they are not consciously attending to it. So in the later two stanzas: the monosyllables first pick out a tune faintly reminiscent of nursery rhyme ('Whose was the hand that held the brush?/And who the guest who came to break . . .'); and then they continue on in graceful simplicity, with the sole exception of two adjoining and logically related 'amphibrach'-shaped formations: 'three hundred' and 'belated' which therefore become points of significant emphasis. It can be all accident; but you have to have a talent for the right accidents. A real artificer knows by feel when the words are coming right, and will sometimes consciously attend to such detail, working over it with minute care.

The poem falls into two main parts of two quatrains each. The internal proportioning is nicely varied: in the first half, the first three lines form a subdivision, and then the next five lines flow on to complete the pictorial effect; whereas in the second half the subdivision coincides with the quatrains. If one looks at the phrasing within these divisions and subdivisions, one sees that the line provides the basic rhythmic unit, and keeps the sense of definite shape, but there is just enough run-over phrasing to provide satisfactory variation. It is within this well-composed structure that the charac-

teristically refined and even slightly teasing phonetic texture provides its own kind of pleasure. Only two of the lines in the quatrains
are rhymed, but other relationships operate ('flask-cask', 'held-hold',
'brush-break', 'tilt-drink'). Of course, all words are built out of a
limited number of sounds, and any utterance has a 'texture' of *some*
kind, which will contain both repetitions and isolated occurrences
of particular sounds. But there are those poets for whom it comes
right, aided as need be by deliberate attention to detail; and there
are those for whom accident and effort add up to nullity; and
those, alas, for whom the accidents are always bad accidents.

But what is the poem about? What does it mean? In the Introduction she wrote to the selection of her poems in the Australian Poets
series (1963) Rosemary Dobson says:

> To a certain extent it is possible for a poet to give this information
> [what the poem is about] simply and satisfactorily, but I believe that at
> the centre of every poem there is a meaning which is supplied by the
> reader in collaboration with the poet, and different readers may find dif-
> ferent meanings, all equally valid, and all probably acceptable to the
> poet himself.

I am not entirely happy with this way of putting it, and the example
she herself gives, in discussing her poem 'The Raising of the Dead',
should not really encourage a reader to *supply* a meaning which the
poet would *probably* find acceptable. Readers should be firmly encouraged to find only the meanings that the poet provides, which are
there if the poet has succeeded in his undertaking. What her discussion does point to is that there can be a plurality of meanings,
which may in one poem rank from superficial to fundamental, and
may in another co-exist as equally valid aspects of a whole.

'Still Life' obviously describes a picture by an unknown seventeenth-century artist, and says that the modern viewer can receive
what the painter offers just as well as the first viewer did. But in
doing this the poem does much more. It shows us the objects in the
picture, arrested in stillness, as if out of time. The movement of the
poem serves not only to articulate the painter's composition but also
to register the movement of the beholder's mind, as it explores the
work of art and reacts to it and then goes on to sense the mystery of
the hospitality and the communion (the latent sacramental analogy
is surely discreetly intended) that the dead unknown painter still
provides under the species of the bread and wine that he painted
three centuries ago.

The poem recreates, in its own way, part of the problem Keats
tried to grasp in his 'Ode on a Grecian Urn'. Art defeats time by
arresting things within its still duration. But the triumph of art is at
a price: what it rescues—and gives back to us as an image of beauty

or truth or fulfilment—has been taken out of life; though we have it, we have it only in the mode of art, not in actuality. The bread feeds the spirit, but it cannot be grasped and broken and eaten; the wine cannot be poured and drunk. The way the poem reminds us of this distinction is paradoxically by seeming to ignore it, as if one could reach into the picture-space and break the loaf and pour the wine. Rosemary Dobson's poem confines itself to thus setting up the mysterious mind-bemusing relations between the beholder's space and time and that within the picture. It has nothing of the tragic quality of Keats's anguished oscillation between an actuality of warm, breathing, unfulfilled desire and an image of beauty and joy that is silent and cold. The tone of 'Still Life' is one of gratitude and courtesy, expressed in the slightly mannered idiom pleasantly used in the last three lines.

It is in contrast to the triumph over time expressed in this poem that some of the other poems insist on the threat and pathos of time passing. The first volume, *In a Convex Mirror* (1944) has this as a recurring theme. Among several poems one could quote is 'One Section':

At the first doorway a child with a jug held carefully,
The cat with its back arched to a query, and the knocker
A little too high for her hand.

At the next a girl who leant on the iron railing
In a parroty dress with eyes on the tipsy soldiers—
Hands full of bottles and roses, buying a paper.

At the third, with the curtain bellying out from behind her
A woman waiting for something, or nothing—in slippers,
One hand to her eyes to shade the dazzle from distance.

Will you believe what I saw in the late afternoon from the tramway,
Going up William Street from the Past to the Future?
Who can deny it was Death in the final doorway?

Shut, shut, with the wind blowing outside from inside,
The bulb removed from the socket under the lampshade,
And the Vacancy notice swinging loose in the window.

Each tram-stop up William Street marks a stage of life, and at each stop an emblematic figure is presented in a realistic manner, the incidental details being left discreetly suggestive, not manipulated into a definite allegory. The poem is very well handled. The feminine ending of all but two of the lines works in place of rhyme, and also allows the two masculine endings to give unobtrusive variation. The danger of a monotonous list ('At the first' . . . 'At the next' . . . 'At the third') is overcome by the different cast of the rhetoric in the last two lines of the fourth stanza: two arresting questions, followed by the flat repetition of 'Shut, shut' and the final phrases without a principal clause. The poem obviously does not offer itself as a definitive statement about life in general, but as a view, an impression, a tremor of intuition. One notices also that the inner dynamics of the poem include a tension between the observer's consciousness in the tram and the living tableaux observed like pictures.

The curious effect obtained in 'Still Life' by seeming to abolish the difference between the reality within the picture, and our actuality outside it is one that has fascinated Rosemary Dobson. A somewhat analogous effect is gained where the different reality is not a painting but memory: things or people standing in the past, seen clearly as if still there. In a poem called 'Family Progress' (in *The Ship of Ice*) the device of movement in space representing movement in time is applied to memory. We move on a path from the stables down to the orchard and at each turn of the path some family recollection appears:

> Perhaps Cousin Rose shied trembling to the right
> When William's arm stole slyly round her waist
> Without preliminary proprietaries—
> Through the high grass she ran, one hand to heart,
> Till at last, pushing back the ivy-leaves,
> She cooled her blushes at the water-butt.

Farther down the path:

> Then we go on again till James has grown—
> See those dark trees that we avoid—almost a man,
> He took his gun there once and shot himself:
> No, no one quite knew why.

The poet is very good at catching the turn and tone of colloquial speech when she needs it.

One must not so insist on Rosemary Dobson's excellence as artificer, nor on the affinities with painting and other crafts that enter into the thematic material of some of her poetry, that we give a restricted impression of the range of her themes and styles, or of the depth of personal feeling that some of her poems contain. In her work intense and passionate feeling is at times expressed very clearly, but always with a certain decorum and civility which I find wholly admirable. It reminds me of the chastity of expression even in the most poignant things of Mozart, after which an encounter with some nineteenth-century emotionalized music can make one feel one is being interfered with. This quality emerges in a poignant group of poems dealing with childbirth and the loss of a child: including the two poems called 'The Birth' that end *Child with*

Cockatoo, and 'To Meet the Child' in *Cock Crow*. But I shall give
an example taken from a different area of feeling, to which Rosemary Dobson has drawn attention in the Introduction from which
I have already quoted. It concerns the title-poem 'Cock-crow':

> In 'Cock-crow', for example, I have tried to give some idea of the
> dilemma of the poet who, because she is a woman, has responsibilities
> which must absorb her and draw her away from her preoccupation
> with the making of poetry. This is a problem which every woman poet
> or creative artist must work out for herself.

It is a special case of the more general experience people can have of
being trapped in legitimate demands and denied self-realization.
The poem is very clear: it enacts its real but symbolic movements
with a matter-of-fact terseness: the shutting of the door on going out,
the walk to-and-fro between the house and the bridge, the opening
of the door again to go inside. Such movements, even slight ones,
within a poem create a kind of dynamics which can hold and guide
the mind, when a static diffusion of sentiments might fail to keep
our attention.

> Wanting to be myself, alone,
> Between the lit house and the town
> I took the road, and at the bridge
> Turned back and walked the way I'd come.
>
> Three times I took that lonely stretch;
> Three times the dark trees closed me round;
> The night absolved me of my bonds;
> Only my footsteps held the ground.
>
> My mother and my daughter slept,
> One life behind and one before,
> And I that stood between denied
> Their needs in shutting-to the door.
>
> And walking up and down the road
> Knew myself, separate and alone,
> Cut off from human cries, from pain,
> And love that grows about the bone.
>
> Too brief illusion! Thrice for me
> I heard the cock crow on the hill
> And turned the handle of the door
> Thinking I knew his meaning well.

It is always remarkable to me that Rosemary Dobson can use or
omit rhyme freely but keep such a definite sense of lyric shape. The
first and last quatrains vary from the rhyme-scheme of the rest of

the poem. The effect of the absence of true rhyme in the first stanza is to enhance the matter-of-factness of tone. The assonance 'hill:well' in the last quatrain reinforces the invitation to dwell on the meaning of the cock-crow: there is a slight indefiniteness, which does not, however, stop the last cadence from being conclusive.

The poem 'Jack' also in *Cock Crow* opens up the same theme: the jack-in-a-box is an image of the inner self 'coffined up in life' and longing for the chance to get out.

There are aspects of Rosemary Dobson's work which I have not considered here, including her sense of comedy. My chief concern is with the question of meaning which these pellucid poems often raise: a meaning within the meaning, or haunting the meaning, a feeling that what the poem says or does is only a way of conveying something else which is ineffable—an awareness of being, a sense of a mystery, a paradisal rareness—momentarily glimpsed, caught in the still surface of the words or suffused through the apparent subject. It is fairly overt in such different enchantments as 'Country Morning' and 'The Conversation' and 'The Mirror' and 'Dew, Frost and Snow', which are among her best poems. It seems dissolved into the rococo elegance of 'Azay-le-Rideau', a poem ostensibly no more than the heart's dialogue with past beauty, occasioned by a visit to the *château* of that name in the Loire valley, a poem apparently existing mainly for the aesthetic pleasure which the verbal artistry yields, and yet: what *is* it about? Ah, listen:

> What lutes, what notes, what waterfalls of music,
> Voices of summer dying on the wind;
> From the carved balustrades, the formal gardens
> The murmuring laughter eddies to its end.
> Over the paving-stones the lingering crimson,
> Linden and gold, a burden of brocade;
> In the stitched meadows of a thousand flowers
> Pensive as listeners to a silent music
> They dream, enchanted, in the close-leaved shade.
>
> Oh idle hands beneath the falling fountain,
> Gloved fingers resting on the marble urn,
> Hands that withdrew, that speak, that lie together
> Folded like wings upon a shaft of stone.
> Distant as figures dancing in a landscape
> This fabled grace gives back its youth to Age,
> Prisoned and held upon a web of canvas
> Or shut for ever in a Book of Hours
> Between the enamelled and the gilded page.

It is in such work that one feels the force of Johnson's distinction in the *Rambler* (no. 92) between those matters with which the critical interpreter can deal, 'those means of pleasing which depend upon known causes and rational deduction' and those matters in which the finest analysis ends at a loss, 'the nameless and inexplicable elegancies which appeal wholly to the fancy, from which we feel delight . . .' The style of comment I have used in this essay is meant to encourage a critical attentiveness, from which the poems can only gain, and which assures us that we can trust the enchantments, because they are grounded in intelligence and moral care and good workmanship.

1973

NOTE

1 As in the essay on Judith Wright, I am using metrical terms in a secondary sense to describe 'word-build', as explained on page 54.

The dynamics of verse

IN common usage the idea of a poem involves the patterning of language. Patterning can take various forms, and I am not concerned to be prescriptive or restrictive; but I will confine myself to English verse and the standard kind of patterning which has predominated in it. This kind of patterning is called metrical, and the metrical system used can be designated accentual-syllabic.

English metrical verse is a patterning that takes place in the sound of words; and of all the elements that make up the sound of words only one is used for the purpose of patterning, namely variations of stress. To understand how ordinary English verse is organized we need no more than to understand two concepts, 'metrical pattern' and 'variations of stress', to keep them distinct from one another, and to see the way they are connected.

Patterning usually implies repetition of a unit or units according to some rule. Take for example a visual pattern, let us say a black-and-white check. The unit may be stated as a black square and white square adjoining, and this is repeated in the same order in two dimensions.

Note that a pattern of this sort is a semi-abstract thing; it is a set of specifications, which refers to physical arrangements but exists prior to and independent of any particular actualization in a physical medium: on a chessboard, in a dress, by tiles on a floor, in print on a page.

Note also that the rules of a pattern can be expanded to admit variation, either regularly or irregularly: for example the check pattern could admit the substitution of another colour for black at fixed intervals, or at random.

Metrical pattern is similarly a semi-abstract thing, a formula. There is a unit of repetition, and certain variations are allowed at will.

The units of repetition used to make standard English verse are five and only five. They are called 'feet' as in Greek and Roman verse, and their names have been borrowed from the same source: iamb, trochee, anapest, amphibrach, dactyl. These feet are composed on definite principles: there are either two or three components in the foot, neither more nor less; one and only one of these components is the 'metrical accent' (marked /) the other component or components being designated as 'unaccented' (marked x). Each foot

48

is characterized by the number of its components, two or three, and by the position of the unaccented components relatively to the metrical accent. In diminishing frequency of occurrence the units available for metrical patterning in English are these five feet:

disyllabic
- x /   iamb
- / x   trochee

trisyllabic
- x x /   anapest
- x / x   amphibrach
- / x x   dactyl

By the repetition of one of these units one of the normal English metres is produced. The commonest metre is iambic, and the commonest lines are of three, four or five feet. Metrical variation is provided under the rules by allowing any of the other four feet to be substituted at will. 'Substitution of feet' is the proper description, because a variation is not normal and within the rules unless scansion reveals it to be one of the other four feet (that is, it will consist of two or three components, neither less nor more, and one and only one of these will be a metrical accent).

If this is the nature of metrical pattern in English, the question then is: in what physical medium is this pattern actualized? The answer is that it is actualized in *Variations of stress*. Every spoken syllable has some degree of stress: weaker than, or stronger than, or roughly equal to the adjoining syllables. If we take a natural pronunciation of a single word and assign four numerical values from weakest to strongest, we can see a stress profile emerging:

2   3   1   4   1 1
uncomplimentary

Note that in this discussion a degree of stress is a property of every spoken syllable, so that we will not speak of stressed and unstressed syllables but of relatively strong and relatively weak degrees of stress. Note also that stress, being a feature of actual speech, is variable, within limits, according to different speakers and their sense of the semantic and rhetorical requirements.

If we now take a line of verse as an example we can see how stress-variation actualizes the pattern. This is an iambic line to which I give a stress profile as shown (though different speakers might wish to modify this somewhat without disturbing the metre):

x /   x / x   /   x / x /
2   4   1 4 1   2   1 3   1 4
Must all | tradit|ion then | be set | aside |
(Dryden)

The 'components' of the iambic foot are now seen as metrical values assigned to syllables. The iambic pattern (unaccented-accented) is actualized in a row of syllables by a weaker-stronger relation of syllables within each foot. Specifically, any one of these ratios will actualize the iambic pattern: 1,2; 1,3; 1,4; 2,3; 2,4; 3,4.

In many cases roughly equal degrees of stress will occur within the foot (that is, approximately 1,1; 2,2; 3,3; 4,4). It is a matter of observation that equal stress satisfies the mental expectation set up by the iambic pattern. So the rule can be stated that *equal degrees of stress satisfy the prevailing metrical pattern.* For example:

$$x \ / \ x \ / \ x \ / \ x \ / \ x \ /$$
$$2 \ 2 \ 4 \ 4 \ 14 \ 1 \ 1 \ 1 \ 4$$
Or o'er | cold coff|ee trif|le with | the spoon |
(Pope)

Metrical variation by substitution of feet can occur at will, but in practice some forms of substitution are preferred and some positions of the line are more favoured. This line illustrates two common variations:

$$/ \ x \ \ x \ / \ \ x \ / \ x \ / \ xx \ /$$
Labour | and rest | that equ|al per|iods keep |
(Pope)

Two minor rules complete the system. In iambic verse a 'feminine' ending can be produced by an unaccented syllable which is conventionally regarded as 'hypermetrical' or not counting:

$$x \ / \ \ x \ / \ \ x \ / \ \ x \ / \ \ x \ / \ (x)$$
Farewell | thou art | too dear | for my | possessing |
(Shakespeare)

On the other hand in trochaic verse a 'masculine' ending is produced by dropping the unaccented last syllable, making the line 'catalectic':

$$/ \ x \ \ / \ x \ \ / \ x \ /$$
Queen, and | huntress, | chaste and | fair |
(Jonson)

'Catalexis' is a functional peculiarity of trochaic verse, and does not provide the basis for inventing a monosyllabic foot. Standard English verse has no monosyllabic feet. Remember that feet are basic *units of repetition*: there are no one-syllable units of repetition in standard verse, and any monosyllabic variation, outside the case of catalexis, is irregular, exceptional, and very rare.

One further observation must also be supplied. In some cases a line may admit more than one possible sort of stress-profile if the words were read without regard to the fact that they are occurring in a passage of verse. The good reader is a pattern-seeking reader, who will let the prevailing metre guide him to the most suitable reading. This does not mean that the stress-profile is to be distorted: it is the poet's business to see that the metrically required reading is also that which will give the best meaning and emphasis. For example, this line in Shakespeare's Sonnet 40, if looked at out of context might suggest a doggerelish reading:

> Then if for my lòve thou my lòve recèivest

but when it is read in context, the iambic pattern guides us to make the most of the verbal play intended by the poet:

$$\text{x}\ /\quad \text{x}\quad /\quad \text{x}\quad /\quad \text{x}\ /\quad\ \text{x}\ /\ (\text{x})$$
> Then if | for my | love thou | my love | receivest |

The above method of analysis will work for any line of standard English verse. It is simple, consistent, and adequate. It invents no unnecessary entities. It creates no confusion. Confusion arises only if we fail to keep distinct the two categories and the terminology belonging to each: (1) metrical pattern, involving the terms 'accent', 'unaccented', 'foot'; (2) variations of stress, the syllable being the bearer of a degree of relative stress, weaker or stronger, and the line being a row of syllables with a stress profile.

It is strange what tenacious prejudices and what passions can be disclosed in metrical discussions. One might think that to offer a simple consistent and adequate account of the way the largest part of English poetry is metrically organized would evoke mild gratitude. But in fact there are two common forms of resistance.

One comes from people who feel that there is something wrong, reactionary, and undesirable about such a formal analysis of verse. They are opposed in *policy*—a policy connected with phrases like 'creative spontaneity', 'free expression', 'organic form', and so on. It is especially unfortunate when this prejudice is found among teachers. For if the main body of English poetry involves formal patterning as an essential ingredient, and if this patterning is produced by a particular use of speech-sound, how is the student to be brought closer to the experience of poetry as live utterance if he or she is discouraged from any real understanding of the nature of metrical sound-patterning?

The other main form of resistance comes from within the formalist camp. It consists of a tenacious clinging to two pseudo-metrical fictions produced chimera-like by a confusion between the categories of 'metre' and 'stress': namely the so-called spondee and the so-called pyrrhic. The doctrine of these dissenters is that equal strong stress within the foot can be properly explained only by inventing a two-accent foot (//), and equal weak stress within the foot can be properly explained only by inventing a no-accent foot (xx).

But attempts to validate spondees and pyrrhics are unnecessary, first, because the rule that equal stress-values satisfy the prevailing pattern works quite adequately. Again, spondees and pyrrhics are anomalies in the system, (a) because they contradict the structural principles of the other feet (that there is one accent and one only, and that the position of the syllables in respect of each other matters), and (b) because they are not, as the five true feet are, units of repetition, since there is no such thing as spondaic or pyrrhic verse in English. Moreover, equality is an approximate measure, variably estimated by different speakers and an insecure basis for fixing new metrical units. Finally, our experience of stress equality in a line is not in fact an experience of the substitution of new feet but simply the satisfaction of prevailing expectations in a particular way.

Having established a precise and limited meaning for 'metre', we can reserve the word 'rhythm' for a different use. Let rhythm stand for the sum effect of the factors governing the movement of the line when actually spoken in some particular instance. A line does not have an absolutely fixed rhythm, the same for all speakers, in the way that it has a definite metre. But a natural and appropriate reading of the line will, while satisfying the metre, be true to phonetic usage, and responsive to the semantic, syntactical and rhetorical requirements. Good readings will therefore vary only within limits. The best reading of the first line of *Paradise Lost* has been much discussed, and no one true rendering can be precisely prescribed; but it is arguable that logical and rhetorical considerations favour an approximation to the following stress-profile:

$$2 \quad 4 \quad 3 \quad 3^1 4 \, ^2 \quad 1 \quad 1 \quad 4$$
Of man's first Disobedience, and the Fruit

Rhythm, being the way the line moves, clearly involves first of all the two factors we have already correlated: metrical pattern and stress profile. An endless variety of rhythms can be produced on a single metrical basis by different dispositions of stress. Consider the following iambic pentameter lines, metrically the same, but so different because of the stress profiles (the main peaks of stress are indicated):

$$3 \quad 4 \quad 4 \quad 3 \quad 3 \quad 4$$
He cried cock, cock, and gave a sudden start.
(Dryden)

$$4 \quad 4 \quad 4 \quad 4$$
A pleasurable feeling of blind love
(Wordsworth)

$$4 \quad 4 \quad 4 \quad 4 \quad 3 \quad 4 \quad 1 \quad 3 \quad 4 \quad 4$$
Slow, slow, fresh fount, keep time with my salt tears
(Jonson)

('Fresh' and 'salt' are upgraded in emphasis by being in significant contrast.) The main peaks of stress can give an effect comparable to 'beat' on music. The rest of the line tends to hang from these points, and a good reading is one which uses these points of emphasis or propulsion to give a natural swing:

$$\overset{4}{\text{In pious}} \overset{4}{\text{times ere priest}} \overset{3}{\text{craft did begin,}}$$

$$\overset{4}{\text{Before poly}} \overset{4}{\text{gamy was made a sin}} \dots$$

(Dryden)

One of the remarkable effects possible in iambic pentameter verse is the overlaying of the metrical *ti-tum ti-tum* pattern by a rolling triple movement:

$$\overset{4}{\text{Tomorrow}} \overset{4}{\text{and tomorrow}} \overset{4}{\text{and tomorrow}}$$

(Shakespeare)

$$\overset{4}{\text{Endangered}} \overset{4}{\text{by a brother}} \overset{4}{\text{and a wife}}$$

(Dryden)

But rhythm is governed by more factors than metre and stress. The other determinants are *phrasing* and *variable pace*. By phrasing I mean the grouping of words, and the breaks or pauses, slight or marked, required for a reading that is responsive to the semantic, syntactical and rhetorical requirements. The voice must *dissect* the line, revealing its significant *articulation*, while keeping the general flow. By variable pace I mean that a good reading involves a continual *rubato*, slackening and quickening, shortening and drawing out, so that meaning and feeling take full effect.

When modern critics and poets complain, as some do, of the mechanical character or lack of variety imposed by writing in traditional metres one can only conclude that they have never learnt how to read or write verse so as to realize its marvellous combination of freedom and order, naturalness and art.

This is perhaps the appropriate point to mention enjambment (from the French *enjambement*, 'straddling'). The main structural member of a poem is the line, and no reading that obscures or obliterates the line-structure is a good reading. The voice may pass over more or less quickly to the next line—that is a matter of judgement in each particular instance. But enjambment is not a signal requiring us to rush over to the next line. Essentially it is a grammatical occurrence: a phrase remains obviously incomplete, and the mind is left in suspension awaiting the completion. Usually this will make desirable a fairly rapid transition to the next line—but not always or necessarily: the voice may hang back for heightened effect. Consider this passage from Tennyson's 'Godiva':

> The little wide-mouth'd heads upon the spout
> Had cunning eyes to see: the barking cur
> Made her cheek flame: her palfrey's foot-fall shot
> Light horrors thro' her pulses: the blind walls
> Were full of chinks and holes; and overhead
> Fantastic gables, crowding, stared: but she
> Not less thro' all bore up, till, last, she saw
> The white-flower'd elder-thicket from the field
> Gleam thro' the Gothic archway in the wall.

If 'rhythm' is reserved for the sum of the effects of metre, stress, phrasing, and pace, then we still need an all-embracing term for the sum total of the ways in which physical energy is expended in spoken verse. This may usefully be called the physical *dynamics* of verse. It consists of rhythm, as defined above, plus the phonetic characteristics of the speech sounds: that is, the pitch and quality of the vowels, and the quality of the consonants. These make up phonetic texture. In this category, particular mention should be made of the varied pitch of vowels, which provides the intonation or tune of the line. Pitch in spoken English operates normally within a fairly narrow band as compared with singing. The sense of 'melody' that verse conveys varies widely: in some verse it is not particularly noticeable, in other cases it is quite important; in general it becomes more evident as the poetry approaches the condition of song-lyric.

The progression from metre to rhythm to total physical dynamics brings us to the limits of the physical aspect of poetry. What remains is to observe the multiple interrelations between the phonic system of a poem and the semantic and syntactical elements, as well as the rhetorical or expressive requirements. There is labyrinthine scope here for the linguistic analyst. I want to mention only two obvious features of practical importance to the poet and the reader.

The first is the effect of what I call 'word-build'. From a purely metrical point of view, the line is merely a row of syllables, not a row of words. Yet our experience of the line includes the recognition that it is made up of words, each of which has its own physical form, its own stress-profile. A poet uses this factor consciously or subconsciously, some poets more noticeably than others. I will give only three examples here. Dryden uses the 'trochaic' slope of the two-syllable words in the following line where they are placed athwart the foot-divisions of the iambic line:

> To *lone*|ly *wea*|ry *wand'*|ring trav|ellers |

The psycho-physical effect would be different if the words coincided with the feet in a trochaic passage. Pope uses the important monosyllabic and disyllabic words in the following line in a particular pattern for balance and point:

> They *shift* the *moving Toyshop* of their *Heart*

Herrick employs a word, piquantly borrowed from the vocabulary of science, which ripples out most noticeably in a context of one- and two-syllable words:

> The *liquefaction* of her clothes.

The second feature I want to mention is that though syntax is one of the least regarded elements in the complex of expressive means the poet has at his disposal, it has particularly intimate relations with rhythm because it is a main determinant of phrasing. So stated, this is a mere truism, but the practical implications for the working poet go wide and deep.

1972

E

The languages of poetry

HERE are two lines of verse taken out of context, which any reader might be pardoned for not being able to place from memory:

> Pearl-shells and rubied star-fish they admire,
> And will arrange above the parlour fire.

What might be guessed about them? It is hard to imagine a pre-eighteenth-century poem which would contain them. An early eighteenth-century date is possible, for the first line has something of an 'Augustan' feel about it; but the more informal movement and tone of the second line might make one doubtful. Further reason for doubt is that the people referred to are not merely taking a walk, admiring things in a well-bred way: they are poking about and collecting things in a manner rather beneath the comportment of gentlefolk, and therefore beneath the ordinary notice of the more Augustan sort of eighteenth-century poet—unless these lines fit into some condescending pastoral or burlesque, which does not seem likely. Metre, language and meaning would incline one rather to guess that the couplet comes from some tame discursive piece, late-eighteenth or early-nineteenth century, called 'An Afternoon Excursion' or 'Descriptive Sketch'. A modern academic critic might give the lines good marks for concrete particularity (rubied star-fish, parlour fire) and for non-romantic non-elevation. He may, however, complain that the lines seem to lack complexity, irony and ambiguity—the constituents of an interesting *tension*.

In fact, the lines come from one of George Crabbe's most powerful passages, from Letter XXIII of *The Borough*, published in 1809. The poet presents us with a man condemned to be hanged. Crabbe is not in any doubt that hanging is proper and necessary; but he contemplates, with the soberly sensitive compassion so typical of him, the mental sufferings of the felon awaiting execution. First he establishes the unrelieved dread and despair which dominate the man's waking hours, destroying all other thought and feeling. Then he takes us into the man's dreams. Mainly they are troubled ones; but now comes a pleasant dream, in which the man is back in the innocent season of youth and young love, when he and his girl went out walking with another couple. The walk leads through the countryside to the seashore, where the scene is made visible to us by a few well-placed strokes. The young people look out towards the horizon and count the passing vessels—

> Ships softly sinking in the sleepy sea,

Paddling on the water's edge, they

> . . . search for crimson weeds, which spreading flow,
> Or lie like pictures on the sand below.

Our couplet occurs in this part of the dream-sequence, which immediately afterwards closes in disturbance, as outer reality forces its way into the dream, and the man awakes. The outer stimulus—the cry of the watchman—is at first translated into terms belonging to the dream, but not for long:

> Pearl-shells and rubied star-fish they admire,
> And will arrange above the parlour fire, —
> Tokens of bliss! — 'Oh! horrible! a wave
> Roars as it rises — save me, Edward! save!'
> She cries:— Alas! the watchman on his way
> Calls, and lets in—truth, terror, and the day!

The concentrated power of the last line comes first from its internal organization: the dramatic suspension after the first syllable, and then the figure called zeugma, which brings the three disparate objects of the verb into such close contact as to create a composite reality: 'truth, terror, and the day'.

The other reason for the line's power does not lie in itself but is structural. Crabbe has laid the foundation of dread in first describing the condemned man's despair. Having done so, he lures us along an excursus into the dream of an innocent past, until the attentive reader almost forgets, as the dreamer quite forgets, the grim awaiting reality. Then before the distracting absorption is complete, the poet allows the horror, which has thus been held back, to recoil with dreadful force.

This strategy could not have been executed so well in most kinds of prose narration. The economy which verse favours enables the poet to take us through the whole afternoon ramble of the young lovers in a few lines, where each detail is rendered more effective by the resources of sound and image.

The couplet we started with, when set back in its context, earns a far higher commendation, precisely through that direct simplicity which was all we could see in it when taken on its own. Now the words function as part of a structure of suspense—a structure which at the same time provides an implicit moral comment, in the contrast between innocent happiness and guilty suffering. The lines thus exhibit in their own way two of these three qualities I mentioned above as ones that modern criticism prizes highly: complexity and irony. They lack only that modern ambiguity which comes from un-easiness about one's standpoint and values. Crabbe knows where he stands, and has said so earlier:

> No! he must suffer: pity we may find
> For one man's pangs, but must not wrong mankind.

The tone is under complete control because the poet does have a firm standpoint and clear canons of judgement.

It is, of course, still possible for a negative critical opinion to be passed on the couplet and the surrounding passage. The average cultivated reader of an earlier age than Crabbe's might not have tolerated the poet's abandonment of the Augustan habit of using rhetorical devices for keeping class-differentiation visible: he would have wished for a treatment which kept the felon at a greater social distance, and was more condescending to the simple pleasure of lower-class courting couples. On the other hand, a reader with a taste for Romantic enthusiasm might be repelled by the sobriety and (almost) prosaic plainness of Crabbe's style. Where is the glamour? the veil of enchantment? the rush of exalted feeling? Where, more-over, is the awareness of symbolic potentialities? Where the relation of pearl-shell and star-fish and fire to the archetypes? Not here; and we know that many nineteenth-century readers could not abide Crabbe's realistic texture, however well suited it is to his exploration of human motives and feelings.

II

What I am attempting is really an essay in aid of an improved phenomenology both of poetry and of criticism. Let us keep close to particular texts, and the critical questions which they naturally provoke, even if this imposes a somewhat desultory movement on the argument.

Further away from current critical interest and preference is Wordsworth's remarkable poem, 'The Idiot Boy', which he com-posed in 1798 in the first flood of his great period of inspiration. Here are a few lines out of context:

> She's happy here, is happy there,
> She is uneasy everywhere;
> Her limbs are all alive with joy.

One simply does not know what to make of such lines when they are thus presented in isolation. Into what genre of poetry could they fit? They have a movement and slap-dash informality that would do for a poem like 'John Gilpin' or even for a broadsheet ballad. Yet they exhibit a turn of curious psychological observation which one would not expect to find in such poems. Are the lines serious, or meant to be ridiculous; is it pathos or bathos we are dealing with?

'The Idiot Boy' isn't a wholly successful poem. But it is an extraordinary one, very enjoyable when given a chance. The story concerns a mother's love for her mentally defective son. Since there is no one else to do the errand, the boy is set on a pony and sent off by night to fetch the town doctor. The poem tells of the boy's pleasure in riding the pony, his mother's agitation when he is lost for hours, and the happy reunion when he is found: the boy had forgotten his errand and had let his pony stray and feed at will.

No one before Wordsworth, in verse or prose—not even such different cultivators of sentiment, sensibility and benevolence as Cowper, Sterne, and Blake—would have attempted such a thing. The daring and enterprise required, the will to accept the risks involved, are still readily evident after one and two-thirds centuries—courage is one of the strongest factors in Wordsworth's genius. When Wordsworth classified his poems, he put this one into the group called 'Poems founded on the Affections'; justifiably, because we are invited to enlarge our sympathies to appreciate fully the mother's love for her son—even though she is a fairly simple sort of fusspot, and he is what we politely call retarded. But Wordsworth could equally well—or even better—have put his poem in the group of 'Poems of the Imagination', because another task he sets himself is to give us a sense of what the world seems like to the idiot boy.

Doubtless it is true that in writing this poem Wordsworth opened up a line of literary development that leads to Faulkner's *The Sound and the Fury*, and other fiction which accepts the point of view of the feeble-minded, or dopes and punchies, or infants below the threshold of intellectual responsibility. Doubtless, too, many such modern studies are vehicles for primitivism or anti-intellectualism. But Wordsworth has not in this poem surrendered to irrationalism. He doesn't assert or necessarily imply any disrespect for reason; he doesn't mean that idiocy is as good or better; still less that idiocy will save us. All the poem does is to invite us to take seriously the experiences of the boy and his mother. And the measure of our capacity to take them seriously is, paradoxically, our ability to share without reserve the high spirits and untrammelled energy of the poem.

It begins with an evocation of a clear moonlit night and the shouting of the owls. Because of the recurrence of these two images, the whole poem becomes a moon-drenched space echoing with owl-hoots. The movement of the verse is rapid, and the poet does not allow the words to be subjected to complex impulses or weighted with density of meaning. A reader accustomed to demand such inner tension and weighting of the expression may feel that here the words are running like unladen trucks. But the words are doing what the poet needs them to do. For instance, they enact the good-natured bustle and fret of the mother, who repeats things over and over in her anxiety and excitement, as simple folk do. Then they give us some sense of the delight of the boy seated on the pony. We are not taken *inside* the boy's mind—and yet the words give us, as it were obliquely, a sense of the boy's inner world:

> For joy he cannot hold the bridle,
> For joy his head and heels are idle,
> He's idle all for very joy.

The repetitiveness, and the simple charge of elementary meaning, have a particular and valuable use. Here now rides Johnny, his lips going burr-burr with pleasure:

> The owlets hoot, the owlets curr,
> And Johnny's lips they burr, burr, burr,
> As on he goes beneath the moon.

The three lines I first quoted from the poem occur when the mother is beside herself with joy after having found the boy safe after hours of anguished searching:

> She kisses o'er and o'er again
> Him whom she loves, her Idiot Boy;
> She's happy here, is happy there,
> She is uneasy everywhere;
> Her limbs are all alive with joy.

The language corresponds to an experience, both for the mother and the boy, that approaches pure sensation and feeling. Barely enough has been quoted here to enable the reader to become attuned to the special mood of exhilaration and sympathy which the poem tries to create, and which—with some lapses here and there—it quite remarkably achieves.

The tendency of my comment is plainly to suggest that we should not be too ready to limit the way in which language can acceptably be used in poetry. A narrative poem—both my examples so far have been of a narrative kind—requires a handling of words different from a meditative poem or a lyric. Wordsworth has used language to produce a highly original effect. Prose could not have done so well, lacking the pace and exhilarated rhythm and rhyme, and the daring things done with simple means. For example, at the very end, the boy's answer when asked what he was doing all night, and what did he see, simultaneously locks us out from his inner con-

sciousness by its confused inadequacy, and yet in its nursery-rhyme
topsy-turviness somehow gives us a hint:

> 'The cocks did crow to-whoo, to-whoo,
> And the sun did shine so cold!'

III

The two very different uses of language I have so far illustrated
are examples of a rather informal and plain poetic speech, close to
everyday use. Contemporary preference is for an ordinary-language
poetry. Fortunately this is not enforced with complete consistency:
poets who pass other tests are often given exemptions—and anyway
it is not all that clear what the limits of ordinariness are. Nevertheless the poet who professedly attempts a high style tends to find
critical feeling prepared against him. Milton's epic style, for
example, is often adversely criticized for what it does not try to do,
without sufficient consideration of what it does achieve.

The passage of Milton that I want to quote does not go much
beyond the resources of common vocabulary. It is high, formal and
elaborate rather in its tone, its syntactical organization, its large
cadences and rhetorical power. (The high style is often very simple
in its choice of words.) It comes in Book IV of *Paradise Lost*, when
night has fallen in Eden, and Adam and Eve are conversing before
they retire, not only to rest, but also to 'the Rites/Mysterious of con-
nubial love'. Eve says to Adam:

> With thee conversing I forget all time,
> All seasons and their change, all please alike.
>
> (639-40)

Then follows an aria of sixteen lines in which this simple idea is
repetitively expanded; using images already prepared for it by the
famous passage just beforehand, which begins 'Now came still
Ev'ning on'. In Eve's speech there is a markedly formal structure
of parallels between the elements of the first nine lines and those
of the concluding seven lines:

> Sweet is the breath of morn, her rising sweet,
> With charm of earliest Birds; pleasant the Sun
> When first on this delightful Land he spreads
> His orient Beams, on herb, tree, fruit, and flow'r,
> Glist'ring with dew; fragrant the fertil earth
> After soft showers; and sweet the coming on
> Of grateful Ev'ning milde, then silent Night
> With this her solemn Bird and this fair Moon,
> And these the Gems of Heav'n, her starrie train:
> But neither breath of Morn when she ascends

With charm of earliest Birds, nor rising Sun
On this delightful land, nor herb, fruit, flow'r,
Glist'ring with dew, nor fragrance after showers,
Nor grateful Ev'ning mild, nor silent Night
With this her solemn Bird, nor walk by Moon,
Or glittering Star-light without thee is sweet.

(641-56)

The images are not particularized, but rather remain very general. Clearly the poet is relying upon stock responses or habitual associations in using these images, and also upon his power of building a structure of tones and cadences which, though successive in time, creates in the mind the effect of harmony. I do not have to read the passage once for the music and once for the thought, as Eliot complained of Milton's verse—I have less difficulty with Milton in this respect than with Eliot—but I do find that the music is so powerful as to charm and compel assent.[1] One does not judge; the thing imposes itself.

Why this elaborate *aria di portamento*, which adds nothing to the basic meaning of the previous two lines? Why the carefully organized rhetorical formality, and the use of simple words in a conventional and highly generalized meaning?

The answer includes several considerations. Milton is ritualizing the scene and the speech. The first human pair are a paradigm of natural human behaviour. They are presented as an ideal type, and the love expressed for Adam by Eve is not rendered in the peculiarity of some individual consciousness, but as the general form to which pure affection tends. Moreover, the first pair are shown in a state of harmony with the entire cosmos, moving in accordance with its rhythms, delighted with its varied beauties, yet rising above it as the crown of creation, delighted more in each other. Finally, such extended passages as this have an effect of 'amplification', in the old sense of intensifying and rendering more impressive. I have called them arias (ignoring that arias have a ternary structure, not a binary one as here) because the rhythm and phrasing and diction act out in an enlarged and repetitive way the emotional impulses, developing melodic gestures, as an aria in music can do.

To reject the poetic method of this passage is really to object to certain uses of language, namely those which are ritualistic, ceremonious and exemplary. It is especially appropriate for Milton to proceed in this way here, because his subject is the unfallen state of humanity before 'experience' took over from 'innocence'. But Milton did not have to invent his method; it was already well-established for him in theory and practice by his masters: for example, Sidney with his view that the poet makes a 'golden' world from the materials supplied by our imperfect one; and Spenser with his ideal creations.²

Ah but, many modern readers will want to say, isn't this kind of poetry a one-sided simplification, and necessarily a lower achievement than a more densely concrete and complex realistic expression which does not idealize, and does include the disconcerting contradictions and imperfections of actual experience?

It is true that we require great literature to give us a sense that experience in all its contradictions has been faced. But there are various ways in which this may be done. For example, in Milton's large structure, the above passage in Book IV stands in telling contrast with Book IX, in which discord and disloyalty enter the marital relations of Adam and Eve. (Eve does *not* want to converse all day with Adam, and goes off on her own—and so it starts). The real issue is whether literature is to be allowed its high moments of ritual and exemplarism on proper occasions; and if not, why not?

One gets so tired in modern literature of the compulsion to give the bridegroom piles on his honeymoon; to show the priest thinking about his argument with Mrs Fenessy while saying Mass; or have the great statesman squeezing a pimple and examining the result in a mirror while considering whether to start a war. This thin, trivial and boring sort of irony and complexity is supposed to be the mark of an adult mind. It seems rather to be the very thing that adolescent minds arrive at, and pass through. The mark of an adult is to have surmounted the experience of complexity; not to have to call crumpets every time the sanctuary-bell is rung, not to have to demonstrate a callow knowingness, or protect every expression of feeling with the pitiful routines of 'irony'. The young mind and the mature mind can understand the value of the high style and the ideal instance: it is the adolescent in between, or the arrested adolescent, who may not yet have got beyond the disordering shock of complexity and sorted out his responses. There is an analogy between the way in which the ideal type is used in the sociology of Max Weber, as a means of mastering the flux of empirical detail, and the way the poet may seek to discern and express the important and constant features of his experience of value. What Shelley says of Athenian tragedy can have wider application: there are works which 'are as mirrors in which the spectator beholds himself, under a thin disguise of circumstance, stript of all but that ideal perfection and energy which every one feels to be the internal type of all that he loves, admires, and would become'.³ The fear that such transcendence of the accidental must produce a faceless generality by the absence of interesting texture and differentiated feeling is groundless, as is evident even in Milton's quite extreme example.

It was Spenser who showed Milton the way. Spenser's celebration of his own marriage day, 'Epithalamion', has always seemed to me one of the very great things in literature. But much of modern critical opinion is unsympathetic towards it. I would slightly adapt some remarks of Eliot for the occasion, and say that 'Epithalamion' is 'a type of verse for the appreciation of which we are not provided with the proper critical tools. We are therefore inclined to dismiss it, by reference to poetic criteria which do not apply'. Eliot's comment comes in an introduction to Kipling's verse, where he pleaded for a proper consideration of that writer's merits—a plea that was considered scandalous when it was made in 1941, though it has had a better hearing since—and he even goes on to say that before judging poems we should understand the type to which they belong, and should consider what the poet was trying to do, and what he was not trying to do.[4] This is using the language of intentions, about which difficulties are sometimes raised in critical theory; but the practical effect is sound and clear. It means that in judging a literary work we should give it a chance to speak to us on its own terms; but it also allows for the fact that in our final judgement we are not bound to assent uncritically to the author's intentions. There are times when we may be driven to say: Yes, he does this very well, but I don't think much of the kind of thing he is trying to do.

It is at this point that considerations other than purely literary ones are likely to be influencing our judgement. Since Kipling has been mentioned, his poem 'If' will serve as an example. In its own kind, the poem could not be improved: Kipling has stated in a form recognizable to common experience what being 'a man' consists in. The poem is true to reality—far truer than some poems whose literary rating is higher. If we dismiss it, what are we saying? Partly, no doubt, that we prefer a different *kind* of poem, one which gives us a more intimate and subtle sense of moral experience, instead of these general and typical precepts that have a rather coarse-grained vigorous public impressiveness. But I am willing to say this much, and still not dismiss the poem, because I think that in its own way it has real merit. If the critic goes further and rejects it, often sneeringly, isn't perhaps something else coming in: a dislike of the poet's implication that the good life is a life of strenuous commitment and action of the will; a dislike, in other words, of the moral outlook expressed in the poem, of the assumption that at each critical point in life there has to be a hard, uncomfortable simplicity, because one's yes has to be yes and one's no has to mean no?

To return to Spenser's 'Epithalamion': if I think it a very great poem it is because it is not only well done, but also thoroughly well worth doing. In celebration of his marriage day, the poet brings together (and the quality of the language is the medium in which this is done) the values present in the Western and Christian tradition which are relevant to the occasion. So the personal love between the pair, their clarified sensuality, their hopes of fruitfulness, and the accompanying sense of gladly fulfilling a ritual pattern which works outwards from the couple themselves through the social aspects of the solemnities and festivities to the cosmic order itself, an order like that of human marriage in which love, beauty, generation, harmony and rejoicing form a complex mystery whose ultimate meaning is in God. The cosmic dimension of the poem has recently been stressed by the demonstration that the poet has organized his unusual structure in accordance with a numerical symbolism whereby the poem is at once a representation of the shortest day of the year (the actual marriage day) and of the revolution of the heavens through a year.[5] This new feature of Spenser's complex art can be absorbed into one's reading of the poem, and is not mere external scaffolding. The poem, furthermore, has a range in time which includes elements of Roman marriage tradition, the nuptial imagery of the Hebrew Song of Songs, the courtly and popular levels of mediaeval tradition, and the 'modern' world— artistic, social, religious—of the Renaissance. The range of tone and rhetorical level is from the popular and colloquial to high solemnity, without loss of comprehensive unity. In and through all this Spenser makes the occasion of his marriage an ideal type, in which the authentic values of sexual love are splendidly celebrated.

What the poem does not do is to *directly* show these values encountering the weaknesses and adversities that cramp and flaw their fulfilment in the life-history of any couple. The critical question is whether Spenser's work loses value by not doing this. It would suffer, if one felt that the deliberate idealization was too glibly and emptily arrived at, lacking the authority that only a mature mind, tried by experience, can give. My difficulty is not to determine for myself whether the authority is there: my conviction of the poem's worth is immediate and indefeasible. The difficulty is, to explicate this conviction in terms acceptable to modern critical habits of mind, or to stretch those habits so as to induce them to take in new considerations. I would begin with the features of the poem already mentioned above, but also test the mature strength of the poem's relation to life by the tact and control it exhibits over the wide range of tone, the coherence into which the diverse strands are woven, the sureness with which every aspect of the occasion is handled in turn, not least those sentiments of festive joy and sensual happiness which are harder to manage than darker and more reflective moods. The exquisite refining of the 'Fescennine' or ritually obscene ele-

ment proper to marriage festivals is especially noteworthy. It is
along these lines that I would try to convince the objector that the
simplicity is not a false one, but a precious victory; that the artifice
is not an evasion of the human condition, but the fulfilment of
one of our needs in facing reality.

   In the end, continued disagreement would come down to an assertion on each side about the ways in which language can acceptably be used. Behind this sort of literary disagreement there seems
to lurk a disagreement about the way people should behave, what
is worth being interested in, the value of various attitudes and
commitments. Behaviour of language is not the same thing as personal behaviour; nor are they totally unrelated. Literary value is
not the same thing as moral and metaphysical rightness; nor are
they entirely unconnected. Spenser's poem is a good poem if it is all
right for a poet to extract from lived reality the great ritual pattern
he has grasped in it, and present it as such, though with the colouring and temperament peculiar to himself and his circumstances. If
not, not; but in that case one wants to know why: one wants to
uncover the ideological roots of the opposing prejudice.

   A happy opposite to Spenser's high conception is Suckling's
breezy colloquial description of a society wedding, from the assumed
viewpoint of a simple countryman. 'A Ballad Upon a Wedding' is
entertainment, compliment, raillery, and very pretty sensuousness;
it succeeds because it does not tangle with any wider or more serious
concerns. The light touch is carried through to the conclusion:

> At length the candle's out and out,
> All that they had not done, they do't:
>   What that is, who can tell?
> But I believe it was no more
> Than thou and I have done before
>   With Bridget, and with Nell.

   But Suckling's opposite is not a contradiction. What I need in
conclusion is an instance where my plea for tolerance of the various-
ness of poetical enterprises breaks down: where for me the performance is unacceptable, and the limit of tolerance reached. One
of Donne's wedding-poems, his 'Epithalamion made at Lincolnes
Inne' provides me with the example I need. It essays a middle level,
intermediate between Spenser and Suckling: a social vein, in which
what is required is a witty and gentlemanly assurance, with the religious values of the occasion within reach, while the need for Fescennine touches is nicely judged.

   Donne's attempt along these lines is a failure: the tone is wrong,
the taste abominable, the wit forced, frigid and at times repulsive.

Addressing the company, which is composed of London merchant families as well as of courtiers, the poet turns to the ladies:

> Daughters of London, you which bee
> Our Golden Mines, and furnish'd Treasurie,
> You which are Angels, yet still bring with you
> Thousands of Angels on your mariage daies . . .

The unpleasing pleasantry about dowry-hunting is not improved by the undertone of possible obscenity (compare the beginning of another poem, 'Love's Alchymie', 'Some that have deeper digged Love's mine than I'), and the familiar pun on angel (a gold coin). We are far away from Spenser's fresh and vital purity of tone:

> Tell me, ye merchants daughters, did ye see
> So fayre a creature in your towne before,
> So sweet, so lovely, and so milde as she,
> Adorned with beautyes grace and vertues store?

Donne's solecism may, for all we can tell, have passed for an elegant sally on the occasion, and in the company for which it was composed. If so, so much the worse for the company: it is still to me a clanger, not an example of a poised, mature, tough-minded, civilized, urbane 'stance' (to string the vogue-words together).

From this, he moves on to compare the church in which the pair are to be married to a belly hungry for their corpses when they are buried. This gastronomic theme is kept going by other touches, comparing love's delights to food. Then he tells the musicians they can pack up and go home to bed like 'all toyl'd beasts', and goes on to dilate upon an odd notion he has that animals go to bed at night to copulate—making 'dainty feasts' of it, of course. It needs a sudden awkward jerk to pull out of this unprofitable line back to the bride. In regard to her, Donne attempts an analogy between loss of virginity and martyrdom. As a man may submit to death in order to turn into a martyr, so a woman may lose her virginity in order to turn into a mother. Accordingly, the bride lies awaiting the bridegroom—

> Like an appointed lambe, when tenderly
> The priest comes on his knees t'embowell her . . .

By this time, we are not surprised to find that (whether for the want of another rhyme or for queerer reasons) the concluding lines seem to imply that loss of virginity = being maimed.

This is not a poem one would adduce in favour of Donne, whose greatness in other poems can look after itself. My point in quoting it is that, in rejecting the poem, I am not, I think, making a purely literary judgement. I shrink from Donne's social pleasantries as I would from someone's bad breath in my face, and I regard the way in which the erotic theme is developed as 'sick' art: which means that I find, not just the expression, but the attitudes thus expressed inappropriate and unacceptable. Some abler critic may be able to convince me that I am guilty of cross-eyed reading in this case. Yet my point holds, that the poetic uses of language are various; that we should try to accept the poet's work on its own terms; but that in the end every critic reaches a limit of tolerance, and that the limit is determined, at least in part, by one's basic outlook and standards of behaviour, that is, by considerations beyond literary ones.

1964

NOTES

1 T. S. Eliot, 'A Note on the Verse of John Milton', *Essays and Studies . . . of the English Association* (London, 1936).
2 Sidney, *The Defence of Poesy* (1595): 'Nature never set forth the earth in so rich tapestry as diverse poets have done, neither with so pleasant rivers, fruitful trees, sweet-smelling flowers, nor whatsoever else may make the too much loved earth more lovely: her world is brazen, the poets only deliver a golden.'
3 Shelley, *A Defence of Poetry* (1821).
4 T. S. Eliot, *A Choice of Kipling's Verse* (London, 1941).
5 See A. Kent Hieatt, *Short Time's Endless Monument: the Symbolism of the Numbers in Edmund Spenser's Epithalamion* (New York, 1960), pp. 16-30, 83-109; and 'The Daughters of Horus: Order in the Stanzas of *Epithalamion*' in W. Nelson (ed.), *Form and Convention in the Poetry of Edmund Spenser* (New York, 1961), pp. 103-21.

Edmund Spenser and George Eliot

A CRITICAL EXCURSION

I

ONE of the results of the study of literature should be that we can read the work of many different periods with an appreciation not wholly limited by our contemporary habits and demands. By trying to read the works of the past as nearly as possible on their own terms, we are not retreating from our own day. On the contrary, we are doing what is needed to make these works truly present, so that what is vital in them can still speak to us. For it belongs to a full human culture to extend our awareness of the past, as well as to have regard to the future. One sign that, in spite of everything, we are progressing is that we are increasingly able and willing to do both. Nor does this willingness to submit ourselves to the past mean that we abandon our right of finally judging works in accordance with our own present standards: it only means that we are making that judgement after giving the works in question a chance to reach us and disclose themselves.

It was in the context of these reflections that I first thought of bringing Edmund Spenser and George Eliot into unlikely conjunction.

In Cantos 9 and 10 of the Third Book of *The Faerie Queene* there is a story about a beautiful young woman unhappily married to a rich but withered and jealous old man. A young man arrives on the scene and the feelings of the wife are drawn towards him. As thus stated, this happens also to be the central story in George Eliot's *Middlemarch*, where the beautiful young Dorothea is married to the wealthy, but old and futile, scholar Casaubon, and cannot but be attracted towards the handsome young Will Ladislaw. Of course the whole treatment and development of the two stories is very different; though, as I shall try to show, there are certain problems of 'composition'—of combining disparate materials into a unity—faced by the two writers, which have an odd resemblance.

It was the accident of noting this resemblance of compositional problems that was my starting-point. Now, in themselves, these resemblances in the basic story, and in certain formal problems of composition, are not important: they are useful only as a convenient way of making a comparison which proves more interesting and illuminating than might be expected. Our current lines of critical evaluation put George Eliot and Edmund Spenser, I suspect, much further apart in their attitudes, interests and artistic aims than George Eliot herself would have thought necessary. George Eliot is at present at the summit of general critical approval, after a period of relative neglect; while Spenser's critical fortunes have fallen rather low in recent years. Both are great writers, for whom periods of disfavour provide the challenge for a better understanding of their virtues. Both are writers separated from the contemporary reader by some historical distance—wide in Spenser's case, but not negligible in George Eliot's either.

Before considering more closely the two stories I have referred to, some general remarks placing the two writers in relation to one another may be helpful. We may begin with the fact, to which critics have rightly paid attention, that the opening and closing pages of *Middlemarch* contain an invitation to compare the career of the heroine, Dorothea, with that of St Teresa of Avila, the great Spanish mystic who was also a practical reformer:

> Theresa's passionate ideal nature demanded an epic life . . . Her flame . . . fed from within, soared after some illimitable satisfaction, some object which would never justify weariness, which would reconcile self-despair with the rapturous consciousness of life beyond self. She found her epos in the reform of a religious order . . .
>
> Many Theresas have been born who found themselves no epic life wherein there was a constant unfolding of far-resonant action: perhaps only a life of mistakes, the offspring of a certain spiritual grandeur ill-matched with the meanness of opportunity . . . these later-born Theresas were helped by no coherent social faith and order which could perform the function of knowledge for the ardently willing soul.[1]

Thus the epic quality George Eliot finds in St Teresa's career is made a frame of reference which encloses, and measures, the story of Dorothea, the novel's principal character. George Eliot suggests that there in Dorothea went another St Teresa, thwarted only by unfavourable external conditions. She insists on this again at the very end, adding: 'For there is no creature whose inward being is so strong that it is not greatly determined by what lies outside it' (p. 896). The comparison between Dorothea and St Teresa is a strange one, more destructive to Dorothea than the author seems to have wished, but it is significant of the author's underlying intentions.

Now, St Teresa (1515-1582) was an older contemporary of Spenser (1552?-1599). Both stood at the extreme end of the period in which it was still possible to use the tradition of romantic chivalry as a way of expressing the highest aspirations. Both could also use allegory as a normal means of conveying psychological states and recording spiritual adventures, though the long reign of allegory was nearly over. George Eliot was conscious of looking back on all that from the other side—of belonging to a time when romance and allegory in their old forms were no longer available. But she wanted to find a nineteenth-century equivalent for what St Teresa had: namely, a unified world-view, a soaring ardour of heroic self-dedication, and an opportunity to produce significant social results. One way of describing the theme of *Middlemarch* is to say that it arises from, and is about, this search for a nineteenth-century equivalent. And this responsive attitude of George Eliot's to the heroic and religious values she finds represented in St Teresa's dedicated life brings her close at the same time to Spenser's passionate commitment to a Christian humanism of epic dimensions.

Thus seen, the comparison between George Eliot and Edmund Spenser may appear less wilful and irrelevant; for the likenesses are found in the central concerns of each writer, while the differences are in the obvious externals.

Certainly, George Eliot uses, instead of Spenser's romantic epic and overt allegory, the methods of realist fiction, in which symbolism and schematic intentions are not absent, but kept submerged. But in spite of this difference in method, each writer is trying to attain and express an inclusive systematic view of reality, and to show how this becomes the ground of an heroic idealism. Both interweave vast political, religious and moral concerns in their work while portraying psychological states and individual moral choices. Both are by confessed intention 'didactic' writers in the noble and best sense of the word, for they wish to illuminate reality for us, and quicken our responsiveness to reality, through their imaginative creations.

There are more particular likenesses as well. Both writers are very interested in opposing the cult of 'romantic passion', by exposing its falsities and destructive effects, and by presenting in its place an ideal of true love which is at once more genuinely exalted and more realistic. Both are also concerned with the possibility of a feminine vocation to the heroic life: what the virgin-warrior Britomart represents in the idiom of *The Faerie Queene* is very similar to what Dorothea represents in the idiom of *Middlemarch*. Furthermore, both writers exhibit a strong positive feeling for the values which were traditionally attached to the pastoral convention: a humble and retired integrity, sincerity and contentment, and health of mind and body, expressed in the capacity for hard work and joyful play—values represented in *Middlemarch* by the Garth household.

One might also say that the treatment of their themes by both writers suggests that they feel that a certain quixotic high-flying

F

ardour is necessary for the attainment of the greatest heights. Indeed the word 'quixotic' is applied by the author to Dorothea in *Middlemarch*.[2] This may remind us that that other exponent of romantic chivalry, Don Quixote, was also a contemporary of St Teresa and of Spenser. Cervantes (1547-1616) separated out in Don Quixote and Sancho Panza those extremes of soaring idealism and down-to-earth realism which St Teresa united so remarkably in herself. This union of high aspiration with 'lower experience such as plays a great part in the world' (p. 821) is lacking in the generous Dorothea—a lack which George Eliot unconvincingly blames too exclusively on the social conventions and restrictions of Dorothea's milieu.

One final point of comparison will bring us closer to the two stories I am about to consider. In each of these stories there is an unfulfilled young wife yoked to an old man. Spenser is quite explicit about the sexual incapacity of old Malbecco in his story, and about the disastrous effect of this on the wife. He is so, both because the fabliau style of his story demands it, and because the conventions of his time favoured plain-speaking. On the other hand, in George Eliot's story, the reader's impression that lack of sexual fulfilment is an important part of Dorothea's misery after her marriage to Casaubon is not explicitly confirmed, because of the Victorian conventions. Nevertheless, George Eliot does, it seems to me, intuitively find a means of conveying the truth, indirectly and symbolically. The opening pages of Chapter XXVIII show a winter-morning scene at Lowick Manor after the bride's return from her honeymoon; and the contrast is emphasized between the way the subjectively-perceived landscape and domestic interior now appear and the way they appeared during the courtship.[3] The whole passage is needed for the effect, but I shall quote a little:

> The very furniture in the room seemed to have shrunk since she saw it before: the stag in the tapestry looked more like a ghost in his ghostly blue-green world . . . The bright fire of dry oak-boughs burning on the dogs seemed an incongruous renewal of life and glow . . . Her blooming full-pulsed youth stood there in a moral imprisonment which made itself one with the chill, colourless, narrowed landscape, with the shrunken furniture, the never-read books, and the ghostly stag in a pale fantastic world that seemed to be vanishing from the daylight. (pp. 291-3)

The complete passage is an extraordinary evocation of disenchantment, of a withering and shrinking world, of a chill cast upon vitality. It is enough in itself to dispose of the charge that there is no poetry in the work.[4] Not only is this passage poetic both in method and in result: it is so in a Spenserian way, creating a psychic landscape with figures that are meaningful for the inner life of passion and desire and dread.

With these preliminary observations, I shall turn to the episode I have selected from the Third Book of *The Faerie Queene*. It is not chosen to exhibit Spenser in his best advertised qualities but it does show some of his characteristic powers being exercised in an interesting way.

II

In the Third Book the varieties of true and false love are displayed. As Canto 9 begins, we find together, needing shelter for the night: Sir Satyrane, a type of primitive forest-bred virtue, and two knights tainted with lechery, the Squire of Dames and Sir Paridell. Sir Paridell concerns us most. He has knightly qualities and breeding, but is flawed by his addiction to the art and game of love. Descended from Paris of Troy and Oenone, he knows love only as a sterile routine of seduction:

> But nothing new to him was that same paine,
> Ne paine at all; for he so oft had tryde
> The powre thereof, and lov'd so oft in vaine,
> That thing of course he counted, love to entertaine.[5]

These three knights come to a castle and are denied admission by Malbecco, the owner. At this point, the romantic-epic setting and treatment are modified: we become aware that the basic narrative structure has become that of a comic bawdy tale, a fabliau. The master of the castle, Malbecco, who represents Age-Avarice-Jealousy, one-eyed and impotent, is married to a young wife, Hellenore. The castle is really a bourgeois household of which he is 'the good man' (9: 10) who keeps the keys, and 'has no skill of Court nor courtesie' (9: 3). The language takes on a corresponding colloquial tang with undertones of bawdy. There is farcical business and tone when Malbecco pretends to be his own servant answering the door, and later when pretending that his wife is too indisposed to meet them.

The knights are also drawn down perilously close to farce. When they are at first refused admittance, they take refuge from the storm in a shed. Britomart, the Amazonian virgin-knight, arrives; she cannot fit into the overcrowded shed; there is jostling and Paridell ends by fighting with her, which results in both being temporarily stunned, though she has the better of the encounter. Even the expedient of an epic simile at this point hardly saves the dignity of this unseemly scuffle.

When their threats finally gain them entrance, they disarm, and Britomart reveals her womanly beauty, 'like Minerva', as her golden hair streams down when she lifts her helmet. In these stanzas the treatment reverts to the epic level, with a splendid

High-Renaissance picture, mounted with appropriate classical references.

Sir Paridell now sets out to seduce Malbecco's young wife Hellenore in the approved style of such courtship: looks are exchanged, sign language is employed.[6]

Meanwhile, when supper is finished, the knights tell of their experiences and of their lineage. Sir Paridell reveals his descent from Trojan Paris. Thus Paridell-Hellenore-Malbecco is parallel to Paris-Helen-Menelaus. But the immediate relevance of this Trojan theme is not in this parallel, but in something quite different and surprising. Britomart is also of Trojan descent; so she and Sir Paridell share between them an account of how men of Trojan stock founded Rome, which thus became a second Troy; and how a third Troy or 'Troynovant' is yet to rise—London, founded by 'Trojan Brutus'. This lofty-quaint rehearsing of legendary history has a core of topical purpose, because it is part of an elaborate Tudor political myth. The idea of London's imperial destiny as the third Troy is parallel to the German myth of a Third Reich, and the old Russian idea of Moscow as the Third Rome.

The canto ends with a brief reminder that in the midst of these high matters the seduction is progressing, as 'faire Dame Hellenore' listens to Paridell's discourse, 'Fashioning worlds of fancies evermore/In her fraile wit', while the old husband is interested only in sleep.

As Canto 10 opens, the other guests ride forth, but Sir Paridell contrives to stay behind, pleading the hurt received in his scuffle with Britomart. The love-game is now played out, with Chaucerian echoes in the phrasing. Hellenore steals part of Malbecco's wealth and then sets fire to the rest. As the flames rise she pretends that Sir Paridell is carrying her off by force. Malbecco is torn between saving wife or money, and the money wins as he turns back to put out the fire. In this comic presentation of Malbecco as Avarice, Spenser is perhaps inconsistent, because Malbecco ends by becoming a pure personification of Jealousy.

Malbecco subsequently decides to set out to find his wife ,and takes a considerable amount of wealth with him. He comes upon the cowardly bully Braggadocchio, and his servant Trompart, and relies on their help. They come across Sir Paridell, but he has already deserted Hellenore:

> Alone he rode without his Paragone;
> For having filcht her bels, her up he cast
> To the wide world, and let her fly alone,
> He nould be clogd. So had he served many one.
> (10: 35)

Thus Hellenore's abandonment points one sort of moral. But this is not the last stage of the story, and a different sort of moral is yet to be drawn, as the tale moves on to an extraordinary final development.

Paridell says that Hellenore is somewhere in the forest. So Malbecco buries his money and ventures into the forest in search of her. In fact, she has taken up with the wild satyrs, acting for them as housewife and partner in common:

> To milk their gotes, and make them cheese and bred,
> And every one as commune good her handeled.
>
> (10: 36)

So at last Malbecco draws close:

> Now when amid the thickest woods they were,
> They heard a noyse of many bagpipes shrill,
> And shrieking Hububs them approaching nere . . .
>
> (10: 43)

These satyrs are a transformation of the wild Irish of Spenser's observation. Malbecco's two cowardly companions, Braggadocchio and Trompart, run away—and steal the money he has buried. The old man remains to watch the satyrs from his hiding-place. Here a Pan and Mayday motif is woven in to form a texture of rustic pagan sensuality:

> The iolly Satyrs full of fresh delight,
> Came dauncing forth, and with them nimbly led
> Faire Hellenore, with girlonds all bespred,
> Whom their May-lady they had newly made.
>
> (10: 44)

At dusk Malbecco inserts himself amongst the satyrs ('like a Gote amongst the Gotes did rush'), the more easily because he has a goatee beard, and because he, too, wears horns (the metaphor of cuckolding taken literally). His wife lies partnered with a satyr:

> At night, when all they went to sleepe, he vewd,
> Whereas his louely wife emongst them lay,
> Embraced of a Satyre rough and rude,
> Who all the night did minde his ioyous play:
> Nine times he heard him come aloft ere day,
> That all his hart with gealosie did swell;
> But yet that nights ensample did bewray,
> That not for nought his wife them loued so well,
> When one so oft a night did ring his matins bell.
>
> (10: 48)

Creeping nearer when the satyr has at last fallen to sleep, he pleads with her to come back to him, but she refuses, preferring the vigour of the coarse satyrs to all that he can offer. Thus Spenser reads his second lesson, on the evils of mismatched couples, and the moral peril of those who are

> Depriv'd of kindly joy and naturall delight.
>
> (9: 5)

This emphasis on the sensuous fulfilment needed as the basis of the healthy virtuous life is a characteristic Spenserian note.

Discovered in the morning, the spurned old man is butted and trodden down and driven out. He finds his money gone. But now he is ceasing to be a man and is transformed into a pure emblem. He creeps at last into a cave and there:

> Is woxen so deform'd, that he has quight
> Forgot he was a man, and Gealosie is hight.
>
> (10: 60)

Even this rather detailed account has had to omit much for brevity's sake. But enough has been told to make it evident that the episode is of very complex construction. I shall summarize what seems to me the chief elements:

1. There are the high-romance figures of moral virtue, Sir Satyrane and Britomart, drawn from the highest stratum of the epic, and presented in the high style, e.g. by the splendid High-Renaissance pictorial image of Britomart disarming, 'like Minerva'.

2. The 'Trojan' material of the Tudor political myth is woven in, its genealogical threads linking up with the personages of the land of Faery.

3. These high-value elements in the structure are not here set against their conventional opposites in the form of dragons or wicked enchanters or paynim knights. Spenser is doing something else at this point. He is finding a means within his romantic epic of glancing at the seamy side of the tapestry of Elizabethan court life and gallantry. The opposites of virtue here are figures claiming knightly status, who are shown to be tainted with vice—Sir Paridell and the Squire of Dames—or are wholly vicious like the cowardly Braggadocchio.

4. But also the Court interacts with the City, and we have what is essentially a fabliau, telling how a merchant's wife was seduced and abducted by a dissolute courtier.

5. This fabliau-style comedy opens out unexpectedly into the adventure among the satyrs in the fabulous forest, and ends by the reduction of Malbecco to an abstract emblem of Jealousy. The satyr-scene, different as it is from what has preceded it, nevertheless by language and situation retains links with the earlier part of the story. Only an historically-attuned and alert reading will bring out the

different modalities of this multiplex composition. The shifts of level from 'base' to 'high' styles, and the composite effects, are tricky and require skilful adjustment by the poet, as he first insinuates a comic tale into the romantic-heroic framework, and then inserts within it such materials as the unhelmeting of Britomart and the 'Trojan' political myth, thereafter again transforming the mode to accommodate the satyr-scene, and ending in pure allegory. The diction is a main instrument in adjusting these disparate materials, but the syntax, in the wider sense of the word, is also important.[7]

The elements thus brought into a precarious unity vary in their *distance* from the actual world which is presupposed throughout the whole poem. There is a continual shifting along a scale whose extremes could be marked realism—fantasy. But even this is too simple, because the elements of the episode are not only at varying distances from reality, they also have different *kinds* of relation to reality. For instance, Malbecco transformed in the end to an abstract emblem-figure representing Jealousy has a different kind of relation to the real world from that of Sir Paridell, in whose person Spenser is attacking fairly directly the mores of court gallants, and may be pointing at a particular individual. And different again in their bearing on actuality are ideal figures like Britomart and Sir Satyrane; or the Trojan material which manages to be invested with legendary charm while giving out the Tudor line.

I have called the unity Spenser achieves 'precarious'. One would expect a unity created from such disparate elements to be precarious. One must take into account the conventions of the work. No doubt under a hostile glare the unity could come quite unstuck. People sometimes forget that no fiction—even one that attempts verisimilitude—can have the unity and coherence in depth of reality. And all 'serious' fiction is created because it renders a vision of reality in a particular way which is meaningful and satisfying for particular minds at a particular time. Fictions operate by varying codes and serve different intentions. Modern realism is not the only way of being faithful to reality.

In Spenser's case, one might judge that his composite performance presents us with childish incongruities. But Spenser was a mature, serious and sophisticated artist, and it seems to me that one should seek, and one can find, a point of view from which these incongruities achieve a sufficient congruence, though I have indicated a couple of possible faults. Perhaps the distinguishing mark of Spenser as a creator and stylist is the *inclusiveness* he strives for. He uses much dexterity, but also has the courage to take great risks, in order to keep present in his work all the relevant frameworks and contexts and resources and resonances: classical, mediaeval, renaissance; pagan, Christian; courtly and popular; learned and naïve. This am-

bition of inclusiveness is the key also to his language. Both in matter
and diction the episode I have been discussing illustrates this feature
of Spenser pretty well.[8] Here as elsewhere Spenser is trying to sound
together, or in close proximity, a number of themes and tones which
have their full resonance only within the whole poem, and which
make up the complex world of Spenser's art.

III

The complex world of George Eliot's art is developed by a different fictional code from that of Spenser. The implied relation to
reality is generally the direct one of verisimilitude, the probability
rating of events has to be relatively much higher, and spatio-temporal and causal connections have to be more strict and definite.

Nevertheless, *Middlemarch* is not as homogeneous and univocal
as this may suggest, and by observing the composite character of the
work we may get close to some of the problems, and perhaps limitations, in George Eliot's achievement.

By speaking of composite construction, I am now referring to the
fact that *Middlemarch* came about by weaving together one set of
characters and events already existing in an uncompleted draft
called 'Miss Brooke' with another set of characters and events, thus
enabling the final work to give a wide panorama of Midlands society
in the years just before the Reform Act of 1832. This complexity of
character-groupings and interlocking events might nevertheless all
exist on one uniform level of significance and probability.

More to the point is the way in which political and religious concerns introduce a complexity of wider meanings, and open up deep
perspectives behind the forefront of the novel. These issues are discreetly handled, and remain secondary. No one character, no one
event, takes the full weight of these issues, nor does the society por-
trayed do so as a whole. This is as the author intended; and it
might also seem inevitable in a novel of provincial life. However,
it is one sort of limitation upon the range and depth of the book;
and one may point out that a provincial setting did not prevent
Dostoievsky in *The Possessed* and *The Brothers Karamazov* from
bringing the full weight of political and religious problems to bear
upon his fiction.

However, the chief kind of complexity I want to look at consists
in the fact that not all the characters and events have the same relation to reality, or operate under the same fictional code.

One may distinguish three groups of characters without drawing
unnecessarily fine distinctions:

  1. Let us accept the bulk of the characters in the book as being
'real people', presented according to the verisimilitude required by
nineteenth-century social realism. This applies to the Vincys and

Lydgates and Chettams and so on; and I should be content to include the more simplified comic characters like Mr Brooke and Mrs Cadwallader, and the slightly idealized Garth household, in this category.

2. On the other hand the catastrophe that affects Lydgate and Bulstrode and others comes about by the agency of characters that have a different feel: Raffles and Rigg and old Mr Featherstone. Critics have pointed out that these are grotesques and gesticulating humours imported from Dickensian melodrama. Bulstrode himself, a major figure in the book, the evangelical banker, belongs in part to this world of melodrama through his murky past, in which probabilities are uncomfortably stretched.

3. Different again is the status in reality of the book's heroine, Dorothea, and of Will Ladislaw whom she eventually marries. Ladislaw is just a lady-novelist's beau. The objective indications would lead us to expect him to turn out to be a spiv, as Sir James Chettam regards him, rather than a character moved by an unusual nicety of gentlemanly honour. George Eliot, who insists so strongly on the influence of social conditioning on individual character, fails to show us anything in Ladislaw's formation that makes his performance likely or convincing. Dorothea, on the other hand, is at least partly real. The ironies by which the self-centred and wilful aspects of her personality are illuminated in the early chapters help greatly; but, alas, these ironies are allowed to disappear, and Dorothea becomes a character whose ardours and idealism are themselves increasingly idealized. Certainly, they are not fully subjected to the critical controls that operate so finely over the greater part of the book.

Here, then, is a compositeness which is also in its way quite precarious; all the more because the third element I have mentioned, the idealization of certain characters, is not recognized and intended as such by the author. The relation between fiction and reality is here not fully under control.

What happens in regard to the characters happens also in the action they are involved in. In one view, the structure and dynamics of *Middlemarch* can be seen as the slow accumulation of events and pressures, so organized that their full weight is brought to bear on a few decisive moral choices, in which one or more individuals experience a true *crisis*. But in fact some of these moral choices are the weakest part of the novel.

For instance, Dorothea faces a crisis when her aged husband Casaubon asks her to bind herself to his wishes. She is afraid that he will ask her to consecrate her life after his death to writing the book in which his enormous, futile and erroneous labours of pseudo-scholarship are to be embodied. Actually, he is also going to ask her not to re-marry, because he is jealous of Will Ladislaw. Dorothea is torn between horror at the prospect of a living death if she is condemned to labour on the treadmill of Casaubon's scholarly futilities, and a shrinking from the hurt she must give him if she refuses to be bound, and thus reveals her judgement that he is a failure. We must also concede some weight to the convention of a wife's subservience and loyalty to the husband, beyond the point that we would take for granted today.

George Eliot allows Dorothea to decide to bind herself as an act of self-abnegation. While admitting the possibility of another view, she endorses Dorothea's choice in the following passage, in which compassion and an extreme view of marital loyalty are both given as reasons:

> Neither law nor the world's opinion compelled her to this—only her husband's nature and her own compassion, only the ideal and not the real yoke of marriage. She saw clearly enough the whole situation, yet she was fettered: she could not smite the stricken soul that entreated hers. If that were weakness, Dorothea was weak. (p. 513)

The challenge of that last sentence must be taken up. For there *is* weakness in Dorothea's choice: understandable as it is, and admirable as her compassionate feeling may be, such a decision is far from ideal. One may apply the measure George Eliot has invited us to use, and ask what would the shrewd, humorous, practical, affectionate St Teresa have done in this situation. Well, first, she would not have let it arise in this way; and, second, if it had arisen, she would have jollied the poor old thing out of it, humoured and soothed and mothered him, while gently but firmly refusing to listen to his nonsense. Abundantly capable of self-abnegation, she would have found a better cause for it than to shut herself in the trap of a false relationship with Casaubon (pretending to believe in him) and to write a book she knew ought not to be written.

It is significant that George Eliot had to rescue Dorothea from the consequences of her choice, by letting the old man die in the nick of time. Otherwise the novel would have foundered then and there, as we left the heroine settling down to a decade's work of compiling the 'key to Mythologies'.

Another moral fulcrum which, even less, will bear the weight put upon it occurs towards the end of the book. Dorothea, now a young widow, comes in upon Will Ladislaw while he is clasping the hands of Rosamond Lydgate, and fervently talking to her. She jumps to the conclusion that Ladislaw is making love to his friend's wife. Actually, it is the other way round: Rosamond wants to leave her husband and go off with Ladislaw, and he has been pleading with her to come to her senses.

Dorothea walks out in high indignation. It seems that the incident has irremediably blighted the relationship between her and Ladislaw. Why? Why can't he simply explain? Impossible: according to the chivalric code Ladislaw accepts, and George Eliot does not question, he must remain misunderstood:

> 'Explain! How can a man explain at the expense of a woman?'
> 'You can tell her what you please', said Rosamond, with more tremor.
> 'Do you suppose she would like me better for sacrificing you? She is not a woman to be flattered because I made myself despicable—to believe that I must be true to her because I was dastard to you.'

So high is the chivalric standard applied to this situation, with the author's endorsement, that Ladislaw even has to be excused for having thus spoken in furious anger to Rosamond: 'how could he tell a woman that he was ready to curse her?' (p. 534).

The issue that arises here involves an historical question. I should say flatly that from our point of view today the whole problem is unreal. We would regard it as simply absurd and unjustifiable to allow such a misunderstanding to blight friendship or love—Ladislaw would have the right, almost the duty, to tell as much of the truth as was necessary. And secondly, the best thing that Ladislaw could do for Rosamond was just what he did: speak with such bitter anger that Rosamond's shell of blind egoism was cracked. This prepared the way for Rosamond's responding to Dorothea's generous approach and telling Dorothea the truth. Now, evidently, if we are to see the situation as George Eliot intended, we have to make an historical adjustment in our vision. It is for the social historian to tell us how far this high-pitched chivalric code was really and effectively operative in English society around 1830, or still recognized in 1871-72 when the novel was published. The novel gives at least this much testimony, that George Eliot assumed a familiarity with such a code, and an acceptance of it as an ideal standard of conduct—however much we may feel sure that it would not have been observed very much in practice.

But the attempt to make historical allowances in this way, while right and necessary, does not solve the whole problem. For in the end we must reserve the right to measure what is presented against what we feel to be the true requirements of human conduct, even while making allowances. And in this regard, we cannot but be oppressed by the sense that unreality has again got into the staging of moral issues at a critical point.

This brief examination of two moral crises came by way of illustrating my contention that *Middlemarch* is not as homogeneous as it at first appears. In addition to the large element of social-realist verisimilitude and shrewd analysis of motive—which is the great and wonderful strength of this novel—there is the melodramatic ingredient furnished by the Bulstrode-Rigg-Raffles-Featherstone group, and also the idealization which occurs in the handling of Ladislaw and of Dorothea herself.

George Eliot has used great skill in combining these materials, and smoothing over the incongruities. In the case of the melodramatic ingredients, the minor characters function satisfactorily in the plot; while the major character Bulstrode is quite a triumph. He has the outline of a hypocritical villain of melodrama; but George Eliot has filled in this outline with such a degree of psychological realism and pathos that she practically brings him over into the camp of the 'real' people.

The idealized and chivalric elements cause greater trouble. F. R. Leavis's remarks are very searching at this point. He observes that 'the irony seems to be reserved for the provincial background and circumstances, leaving the heroine immune' (which after the first few chapters is true); and says of Dorothea and Ladislaw that 'we are expected to share a valuation of them extravagantly higher than any we can for a moment countenance'. And of the situations which are presented to illustrate the noble feelings of these two he says that they 'have the daydream relation to experience; they are generated by a need to soar above the indocile facts and conditions of the real world'.[9]

This is a reasonable and accurate view of the flaw in George Eliot's performance, applying the criteria of the realist novel. But that is not the only way of looking at it. George Eliot has an unstilled hunger for the transcendental and the ideal. Within the terms of her beliefs and her art she has no way of giving these aspirations satisfactory form and expression.

Once again the comparison we have been making with Spenser is illuminating. Spenser's fiction has, in a sense, a 'daydream relation to experience'—but it is a daydream that is disciplined, organized and significant. It also can be said to be 'generated by a need to soar above the indocile facts and conditions of the real world'—but it does so without denying or ignoring those facts, and it preserves a real and illuminating relation to those facts. In the terms of his beliefs and his art, Spenser could present ideal types and transcendental perspectives validly. But George Eliot's fictional code requires life-like, imperfect characters, exposed to all the rubs and checks and flows of everyday circumstance. If she tries to present a lofty ideal in a state of purity, she begins to violate the canons of her art and falls into uncertainty and confusion. For example, when she first presents Will Ladislaw she makes a show of applying to him the critical ironies (pp. 83-4) which are so effective in the book generally, but it is a mere show, and Ladislaw remains unreal and uninteresting.

Spenser's method, in this respect at least, makes for the greater realism, simply because the fiction and the actuality are held apart in an intelligible relation, not crushed together in perilous confusion.

We have not paid much attention to the virgin-warrior Britomart in our account, though she figures in Canto 9. When she reveals herself to the company, they are enraptured with her beauty, but even more with her 'chivalry' and 'noble prowess'; so 'everyone her likte, and every one her loved'; even Sir Paridell is won over by her graciousness and forgets his annoyance that she had had the better of their fight. Now in all this there is no touch of sentimentality, no gush of self-indulgent feeling, no false note: it is proper to the ideal mode in which Spenser is writing, and there is no difficulty in seeing the meaning of this ideal type in terms of actual life.[10]

On the other hand, when George Eliot wants to show Dorothea similarly admired by all, and conquering all with her beauty and nobility and fine feeling, sentimentality and gush and unreality flood in. It is Leavis's comment that is again sharply accurate here; and among the passages he quotes is a short one that will serve for an illustration: it tells how for Lydgate the 'childlike grave-eyed earnestness with which Dorothea said all this was irresistible—blent into an adorable whole with her ready understanding of high experience' (p. 821). And shortly after comes that embarrassing passage in which George Eliot really goes overboard:

> As Lydgate rode away, he thought, 'This young creature has a heart large enough for the Virgin Mary. She evidently thinks nothing of her own future, and would pledge away half her income at once, as if she wanted nothing for herself but a chair to sit in from which she can look down with those clear eyes at the poor mortals who pray to her.'
> (p. 825)

This would be going a little far even in the worst sort of pious hagiography; but George Eliot lets it stand without any critical check, and thus virtually endorses it. Yet having picked out these weaknesses to further our argument, one must also say that it is surprising how little damage to *Middlemarch* they really cause; and this is because of the strength of the book's positive virtues.

Let me comment briefly in conclusion on the critical principles I have been implying. I think the soundest way of developing a critical approach is, not to reason out a system in advance, but to engage in criticism, make the judgements that seem appropriate, and then reflexively consider what it is one has done, how consistent one's implied bases of judgement seem to be, and what general issues are thus raised.

One thing that has arisen at several points is the importance of historical attunement in our reading of literature. I am inclined to the view that the essential *academic* component in literary studies is not the pretension of shedding the white light of final critical judgements, but the obligation to make the work as fully *present* as possible by interpretation and analysis. To put it very formally: it is chiefly as hermeneutics and exegesis that literary study becomes an academic discipline. By putting things in this order, I am not saying that this essential academic task does not need to be completed by critical judgement, within and without the academy. For the vital question in literature is very simple: *Do I like this, and why or why not?* Don't be deceived by the word 'like'; it does not reduce everything to mere feeling. We are partly and imperfectly rational beings and our liking is in part and imperfectly an intellectual judgement. That is the best it can be, have regard to the complexity of literature and its involvement in the human situation.

The good critic is precisely the one who can truthfully use the phrase so often sneered at, 'I know what I like'. For really to *know* the work, and to discover what one's responses *genuinely* are, are two difficult things: they are not the beginning, they are the crown of our endeavour.

But before we try to fix the degrees and directions of our genuine likes and dislikes and our reasons for them, let us be sure we have seen the works in question as nearly as possible in their full reality. This is why scholarship is an essential part of humanism. We cannot know unless we are docile; we cannot understand unless we are willing to let works of art first speak to us on their own terms. If there is a degree of historical relativism in this, it is only so much as commonsense and justice seem to require.

1963

NOTES

1 World's Classics edition, p. 1. Subsequent references included in the text in parentheses are to this edition.
2 'Lydgate did not stay to think that she was Quixotic', p. 820. The same word is applied to her by Casaubon: 'her Quixotic enthusiasm', p. 458.
3 Cf. p. 74.
4 One of the remarks in the unfortunate introduction by R. M. Hewitt. Other blunders committed are: 'neglect of construction', 'little of the usual kind of plot-interest and nothing of accident or coincidence', 'the author seems indifferent to beauty'.
5 Canto 9: stanza 29. All references are similarly cited by canto and stanza.

6 Writing love-pledges in spilt wine is referred to, in a greatly admired line, as 'A sacrament profane in mystery of wine' (9: 30). This has resonances more suited to the similar intensities of the House of Busirane, where the worship of erotic passion prevails.

7 Within the stanza the units of meaning are subordinated into fairly elaborate syntactical wholes. Between stanzas the degree of connection varies. The cartographic and chronological canons of Faery admit a good deal of looseness in spatio-temporal, and at times even in causal, relations. Consider, for example, the indefiniteness of the time indications in 10: 3-20 and 10: 34-7.

8 By stressing Spenser's will to inclusiveness I do not maintain that he kept all these resources completely alive, understood and integrated. Mediaevalists may well lament how much of the mediaeval tradition has *not* survived in Spenser. But if we take into account the full range of his complex resources we must surely admit he has done remarkably well.

9 F. R. Leavis, *The Great Tradition* (London, 1948), pp. 74, 75, 79.

10 It remains true that the typical modern reader does not have, and cannot fully recover, the sense of pleasure and profit which the typical sixteenth-century reader could evidently have in contemplating ideal types and their relation to actuality. The popularity of pictorial emblems, and moral allegories in painting, are evidence of this disposition, which we do not readily share.

Politics versus Art in the Fifth Book of 'The Faerie Queene'

RECENT interpretations of *The Faerie Queene* have been more concerned with symbolic structures of general import than with the poem's allegorizing of political events. This is partly because earlier commentators had already pointed out the obvious and unmistakeable historical references; and in the more doubtful areas their readings had been ingeniously unsatisfactory, so that the vein seemed unprofitable. Nevertheless, in two books of the poem, the First Book and the Fifth Book, the historical meaning is very important: it is in and through particular political situations that we are asked to see the general truths about Holiness and Justice.

In the First Book, Spenser based his allegory on the 1559 religious settlement which created the Anglican Church. This book has always been regarded as poetically successful. In it Spenser achieved the correct distance from the political-religious actuality to which he alludes. The topical references are well integrated with the general allegory of the progress of the militant Christian. Moreover, the real-life material Spenser has used has undergone a marvellous transformation: it has truly passed into the depth of Spenser's creative imagination, and comes forth as the coloured images of a popular yet sophisticated picture-book world.

The Fifth Book is by common consent much inferior in poetic interest and even in the moral-psychological illuminations it offers; and this artistic inferiority seems bound up with the way it handles its topical references.[1] I want to ask why this is so, and also to find what sort of interest the historical meaning might nevertheless offer.

The Fifth Book is concerned with the politics of the 1580s and '90s: the trial and death of Mary Stuart, the interventions in the Netherlands and France, the war with Spain, the Irish problem. The events in the poem are rather miscellaneous: they do not offer the unity of design which the First Book preserves amid its complexities. But this is not the main trouble. In the Fifth Book, Spenser has not achieved the necessary distance from his political material. He is working on current affairs, or events of the recent past, partly within his own experience. The impulses of the partisan pamphleteer and propagandist are not sufficiently sublimated in the work of the poet. The interest depends far too much on a mere recognition of historical persons and events. The general doctrine and allegory of the virtue of justice is not well developed, and offers little countervailing sustenance to the intellect and imagination. The transformation of reality has not occurred in depth: it is a contriving, perfunctorily disguising, officiously fabricating kind of activity that has produced the Fifth Book. And there are features which are apt to arouse quite negative reactions: Artegall is either a bore or repulsive much of the time, and the visit of Britomart to 'Isis Church' (the counterpart in this book of the sojourn in an allegorical house which occurs in other books) offers a Renaissance-style 'mystery' that chills and disgusts by its grotesque contrivance, a cryptogram devoid of imaginative attraction.

I shall comment first on some of the main episodes in the book which are obviously transcriptions of historical situations; and then on one episode which stands out as not having an obtrusively obvious counterpart in actuality, the story of Radigund.

In Canto 2 there is an argument about social justice between Artegall and a foolish demagogic Giant, who has frequently been dubbed Communism, though Egalitarianism would be a better word, since the abolition of private property is not mentioned. The background of this episode is undoubtedly the strong and widespread, but mainly submerged and inarticulate, tide of popular 'levelling' sentiment that wanted a 'commonwealth' instead of an England where the Haves lorded it over the Have-nots. In this latent radicalism there were confused currents of Anabaptist enthusiasm; and these were reinforced by the arrival of refugees from Alva's persecution in the Netherlands. Already, under Henry VIII in 1535, fourteen Anabaptists had been executed. Under Edward VI a number of Anabaptists were imprisoned and some were executed. Elizabeth burnt two Flemish Anabaptists in 1575 and four more in the following decade, and also deported a considerable number. Not all those classed as Anabaptists were socially radical or revolutionary, but undoubtedly many did hold communist or anarchist doctrines. The fear of Anabaptist ideas was enhanced by the lurid memory of the Anabaptist millennium in Münster in 1534, and other disturbances at that time: no legend was required to make this horrifying. Still vivid in memory also were the large waves of popular unrest in Edward VI's time, especially in the Norwich 'soviet' under Ket, which ended in the 'white terror' enacted by John Dudley, Earl of Warwick, with foreign mercenaries. This John Dudley, later Earl of Northumberland and for a period a dictator of England, was the father of Leicester: father worthy of the son, son worthy of the

G

father. Whether or not Spenser was specifically paying a compliment to the Dudley family in showing how Artegall concluded his argument with the Giant by having Talus throw him off the cliff and use his flail upon the 'raskall rout' of his supporters, Ket's movement has probably left its impress on this Canto.

Nor should we overlook a more recent event, which commentators have neglected: Willemsen's movement in the Netherlands 1567-80. Willemsen was a cobbler who set up a New Jerusalem in Westphalia with three hundred followers, some being survivors from Münster. Polygamy was practised. The anarchist ideology of the Free Spirit was revived. They claimed that all things were rightfully theirs, and attacked the house of nobles and clergy, becoming in the end a robber-band practising unbridled terrorism. Willemsen was captured in 1580 and burned at Cleves. Such a contemporary movement must have amplified the horror with which Anabaptists were regarded in England.[2]

The debate between Artegall and the Giant is one of those puzzles concerning Spenser's methods and intentions which have continued to elude commentators, in spite of the efforts of some recent interpreters endowed with both scholarship and sympathy. It reads like a dream-impression of an Aristotelean argument, defying any attempt to reduce it to a logically coherent paraphrase. It has the appearance, not the reality, of eloquence overcoming error. Its best defence is that it is a peculiar case of that transmogrification of all things into Faery mode which is the overruling method of the poem.

What in any case one misses, here and in other parts of *The Faerie Queene* where social justice is treated, is some expression of real feeling for the plight of the poor. Let the fallacies of the theory, and the horrors of the practice, of egalitarianism or anarchism be what they may. Let it be admitted that an England given over to such a theory and practice might have become a Münster writ large. Let it be granted that the gentry were justified in viewing popular radicalism with alarm, even though their reasons were too often merely selfish. Let it further be said in extenuation that people in the sixteenth century could not clearly understand what was happening to the English economy; and that the area of feasibility within which social reform could move was very restricted: so that many an intelligent sensitive man, who saw the evils, may have seen also how discouragingly doubtful and difficult were the remedies that reformers and theorists offered. Nevertheless, we are left with Spenser's inadequacy of response. He insists in The Fifth Book very starkly that justice is a matter of having a strong autocrat who has the correct answer in his mind, and sets the executive arm flailing about remorselessly to enforce it. What we miss is some sign that Spenser could see more deeply into the wretchedness of the 'poor commons', some touch of passionate compunction or protest in the name of Christian brotherhood and charity. Shakespeare could reach this in Lear's outcry:

> O, I have ta'en
> Too little care of this! Take physic, pomp;
> Expose thyself to feel what wretches feel,
> That thou mayst shake the superflux to them,
> And show the heavens more just.
>
> (iii. iv)

Nor is this a passing comment of little weight, for Shakespeare doubles its force with Gloucester's plea—framed like Lear's on a traditional and perhaps inadequate model of distributive justice, but touched with humane feeling:

> Heavens deal so still!
> Let the superfluous and lust-dieted man,
> That slaves your ordinance, that will not see
> Because he does not feel, feel your power quickly;
> So distribution should undo excess
> And each man have enough.
>
> (iv. i)

This is the note that is lacking in the Fifth Book. In the poem, Spenser gives justice a traditional definition (*suum cuique*) when he looks back to a golden age 'when all men sought their owne, and none no more'; he also involves justice on earth with the order of the heavens, using an astronomical metaphor at some length. But one misses Shakespeare's compassion, and his admonitory perception that, to the common man, the rightness of God's order, the fact of God's providence, will tend to be evident, or not, depending on the justice or injustice he experiences in society at the hands of those above him on earth. It is man that must 'show the heavens more just'. The sixteenth century sought to justify the ways of God to man by theological argument, by apostolic blows and knocks, by the rack and gibbet and stake, but not so often by showing God's fatherhood reflected in social brotherhood.

Spenser reacts more sharply and clearly to evils he could recognize within his own social sphere. He hates the jobbery in Church and State, the black market in privilege and place, the conscienceless scramble up Fortune's Hill. He had already treated this with bitter gaiety in *Mother Hubberds Tale*, and with a different sort of effectiveness in the Mammon episode in the Second Book, where he had shown people climbing Philotime's golden chain by every disgraceful means (II: 7: 47). He does not succeed in adding much of value to this theme in the Fifth Book. In Canto 2, Artegall quells Pollente and Munera. Pollente represents various kinds of unjust toll or extortion, such as were made possible by the farming of customs, by monopoly, by import and export licences—abuses which enriched his patrons Leicester and Raleigh and others. Munera represents the bribery and corruption which were taken for granted in the system.[3] Spenser's remedy is to have Talus chop off Munera's golden hands and silver feet and nail them up to public gaze, an image that conveys a queer shock of cruelty but does not illuminate anything very much. One is reminded that, under Gloriana, a hand could be chopped off for writing criticisms of the Queen's policies—as happened to Philip Stubbes—not for taking bribes.

One of the most important episodes which depend on recognition of an historical situation is the treatment of Queen Elizabeth as Mercilla in Cantos 9 and 10. Here, with a light veiling not meant as a disguise, is a view of the Court at the time of the decision to eliminate Mary Stuart. The palace is impressive with 'many towers, and tarras' (terraces). It has the giant Awe as porter, who keeps out those evils which Spenser in other poems has found particularly characteristic of the real Court: 'guyle, and malice, and dispight'—the last meaning something like 'cruel and humiliating disregard for people'. As Artegall and Arthur enter, they see the slanderous poet with his tongue nailed to a post—no secure identification of this poet has been made. It is Mercy who sits enthroned in semi-divine queenly splendour.

Duessa has now become Mary Stuart, and her trial proceeds. Spenser adopts the government propaganda against her. He also gives us a glimpse of Cecil in a role not elsewhere conceded to him in Spenser's work, as a silver-haired venerable sage called Kingdom's Care. The chief crime urged against Mary Stuart is the Babington Plot (one of the more artistic contrivances of the agent-provocateurs employed by Cecil and Walsingham). Mercilla-Elizabeth is represented as being overcome with tender compassion: convinced of the guilt of Duessa-Mary, she will nevertheless not allow 'just vengeance' to have its way, but weeps in pity and adjourns the session. So Canto 9 ends.

This highly edifying exhibition of womanly emotion, which has no effect on the eventual result, is as far as the poet allows mercy to operate. Throughout the Fifth Book clemency is afforded very little scope: the poet is more often found frowning anxiously on the dangers of misplaced pity.

Canto 10 opens with a short poem discussing the relation of mercy to justice. Huddled into it almost as an aside is the brief disclosure that Duessa-Mary has been put to death, Mercilla's reluctance having caused no more than a delay:

> Till strong constraint did thereto enforce.
> (10: 4)

The general discussion of the virtues of mercy and justice at this point is one of the most opaque passages in the whole poem; not surprisingly, since the poem fears mercy as a vice. Spenser begins by raising the question whether mercy is a part of justice, or else 'drawn forth from her by divine extreate'. The alternative thus expressed is obscure: it may mean that mercy is not a natural part of justice yet not inconsistent with it—in fact a kind of higher justice produced by the operation of heavenly grace. It is the next stanza that is truly baffling. If, he says, Justice is such a great thing, even though in its rigorous application it often 'spilles the principall, to save the part', how much greater a thing is mercy, which manages to save the part without spilling the principal, yet without departing from the requirements of justice. The metaphor seems to be a medical one, but its application is not clear, particularly since the practical case before us is one in which Mary Stuart's head is cut off on grounds of political necessity: surely an instance of spilling the principal.

What really emerges from the Mercilla episode, however much muffled in compliment, is a censure of Elizabeth for her imprudent weakness in not eliminating Mary Stuart more speedily.

The historical truth is, of course, that Elizabeth's hesitations were governed by political caution, not by tender feeling. The repercussions in Scotland and France had to be weighed. She had imprisoned Mary unjustly in the first place. The trial of a foreign prince was of highly doubtful legality. The Babington Plot was a government artefact, a painstakingly woven trap into which Mary was lured by Walsingham's agents: whether or not Elizabeth's subjects would swallow the story (and many obviously did not) it was not likely that well-informed governments in Europe would be much deceived.[4] Above all, Elizabeth wanted Mary dead without having to bear public responsibility for her death. She had long since tried to arrange for her death by means that would not let the blood show on her hands. In 1572 she sent Henry Killigrew to Scotland on a secret mission to negotiate with the Regent, the Earl of Mar, and the Earl of Morton, for the handing over of Mary Stuart to them, if they would undertake to have her put to death without fail—this point being so vital that they were to supply some of their own children as hostages to guarantee performance of the deed. The negotiation did not succeed. After Mary's trial, Elizabeth's delay in proceeding to execution was because she was still trying to avoid accepting the responsibility. She wanted Mary murdered without warrant. Archbishop Whitgift favoured this, and a man named Wingfield was said to be ready to do it. She sounded out Mary's keepers, Paulet and Drury, about getting rid of Mary. They jointly replied in a letter written by Paulet: 'God forbid that I should make so foul a shipwreck of my conscience or leave so great a blot to my poor posterity to shed blood without law or warrant.' Elizabeth, according to Mr Secretary Davison's account, stormed against 'the niceness of those precise fellows (as she termed them) who in words would do great things but indeed perform nothing'.[5] She then made it clear to Davison that she wanted the execution carried out according to the warrant, but that her officials were to do it without further reference to her. When it was over, she enacted a charade purporting indignation against her officials, sent Davison to the Tower and coldly destroyed his career but, significantly, his fee as secretary continued to be paid till his death—and kept up a show of anger against Burghley for about four months.[6] We do not, of course, know what private feelings she may have had as an individual; she may have been reluctant and distressed: what we know is how she acted as a politician.

The point is that Spenser's candied but incoherent view of the Queen's mercy is not very interesting as compared with the truth. Of the full truth he was of course ignorant; but he had no need, except for partisan blindness, to be so uncritical of the government's propaganda story, which did not by any means win universal credence. Spenser himself admits that public feeling did not accord with the ruthlessness of the Government and the Puritan-dominated Parliament, when he says of the victim:

> She did sure
> The peoples great compassion unto her allure.
> (9: 38)

It may be that Spenser's literary form would not have enabled him to deal with the complexities and ironies of this case even if he had wished. In an allegory we have to take sides and the issues must be simplified. Spenser has scope for ironies and complexities of other kinds, but not in a matter of this sort. Likewise in the First Book, the allegorical treatment of the historical theme required him to simplify the English Reformation to a struggle between goodies and baddies; we accept this, because on this simple framework is based the general moral and religious significance of the militant Christian's progress. But in the Fifth Book the amount of general significance that gains any real effect on our minds is, in my assessment, low, as is the artistic achievement. Our noses are held down to tracing the topical allegory, and the value of the composition is, to too large an extent, the value we can place on Spenser's presentation of the contemporary historical issues. Or, even if we do not worry about the bad history he offers—even if we reject as irrelevant a comparison of the poem's version with the historical facts (though the journalistic-propagandist slant of the Fifth Book invites such a

comparison as a legitimate response to the author's intentions)—
nevertheless the verdict is the same: the cartoon Spenser offers in the
passages we have considered is philosophically and artistically crude
and lacks intrinsic interest; it achieves no vision of politics worthy
of deeper regard; the imaginative transformation of actuality has
not taken place.

The same conclusion arises from a consideration of Cantos 10-11,
in which the principal subject is English intervention by land in
Europe against Spain. The references stretch from Leicester's
expedition to the Netherlands in 1585 to Henry of Navarre's de-
sertion of Protestantism in 1593 while English troops were aiding
him. What concerns us is the jejune mechanical quality of the presentation—which is felt all the more sharply if it is compared with
the more interesting truth. For example, Leicester did not turn
out to be a victorious Prince Arthur as the poem claims. He began
his mission with a colossal misdemeanour. Fired with enthusiasm,
the Dutch offered him all the powers and the title of Stadholder, as
borne by William of Orange, whose death by assassination had
caused the crisis that led to English intervention. This supreme
civil and military authority he was to exercise as Viceroy of Elizabeth. Leicester knew perfectly well that to agree was to ignore Elizabeth's wishes, but he accepted the Dutch offer and took the oath of
office at the beginning of 1586. When Elizabeth received the news
she was furious. Her policy was not to let herself be drawn in too
deeply, and certainly not to become committed to Dutch independence. Leicester had plainly attempted, not merely to gratify his
own vanity, but also to force Elizabeth into a more forward and irre-
vocable position. When the Dutch in turn became aware of Elizabeth's repudiation, they not only realized that the Queen was not in
accord with their aim of independence from Spain, but also began
to distrust Leicester personally. Thereafter he made a mess of his
political and military mission until he resigned.

No less inflated and unreal is the Burbon episode tacked on as a
late final extra to Canto 11, which deals with Essex's expedition to
Brittany to aid Henry of Navarre—Artegall being momentarily Essex
for this purpose. Once again a fable of victory covers the reality of
failure; once again Spenser's poetic, so splendidly realized in other
parts of *The Faerie Queene*, succumbs here to the raw immediacy of
politics and partisanship. The chief interest offered by the historical
allegory is not intrinsic, it is not provided by Spenser; it is supplied
by the reader if he cares to compare Spenser's bad history with the
truth. I am not implying that the book is poetically poor because
the history is bad; merely that the disappointment of artistic interest
is not compensated for by historical interest, except in the indirect
way I have suggested.

Perhaps the most effective part of the Fifth Book is the mysterious Radigund episode, which extends intermittently from Canto 4 to Canto 7 and, unlike the episode we have been considering, offers no obvious reference to a particular situation. Artegall engages in combat with the Amazonian queen, on the rash agreement that the vanquished shall wholly obey the victor. Artegall overcomes Radigund, but is disarmed by her beauty when he unlaces her helmet in order to despatch her. She takes advantage of the chance to overpower him while he is weaponless. Then she puts him to woman's work, spinning a distaff, somewhat as Hercules spun for Omphale. Radigund becomes infatuated with him. The maid Clarinda, whom she uses as an intermediary, betrays her trust because she too falls in love with Artegall. Meanwhile Britomart has learnt of Artegall's mishap from Talus; she arrives, quells Radigund and cuts off her head.

In one aspect, this story is another of Spenser's warnings against misplaced pity, which are frequent in the Fifth Book. Artegall should not have been so 'empierced with pitiful regard' that, instead of cutting off Radigund's head, he threw away his sword, and enabled her to triumph over him.

In another aspect, the story concerns a topic much discussed in England at the time. France had virtually been ruled by Catherine de Medici, Scotland by Mary Stuart—and Elizabeth was on the English throne. The question was whether rule by a woman was 'unnatural', a violation of right order. John Knox had certainly decided to think so when he inveighed against Mary Stuart in his *First Blast of the Trumpet against the Monstrous Regiment of Women*; and other exiled Puritans had taken the same view in principle. Catholic controversialists, on the other hand, admitted that a woman could legitimately exercise secular authority; but said that it was a monstrous aberration for a woman to rule in things spiritual, as Elizabeth was doing. Both kinds of objection were an embarrassment to the first generation of Elizabeth's apologists. John Aylmer ('Morell' in *The Shepheardes Calendar*) sought a way out in his *An Harborowe for Faithful and Trewe Subjects* (1559) by appealing to those cases in which women had been divinely called to an exceptional role: Deborah, the prophetess (Judg. 4), and Judith in the narrative named after her. These were examples on Elizabeth's side, against Knox's evil examples, Athalia (2 Kgs. 18) and Jezebel (2 Kgs. 9-29).

Spenser's formal position in his poem is governed by the fact that Gloriana is Queen in Faery land as Elizabeth is in England. Nevertheless, he agrees that the exercise of rule by a woman is in general a thing unnatural, and therefore wrong unless legitimated by divine providence. This vital exception to the general thesis is stated rather perfunctorily and unemphatically in one line of a narrative otherwise given over to abhorrence of female sovereignty:

Unlesse the heavens them lift to lawfull soueraintie.

(V: 5: 25)

Not only the question of political rule is involved in Spenser's fiction. Radigund's Amazons represent the spread downwards of unnatural female dominance throughout society. When Britomart has rescued Artegall, she changes the constitution of Radigund's State, acting as ruler only so long as Artegall is recovering from his wounds, after which she resigns authority to him. She repeals 'the liberty of women, which they had long usurpt'.

One looks of course for some historical event to which the Radigund episode might correspond. Inevitably commentators have tried to fit Mary Stuart into the part, but without success, even though one or two features may fleetingly evoke her.

What stands out is the ease with which the Radigund episode can be read as a parody of the Gloriana-Elizabeth conception, and the little care Spenser takes to steer one away from this temptation. One or two commentators have very gingerly raised the question whether Radigund is not mainly Elizabeth.[7] For my part I take this to be the main intention of the episode, which gives it an important function in the poem and prompts some general reflections.

Many of the golden ages of literature have occurred under despotisms. It is true that the extreme phases of totalitarian dictatorship in modern times have suppressed literature. The assumption of many contemporary critics opposed to totalitarianism has naturally been that the best conditions for literature are to be found at the opposite end of the scale, in the conditions provided by liberal democracy. This is an assumption far from being verified. In the past there have been fruitful situations intermediate between these extremes, in which literature has been under pressure and threatened by penalties, yet with sufficient room for discreet manoeuvre to enable much to be said by using indirection and transparent reticence. Some of the very forms of literature—e.g. fable, allegory, historical play with latent parallels—have been to some extent moulded by the need to avoid a direct collision with those in power (though these forms can also serve the writer's artistic need to stand back from actuality in order to contemplate the meaning of his experience). Elizabethan literature is an example of a literature produced under fairly strong pressures, yet with enough freedom to manoeuvre for the canny writers. Only a small proportion of work had to be 'for the bottom drawer', e.g. Donne's satire in which the lustful and murderous soul passed by metempsychosis into the Queen. Spenser had tacked into the wind successfully with *The Shepheardes Calender*, in which the Queen's ecclesiastical policy was censured, as well as her supposed matrimonial intentions. He did not venture to publish *Mother Hubberds Tale* until 1591, when he may have felt more secure, but this 'Aesopian' performance fell foul of Cecil, and the publication was suppressed by government order. In *Colin Clouts Come Home Again* he shows how much can be done by a kind of *duplicity* or double view. On the one hand he gives an idealized picture of Elizabethan's England; but on the other hand he sets within it a view of the baseness and licentiousness to be found at the very centre, at Court.

It is notable in Spenser's case that he combined an outstanding firmness of loyal belief in the Elizabethan 'idea' with an almost invariable habit of disagreeing with Elizabeth's actual conduct of affairs. Such a tension requires, in a poet so given to expressing his political sentiments, a disguised avowal, a sideways escape.

Radigund is herself a lawful prince. When Spenser makes his reservation that there can, if heaven so ordains, be a lawful sovereignty of a woman (V: 5: 25), he does not discuss the basis of Radigund's rule; but Artegall explicitly acknowledges that her title is sound:

> For well I may this weene, by that I fynd,
> That she a Queene, and come of Princely kynd,
> Both worthie is for to be sewd unto;
> Chiefely by him, whose life her law does bynd,
> And eke of powre her owne doome to undo,
> And als' of princely grace to be inclyn'd thereto.
>
> (V: 5: 41)

Radigund is represented as being disappointed in her love for one of the Knights of the Order of Maidenhead, and so having turned cruel to all knights. They must submit to her will—in which case she humiliates them and sets them to women's work—or if they refuse she executes them, as she executes Sir Terpin. She overpowers the knights by force or guile and then tyrannizes over them. The ruthless unfairness with which she uses her feminity to bring them into subjection is illustrated by the way Artegall is defeated. Thenceforth he may resent his situation but he is bound by his pledged word.

> How ever it his noble heart did gall
> T'obay a womans tyrannous direction . . .
>
> (V: 5: 26)

She is passionate, cruel, subject to rages, but subject also to love. Throughout she remains impressive and queenly. Her appearance is reminiscent of Belphoebe (cf. II: 3: 26-27 and V: 5: 2-3), who is an image of Diana and explicitly from time to time represents Elizabeth. The moon-image—so closely connected with Elizabeth—is first impressed on us in describing Radigund's shield:

> And on her shoulder hung her shield, bedeckt
> Uppon the bosse with stones, that shined wide,
> As the faire Moone in her most full aspect,
> That to the Moone it mote be like in each respect.
>
> (V: 5: 4)

Then Artegall shears off half her shield and finally shatters it, depriving her of her essential defence. Yet when he seeks to finish her off, he finds that she is once more armed with a moon-like defence: the beauty of her face, which shows through the blood and sweat of the battle

> Like as the Moone in foggie winters night,
> Doth seeme to be her self, though darkened be her light.
>
> (V: 5:12)

Radigund has a conspicuous opposing counterpart in Britomart, an ancestress of Elizabeth and professedly in the poem one of the mirrors of the Queen. Britomart and Radigund are both beautiful virgins dedicated to prowess in arms, and both love Artegall with jealous passion. Both conquer Sir Artegall in fight, and in both cases it is the sudden revelation of feminine beauty that overcomes him. Britomart's face appearing from the helmet whose ventail has been sheared away is likened to the sun appearing at morning.[8] In both cases also, the female warrior is in turn smitten with love for Artegall after she has been conquered (IV: 6: 26-27, and V: 5: 26-27). So when Britomart at last does battle with Radigund it is as if the two images of a valiant royal virgin were contending which should prevail, the good or the bad. When Britomart wins, her first action after freeing Artegall is to repeal the liberty of women and install Artegall as ruler of that city. Britomart thus chooses to reign only long enough to hand over authority to her beloved consort; and for this restoration of right order she is adored by the people as a goddess of wisdom (V: 7: 42). Spenser is saying pretty bluntly that the best service a woman ruler can do is to find a male consort and hand over to him.

As always, in urging an interpretation of part of *The Faerie Queene*, one must allow for the multiplicity and ambiguity in which Spenser works, and above all the fading suggestiveness which he often prefers: that Parthian tactic which Cory noted, by which he looses his shafts in retreating.[9] One cannot starkly *prove* that Spenser meant such and such a thing, unless he says so pretty explicitly. This is not a case in which he is likely to have made such an admission, or to have allowed his intention to become too sharply focused.

98 *The Grammar of the Real*

Nevertheless, it seems to me difficult not to see the Radigund episode as a sideways escape of his accumulated criticism of the Queen.

1973

NOTES

1 Some recent commentators have tried, unsuccessfully in my view, to establish a higher valuation, notably Jane Aptekar, *Icons of Justice: Iconography and Thematic Imagery in Book V of 'The Faerie Queene'* (New York, 1969) and T. K. Dunseath, *Spenser's Allegory of Justice in Book V of 'The Faerie Queene'* (Princeton, 1968).

2 The movement is described by Norman Cohn, *The Pursuit of the Millenium* (London, 1957), p. 306.

3 J. E. Neale, in 'The Elizabethan Political Scene', *Essays in Elizabethan History* (London, 1958), describes the sale of royal favours by courtiers in a position to obtain them. The phrase 'black market' is used by W. T. MacCaffery, 'Place and Patronage in Elizabethan Politics', in the symposium *Elizabethan Government and Society* (London, 1961), p. 125. He comments that as prices rose and competitors became more ruthless 'the frenetic and reckless character of Elizabethan political life was thereby increased proportionately'.

4 See the evidence assembled by L. Hicks, *An Elizabethan Problem* (London, 1964).

5 Quoted by Conyers Read, *Lord Burghley and Queen Elizabeth* (London, 1960), p. 367.

6 Not only careers but lives could be forfeit to the convenience of great ones. Dr William Parry, an agent of Burghley and Walsingham, ended by being hanged, drawn and quartered in 1584 for a so-called plot; he died declaring the Queen knew he was innocent. In 1594 Dr Roderigo Lopez, the Queen's physician and also a government agent, was sacrificed to Essex's ambitions and the need for another plot.

7 Notably Kate Warren: 'It is just possible that Queen Elizabeth herself, in some of her many moods, may have partly been Spenser's original for Radigund—though, of course, he gives no open clue to this.' (*The Works of Edmund Spenser, a Variorum Edition*, ed. E. Greenlaw et al., rev. edn., Baltimore, 1958, vol. 5, p. 202; see also pp. 273-4). Edwin Greenlaw edges near this view in seeing the sad case of Terpin and of Artegall as 'an arraignment of womanish methods applied to the solution of the Irish problem' (*Variorum*, vol. 5, p. 304).

8 IV: 6: 19. The sun image for Britomart and the moon for Radigund are paralleled by the lioness and tiger images used in V: 7: 30 when they fight. Both sun and moon images were often associated with Queen Elizabeth. Radigund is also identified as a 'Goshauke'; Queen Elizabeth's badge was a falcon. Queen Elizabeth, reviewing troops at Tilbury in 1588, wore a silver breastplate and J. E. Neale (*Queen Elizabeth*, London, 1934, p. 297) quotes a contemporary description of her on that occasion as 'like some Amazonian empress'.

9 H. E. Cory, *Edmund Spenser, a Critical Study* (Berkeley, 1917), pp. 16, 55.

Milton's difficulties in 'Paradise Lost'

LIKE many of the great works of literature, *Paradise Lost* is based on a fable which nevertheless is the vehicle for a profound realism.

The story in Genesis 2-3 has a very primitive feel. God is frankly anthropomorphic as he shapes man from mud and animates him with his breath; or as he walks in the garden in the cool of the evening and calls out to Adam and questions him. The serpent is very much the animal trickster of primitive folklore.

But this primitive traditional material is clearly being worked upon by a rather sophisticated theologically-minded final author or redactor, who asks certain questions of the material, and doubtless manipulates it to elicit answers. For example, the creation of the woman from Adam's rib is so presented as to show that the woman is not of a lower or different nature, but made of the same substance and meant to be his companion. The man ruling or 'lording it' over the woman is specifically mentioned later (3.16) as one of the bitter consequences of the Fall, presumably not 'as it was in the beginning'.[1] The story is suspended in order to bring out the mysterious oneness of man and woman: they are 'one flesh' or 'one body'. Features of this sort support the view of recent biblical scholars who, in seeking to identify the literary genre of these two chapters, have thought it best to bring them under the general category of wisdom literature. There is much wisdom literature in the Bible, and it takes various forms, as different as Ecclesiastes, Proverbs, The Book of Job. Genesis 2-3 may be seen as wisdom literature which makes use of traditional materials of a fabulous or mythic kind.

But the story as we have it remains disconcerting, as primitive narrative often is: it is abrupt, laconic, enigmatic, full of puzzles and loose ends. It will not answer inappropriate questions. For example—one relevant to Milton's problems—when the woman is convinced by the serpent, she eats some of the fruit. Then she gives some to her husband, and he eats. Was he standing by? What persuasion did she use? Did he have the same motive as she did? The story is not a work of modern fiction and offers no answers.

The task Milton set himself in *Paradise Lost* was to produce a

99

blow-up of this ancient fable, and project it in colour on the stereo-scopic wide screen of his modern epic with stereophonic sound. Though Adam and Eve are not taken as far as becoming characters in a modern realistic novel, they are taken as far as becoming charac-ters in an epic poem, whose thoughts and motives and utterances are developed extensively and in some depth. The creator God, too, becomes an epic character: a celestial king who consults with his court, explaining and justifying his policy. And the serpent is not just a serpent: it has been entered by Satan, who is one of the most brilliantly presented personages in literature.

The epic form gives Milton scope to get a tremendous amount from his material. For instance, the detailed examination in Book IX, first of Eve's motives, then of Adam's reaction to Eve's fatal act, then of the behaviour of the pair after they have both eaten the fruit is moving, intricate, full of drama and pathos and irony. The treatment sharpens to an agonizing point the question Milton pro-poses: What was Adam to do, torn between duty to God and love of his wife? Yet there was a price to pay for the achievement: fea-tures of the original story become difficulties when it is transformed into epic. I want to consider some of these, and then look at one even larger problem which grows out of Milton's personal relation to the traditional material.

Questions which the original story did not invite tend to arise as inescapable queries in the quasi-realistic narrative Milton offers. For example, one magnificent artistic stroke in Book IX is that Adam does not ask himself what he will do now that Eve has in-curred death through disobedience. He does not argue at all: he at once knows that he will die with her. But by making Adam decide immediately, in a passion of anguished love, Milton cuts off any discussion of the alternative. Suppose Adam stood firm and said that he must continue to obey God. If Eve alone sinned, must they be separated by her death? When he starts to rationalize subse-quently, he conceives a hope that God will not really destroy them both; nor does God do so, in spite of the threat that on that day they shall die. Evidently we must take the view that Adam's duty was to leave the solution to God and that God would have found a way; but Milton does not develop the point for us.

The whole matter is complicated anyway by the indecision and ambiguity attending the word 'death'. They do not die physically on the day they eat the fruit. What happens to them physically is that they become subject to eventual bodily death: they are now mortal. Adams broods on this later, when he says he is beginning to suspect that the sentence of death will be carried out in a pro-tracted way, 'a slow-pac't evil . . . to augment our pain' (X. 963-4). In an extraordinary phrase he speaks of life as 'a long day's dying'

(X. 964). Of course the word 'death' can also have a spiritual sense; Adam and his posterity have become dead to God, the prey of Sin and Death, until redeemed by the Son of God.

Another one of Milton's problems arises from the treatment he gives of the serpent. In the original story it is 'more subtle than any other wild creature that the Lord God had made'. Later tradition identified this serpent with Satan who in Revelation appears as 'the great dragon . . . that ancient serpent, who is called the Devil and Satan' (12.9). Milton has developed the Genesis fable by making Satan enter the serpent and use its organs; and then leave it again when his purpose is effected. When, in Book X, the Son of God comes to the Garden as judge pronouncing sentence, the serpent is once more just a dumb and guiltless beast. Yet a curse is placed upon it. Milton gives a rather muffled explanation (X. 165-74) of why the serpent has to incur the sentence. He cannot ignore the question, because he is now at a point in the Genesis story which is of the greatest importance; for the sentence pronounced upon the serpent contains these mysterious words:

> I will put enmity between you and the woman,
>   and between your seed and her seed;
> he shall bruise your head,
>   and you shall bruise his heel.
>
> (3. 16)

In the traditional Christian interpretation, this is the *protevange-lium*, the first obscure foreshadowing of the Messiah who, as Eve's descendant, will crush the evil one. (It is not, in fact, unlikely that the theologically-minded final author of Genesis 2-3 intended some sort of messianic interpretation.) The very Son of God who is pronouncing the sentence and uttering the prophecy will fulfil it by taking flesh and overcoming Satan. Satan does not hear the sentence spoken, because he has fled away, but he comes back that night and overhears Adam and Eve discussing it. When he returns to Hell and reports to the assembled council of demons, he says that God has passed judgement on him for his successful enterprise— or rather, a puzzling thing, not actually on him but on the brute serpent; yet he takes the sense of it upon himself:

> that which to me belongs,
> Is enmity, which he will put between
> Me and Mankind; I am to bruise his heel;
> His seed, when is not set, shall bruise my head.
>
> (XI. 496-9)

And he thinks 'a bruise' a small price to pay for the purchase of a world.

Just as the serpent presents a problem for Milton, so does another important element in the original fable, the Tree of Life. When Satan enters Paradise first, in Book IV, he leaps over the wall, just as hirelings later will try to enter the Church by irregular ways; and then, changing himself into the likeness of a cormorant, he perches upon the midmost and tallest tree, the Tree of Life, where he sits devising death (IV. 197).[2] There is no prohibition placed on this Tree of Life. It is first seen as having symbolic significance, and is then virtually ignored until the moment comes in Book XI when fidelity to the scriptural account at last compels Milton to refer to it again. This happens in God's council in heaven, when he says that Paradise is no longer a suitable dwelling place for fallen man. The Genesis text runs:

> Then the Lord God said 'Behold, the man has become like one of us, knowing good and evil; and now, lest he put forth his hand and take also of the tree of life and eat, and live forever'—therefore the Lord God sent him forth from the Garden of Eden, to till the ground from which he was taken.
>
> (3. 22-3)

Milton cannot fit this text plausibly into his account: it belongs to the most primitive stratum of the material. In its literal sense it implies that the Tree of Life had intrinsic power to make man immortal, and that there was a danger that Adam might evade God's watchfulness and take the fruit. Milton cannot ascribe an independant occult power to the fruit of the Tree of Life, any more than he can ascribe intrinsic knowledge-giving power to the sap of the other tree; and it is ridiculous for God, as presented in the poem, to have to say:

> Lest therefore his now bolder hand
> Reach also of the Tree of Life, and eat,
> And live for ever . . .

So Milton adds something to God's words, in order to slide away from the literal meaning:

> *dream at least to live*
> *For ever*, to remove him I decree.
> (XI. 93-5)

But the reason for expelling man from the Garden thus becomes thin: it is not that the Tree of Life has any real efficacy, but man might think it has, and we do not want him to have such vain imaginings.

There are more such difficulties that arise for Milton because of his need to be faithful to the original while translating it into a later literary genre—and of course into a later thought-world than that either of the primitive tale in its earliest, irrecoverable, form or forms, or of the tale as we have it in Genesis 2-3. The difficulties are of some interest, and in understanding them we understand the poem better. It is also evident how little these incidental embarrassments affect the power of the poem.

The final larger problem which Milton had to face arises from the fact that the Genesis account does not come to us as a detached piece. It is imbedded in a set of literary works of various kinds which make up a body of sacred scripture. These works were collected together and given this special status by a people who regarded them as containing the hope of man's salvation. In turn the Christians added a New Testament in which, as they claimed, the promise of the Old Testament was fulfilled; so that the final book, the Apocalypse, by its continual reference back to Old Testament prophecy (including not least the prophetic aspects of Genesis) reaches from end to end of 'salvation history'.

Milton proposes in *Paradise Lost* to do the same. He tells the story of the Fall in order to reveal the whole sweep of God's providential plan to the end of time for the world as we know it and beyond into eternity. His purpose was no less than to vindicate God's goodness and justice, to 'justify the ways of God to men' (I. 26).

In attempting this task, Milton was guided by a traditional form of argument, grounded in St Paul, developed by St Augustine and St Thomas Aquinas, and echoed in the Christian liturgy. Why did and does God permit evil? The first part of the argument stresses that man's great gift and dignity of intellect and free will necessarily involves the possibility of man choosing wrongly. The second part of the argument holds that God is justified in permitting evil so long as, out of this evil, he can elicit a greater good. Note that it must be a *greater* good: only if the last happiness man will find is immensely greater than the first happiness he lost can we sing in the Easter liturgy 'O happy fault!' and be glad that Adam was allowed to fall. So runs the traditional argument. I pass by its merits as an argument, having no talent for comprehending the thoughts of God. The mystery of evil remains terribly dark to me, even in the light of faith.

Milton announces his basic thesis early in the poem in a surprising way. He lets Satan perceive God's likely strategy:

> If then his Providence
> Out of our evil seek to bring forth good,
> Our labour must be to pervert that end,
> And out of good still to find means of evil . . .
>
> (I. 163-5)

Milton then reinforces this by saying that God allows Satan to roam

H

at large and pervert the newly created world of man, because in
the end Satan will have been forced to see

> How all his malice serv'd but to bring forth
> Infinite goodness, grace and mercy shown
> On Man by him seduc't . . .
>
> (I. 217-19)

'Infinite' goodness implies the greater good that God must provide
if man's long experience of suffering and evil is to find justification

Milton's view of the extent and horror of man's wickedness and
suffering is displayed in Books XI-XII when the archangel Michael
takes Adam to the mount of Speculation and shows him the course
of history from beginning until Judgement Day. The central event
is of course the Incarnation of the Son and his redemption of man.
But, as we move on from that event, Milton can find no sign that
the redemption has any effect on the evil man suffers in historical
time. War, cruelty, oppression, persecution, hypocrisy and falsity
flourish unabated. The world as we experience it is still a colonial
dominion of Hell. Evil triumphs while truth and virtue are mocked
and slandered and persecuted. And so it will go on, until the end
comes:

> Truth shall retire
> Bestuck with sland'rous darts and works of Faith
> Rarely be found: so shall the World go on,
> To good malignant, to bad men benign,
> Under her own weight groaning . . .
>
> (XII. 535-9)

The words are bitter, dark and heavy. Where then is the greater
good which is to be our hope and consolation, and God's vindica-
tion?

Milton's answer is twofold, and both answers are given in Book
XII of the poem.

The first answer follows traditional doctrine. It has already been
announced in God's discourses in Heaven, and Michael has already
referred to it, foretelling for man a new Paradise:

> far happier place
> Than this of Eden, and far happier days.
> (XII. 464-5)

The greater good will be the state of blessedness enjoyed by redeemed mankind in eternity after the old world has perished by
fire and the judgement has been made by the Son at his second
coming:

> so shall the world go on . . .
> Under her own weight groaning, till the day

Appear of respiration to the just,
And vengeance to the wicked, at return
Of him so lately promis'd to thy aid,
The Woman's seed, obscurely then foretold,
Now amplier known thy Saviour and Thy Lord,
Last in the clouds from Heav'n to be reveal'd,
In glory of the Father, to dissolve
Satan with his perverted World, then raise
From the conflagrant mass, purg'd and refin'd,
New Heav'ens, new Earth, Ages of endless date
Founded in righteousness and peace and love,
To bring forth fruits Joy and eternal Bliss.

(XII. 537-50)

The passage is resounding, oratorical, and uses the imagery of orthodox teaching. But it is not poetry of a high order. If to justify *in a*
poem the ways of God means to make the doctrine not only intellectually convincing but also poetically effective—eloquent, imaginatively and emotionally persuasive and overpowering—then Milton
has not succeeded at this crucial point. In an ordinary experience of
the poem, would any reader single this passage out as one of the
peaks? With the fluctuations natural to reading a large work, might
this passage not pass by without the kind of attention it should command by its importance? For here at last the great poem should
come to rest, all its huge weight should come down upon this passage: here is the greater good stated and God vindicated.

It can be acknowledged that there is an inherent difficulty, that
the greater good as here presented is a supernatural good, beyond
the range of man's experience or imagining, for which all words are
inadequate, all analogies feeble. This is true; failure to that extent
is inevitable. Yet when Dante essayed at the end of his poem to render a vision of final bliss, of the Divine Love and Beauty that shall
be all in all, it is a passage of extraordinary poetic intensity. Milton
did not have to fail so badly. The fact is that he was not, at this
point, fully kindled, fully penetrated and possessed by the rapture
the theme should inspire. The weight of his feeling does not lie
in the supernatural hope he proclaims in accordance with traditional
doctrine.

It may also be observed (as it has been observed) that in regard
to Christ there is in Milton little sign of loving intimacy—in
Paradise Lost or in *Paradise Regained* or elsewhere. Milton remains
at a distance from the Son of God, and the poem does not come alive
in the presence of the Son.

It is the second answer to the question of the greater good that
more fully engages Milton's feeling and impresses us poetically.
This answer emerges in the rest of the dialogue between Michael
and Adam after the final vision of man's supernatural end. Adam

expresses satisfaction and gratitude, and draws conclusions for himself about the proper attitude to life in 'this transient world':

> Greatly instructed I shall hence depart,
> Greatly in peace of thought, and have my fill
> Of knowledge, what this Vessel can contain;
> Beyond which was my folly to aspire.
> Henceforth I learn, that to obey is best,
> And love with fear the only God, to walk
> As in his presence, ever to observe
> His providence, and on him sole depend,
> Merciful over all his works, with good
> Still overcoming evil, and by small
> Accomplishing great things, by things deem'd weak
> Subverting worldly strong, and wordly wise
> By simply meek; that suffering for Truth's sake
> Is fortitude to highest victory,
> And to the faithful Death the Gate of Life;
> Taught this by his example whom I now
> Acknowledge my Redeemer ever blest.
>
> (XII. 557-73)

The words have a quietness, a sense of acceptance. Milton has seen something of the difference between the way that man attempts to shape his world in pride and violence and the way good actually arises from 'things deem'd weak'. Michael then gives Adam his parting words of advice: if you have truly learned the doctrine you have just professed, you have attained a wisdom worth more than all science or wealth or power. What remains is to act upon your knowledge:

> only add
> Deeds to thy knowledge answerable, add Faith,
> Add Virtue, Patience, Temperance, add Love,
> By name to come call'd Charity, the soul
> Of all the rest: then wilt thou not be loath
> To leave this Paradise, but shalt possess
> A paradise within thee, happier far.
>
> (XII. 581-587)

That is the end of the divine message. Michael simply adds some information about their departure. The lines quoted above are obviously very important: they deal in their own way with the hope of paradise regained. Hear then the conclusion of the whole matter: by the practice of the virtues, by an inner integrity, man can in this life experience the greater good, recover a happiness greater than that which was lost by the Fall, even though outwardly he must suffer in an evil world.

This second solution raises an obvious difficulty. In the first Paradise, Adam and Eve had both external and internal happiness.

Now they can have only a precarious paradise within, obtainable if they overcome the effects of original sin and live in patient virtue. How is this a greater good? Milton does not say. The implication seems to be that the form the virtues take when fallen man imitates the example of Christ is of higher worth than the virtues of original innocence. This seems to bring Milton close to what he wrote in *Areopagitica*, that in this fallen world good and evil grow up together almost inseparably and require us to learn discrimination, so that in a sense what Adam's fault doomed us to was not merely the knowledge of good and evil but the necessity of 'knowing good by evil':

> I cannot praise a fugitive and cloistered virtue, unexercised and unbreathed, that never sallies out and sees her adversary, but slinks out of the race where that immortal garland is to be run for, not without dust and heat. Assuredly we bring not innocence into the world, we bring impurity much rather: that which purifies us is trial, and trial is by what is contrary. That virtue therefore which is but a youngling in the contemplation of evil, and knows not the utmost that vice promises to her followers, and rejects it, is but a blank virtue, not a pure; her whiteness is but an excremental whiteness . . .

This preference for Experience over Innocence is all very well, but I am not sure that it is helpful to the thesis of the poem. If the 'paradise within' is to be preferred to the 'garden state' should not God have *wanted* man to fall? This is of course one way of putting a difficulty in the whole argument, because it requires God to have originally intended a *lesser* good for man, the greater good being contingent upon man disobeying God. That is why St Bonaventura supposed that in God's original plan Christ would have come anyway, even if man had remained unfallen, so as to raise man to a higher perfection and happiness.

But, whatever the difficulties, it will surely be agreed that the poetic level of the passage under consideration is higher than in the passage that proclaims the first solution. Milton's heart is in the this-worldly solution, not in the other-worldly solution, in the contemplation of human virtue rather than the beatific vision.

It has never seemed to me that the poem suffers very much from the flaws, real or supposed, that critics have found in its attempted justification of God. Great works have a power to involve us even when we do not accept all their doctrine. Homer, Virgil, Lucretius, Dante, Shakespeare, Milton, Tolstoy, Dostoievsky—the Titans do not agree amongst themselves. Their power is that they wrestle faithfully with the dark riddle of man's existence; they show us, in the magic mirror of art, man foolish and failing and seemingly overwhelmed by appalling forces, yet somehow preserving hope and love. From the doctrinal conclusion we have been looking at, Milton proceeds with artistic sureness to the great poetry of the poem's last scene. How is such a mighty poem to end? With what sublime chorus of angels shouting jubilee, with what organ tones, with what double fugue of brilliant virtuosity closing with mighty chords? With none of these. Milton has Michael hurrying the human pair through the gate and down the cliff-path to the plain, then disappear. Adam and Eve look back once—and for a moment the vision of the angelic guard, 'the Gate/With dreadful faces throng'd and fiery arms', recalls the earlier splendours of the poem; but then the last long quiet cadence begins. The world is all before them and, sadly but accepting their lot, they walk out hand in hand into history.

1974

NOTES

1 In the Revised Version the phrase is 'he shall rule over you'. In the Jerusalem Bible the rendering is 'he will lord it over you'. Further passages quoted are from the Revised Version.

2 He does not 'enter' a real cormorant as he does the serpent. Why could not Satan in Book IX change himself into the likeness of a serpent, as earlier of a cormorant and then a toad? Because at the judgement scene in Book X, there must be no confrontation directly between the Son and Satan. The biblical curse applied literally to the serpent, and Milton had to respect this, whatever the difficulties. So the serpent had to be a separable vehicle, left there when Satan quitted the scene.

A visit to Bunhill

DRYDEN may have visited Milton several times, as Johnson stated. Aubrey's notes and Dryden's own references certainly imply at least one extended and friendly conversation, which took place in 1674, in the last year of Milton's life.[1]

The house in which Milton lived in retirement is now gone. It was in the road called Bunhill Row, or the Artillery Walk, which was lined on one side by the wall of the exercising ground of the London Artillery Company. This ground is still there, adjoining the Bunhill (Bone-hill) cemetery in which John Bunyan, Richard Cromwell, Isaac Watts and William Blake are buried.

The old blind Commonwealthsman may be pictured as sitting in an elbow chair in a room containing his favourite instrument, the manual organ. (English organs were until the eighteenth century without pedals and gave a clear sound unlike the fuzzy mess created by later organ technology.) Milton was cheerful and civil in conversation, even though he suffered most severely from gout. His hands had the chalkstone deposits of sodium urate characteristic of chronic gout, and he confessed that his blindness was a lesser affliction than the pain from this source. Dryden, as he told Aubrey, noticed that in his speech Milton pronounced the 'r' (*littera canina*, the letter that growls like a dog) very hard, 'a sure sign of a satirical wit': this stray piece of information lights up the phonic texture of many lines in the poetry.

The reason for Dryden's visit was an unusual request. He wanted to fashion out of *Paradise Lost* the libretto of a music drama to be called *The State of Innocence*. It was an ambitious project for the opening of the new Theatre Royal; but it proved beyond the company's financial resources and was never produced. Rather surprisingly Milton good-humouredly gave Dryden permission to 'tag his verses', that is, to turn his epic matter into rhymed dramatic versions. Milton's compliance, and Dryden's courtesy in making the request when he could have gone ahead without consulting Milton's feelings, are equally pleasant to contemplate. Despite their deep differences of attitude and allegiance in political and religious matters, there was a basis for goodwill and conversation. In part it was the truly professional interest they shared in literature generally and in poetic technique in particular. We know from Dryden that they discussed prosody on some occasion; and also that Milton mentioned his large debt to Spenser's work, to which Dryden has also acknowledged indebtedness. But perhaps the main reason for Milton's goodwill was that Dryden was able to offer a sincere and discriminating admiration which must have come agreeably to the older poet. It is reported that when Dryden read *Paradise Lost* he exclaimed: 'This man cuts us all out, and the ancients too!'[2] He has left his praise of Milton on record in several places, but the most certain evidence of his sincerity is that echoes and reminiscences of Milton recur almost obsessively in the work he wrote from 1667 till the end of his life in 1700. Who can say what part Milton's example played in raising Dryden's mind to the great poetic undertakings of his later years? Dryden's generosity and discernment and objectivity in praising so highly the work of an author ideologically so antithetical to him is of a piece with his character and with the quality of his work.

What Milton thought of the poetic merits of John Dryden, Esq., Poet Laureate and Historiographer Royal and leading professional dramatist, we know only from a phrase recollected by his third wife, Elizabeth, that he was 'a good rimist, but no poet', to which she added the comment that 'this was before [he] had composed his best poems'. In 1674 Dryden was forty-three, and still seven years off writing any work which deserves to be called great. He is one of the very late developers: if he had died before writing *Absalom and Achitophel* in his fiftieth year he would be of minor interest today. And this poem visibly and designedly uses references to *Paradise Lost* as a structural element.

II

> Milton! thou shouldst be living at this hour:
> England hath need of thee,

Wordsworth intoned in 1802 in a political sonnet which gives us to understand that Wordsworth is pretty Miltonic himself and regards himself as Milton's natural successor. We have all read this sonnet and perhaps respectfully assented, without quite knowing what political good Milton ever did anyone. On reflection I would amend the sonnet to read: 'Dryden! thou shouldst be living at this hour'. Never did our civilization have greater need of his intellectual virtues. But before confronting Milton with Dryden, we must first see why Wordsworth was wrong about Milton, and why the only use Milton can serve in his political capacity is as an outstanding example of the public nuisance that literary ideologues can make of themselves. The facts need to be sharply re-stated because their

significance keeps getting lost among commentators who stand uncritically in his line of ideological dissent or are just dazzled by the
general idea of Milton's highmindedness.

The truth is that Milton started by being too high-minded altogether. He believed himself to be in a very special sense a dedicated
person, with a peculiar vocation, called by Heaven to play a conspicuous role in the history of human salvation. He saw himself as
ordained to be the prophetic bard whose trumpet voice would an-
nounce the beginning of the reign of God, shortly to commence in
England. This event was of the highest importance because it would
be the prelude to the millennium, the reign of God universally; it
being well known that the English are the new Chosen People, and
that God customarily starts with 'his Englishmen' in bringing about
any new work, as Milton explains in *Areopagitica*. In 1641 his vision
of the coming of the New Order rose to this ecstatic strain:

> Then amidst the Hymns, and Halleluiahs of Saints [meaning the ad-
> herents of the Puritan revolution] some one [guess who] may perhaps be
> heard offering at high strains in new and lofty Measures . . . [looking
> forward to] that day when thou the Eternal and shortly-expected King
> shalt open the Clouds to judge the several Kingdoms of the World . . .

After the revolution, when God's reign will be actualized in the
form of the rule of the Saints—meaning at this time the Presbyterian
party leaders—outstanding services to the revolution will be re-
warded. Such people as himself will be raised to a revolutionary
peerage formed on analogy with the angelic hierarchy: they will receive 'above the inferior Orders of the Blessed, the Regal addition
of Principalities, Legions, and Thrones in to their glorious Titles'.[3]
The merits of our poet would hardly accord with a lesser title than
Principality Milton, of the highest order in the new aristocracy.

The essential task of these heroes of the revolution will have been
to aid in the overthrow of the Anglican bishops and the clergy faithful to them, who are the great hindrance that must be destroyed so
that the reign of God on earth can immediately commence. Milton
had already denounced the ecclesiastical establishment in *Lycidas*,
and prophesied divine vengeance upon it. In that famous de-
nunciation he even inserts some literary criticism of loyalist clergy-
man poets—presumably people like Dean Donne and Bishop Corbet
and Bishop King and the Reverend Robert Herrick—for their 'lean
and flashy songs'. One would like to think that the Reverend George
Herbert was not included in this contempt, but one cannot be sure;
in any case Herbert, if he had lived, would have had to be cast out
with the rest. For Milton metes out rhetorically on God's behalf con-

dign punishment for the noxious episcopalian establishment and its supporters; for they

> . . . after a shameful end in this Life (which God grant them) shall be thrown down eternally into the darkest and deepest Gulf of Hell, where under the despightful control, the trample and spurn of all the other Damned, that in the anguish of their Torture shall have no other ease than to exercise a Raving and Bestial Tyranny over them as their Slaves and Negro's, they shall remain in that plight for ever, the basest, the lowermost, the most dejected, most underfoot and down-trodden Vassals of Perdition.

So concludes the much-admired and anthologized rhetorical prayer at the end of the tract *Of Reformation*.[4] Milton was thirty-three when he wrote this. How did he get himself worked up into such an ideological frenzy?

He had an inordinately prolonged adolescence, of a sort not unlike that which we produce in our universities today. He remained in the children's playground of post-graduate studies, even longer than most of our vulnerable, privileged, and anxiety-ridden students do. Milton's post-graduate studies, however, were not pursued in Cambridge but in retirement with the support of a generous father who was a money-lender. The culmination was a tour of Italy. This prolonged period of deliberate preparation for a great public role fostered in Milton a dangerous combination of three things: a high sense of his moral and intellectual superiority: commitment to a revolutionary ideology; utter ignorance of human nature and behaviour.

The important thing about Milton is not the much-lauded 'idealism'. That consisted, as it usually does, of a set of illusions supported by arrogance and ignorance; armed with this he marched into a series of shattering collisions with reality. What matters is precisely the collisions with reality and the fact that Milton did learn—painfully, very painfully; reluctantly, very reluctantly; and partially, only partially. It was not the great expectations Milton entertained for himself that made him capable of *Paradise Lost*: it was the repeated dashing of these expectations. Though Milton never succeeded wholly in abandoning his pride and stubborn illusions, he tried manfully to bend his will and accept the lessons that are learnt only in the furnace of affliction.

The first collision came when he suddenly, at the age of thirty-three, married a seventeen-year-old girl, the daughter of a Royalist squire who owed his father money. Milton had not at first intended to marry: he had adopted the notion that by celibacy one could sublimate sexual energy into poetic and intellectual power. (This view of Milton's purpose is contested by some scholars, but it seems to me to come out clearly enough in the praise of virginity in *Co-*

mus, the hermetic aspirations of the celibate recluse in *Il Penseroso*, and the odd choice proposed in *Lycidas*, between playing the 'shepherd's trade' of study and poetry and having fun with girls like Amaryllis and Neaera.) Milton's young bride stayed with him a few weeks and then went home, and would not return or answer letters. Civil war had meanwhile broken out, and it widened the gap. By the end of the first year of his marriage Milton had written a pamphlet explaining that when Christ forbade divorce he was actually intending to permit it. This very Miltonic rationalization caused a small furore, and the dominant Presbyterian faction urged Parliament to ban the pamphlet. What action was taken is not clear: it seems nothing of consequence was done. But under the threat of censorship Milton wrote his famous *Areopagitica*.

Areopagitica is a confused and confusing work. The main argument is against *pre-publication licensing* as a method of control. But there is much argument whose effect would be to reject any kind of censorship, before or after publication. Yet Milton more than once affirms that post-publication proceedings against mischievous authors and publications are necessary, without making it clear what classes of authors and writings are not to be tolerated. The only liberty he clearly and consistently pleads for is the liberty of all factions of the Puritan left to circulate their views as contributions to the Revolution, without Presbyterian hindrance. Beyond that, the tract is vague, evasive and contradictory. We may leave this unhelpful performance to the curt comment on it by Samuel Johnson in his *Life of Milton*:

> The danger of unbounded liberty, and the danger of bounding it, have produced a problem in the science of government which human understanding seems hitherto unable to solve.

It need only be added that seven years later, under Cromwell's military dictatorship, Milton accepted the job precisely of pre-publication licenser in respect of the weekly newspaper *Mercurius Politicus*. His biographer Parker bravely says that his responsibility was 'largely routine': the paper was 'semi-official', and *'we may be confident* that Milton's activities as licenser of a newsletter were altogether perfunctory . . . Milton, *we may be sure*, wasted few hours as an editorial supervisor of his friend'.[5] The one thing of which *we may be sure* is that the arguments he applied to others in 1644 he did not apply to himself in 1651.

But what we are most concerned with is the main drift of Milton's political position-taking after his burst of millenarian enthusiasm on the eve of the Civil War. He witnessed with grim approval the beheading of the King in 1649 outside Inigo Jones's Banqueting Hall, and later justified it as government propagandist. (Dryden was a schoolboy in his last year at the Westminster School just down the road.) Milton wanted to believe that the fall of the axe opened the way to the establishment of a virtuous commonwealth: now God alone would be king, and the visible government would be in the hands of virtuous, sober and discreet men in Parliament. It was up to the nation, freed at one stroke from its chains, to rise to the opportunity and lead the whole world into a reign of righteousness.

But of course the godly kingdom was not founded in the blood of royal Charles. Parliament was a confused medley of sectarians and men on the make. Cromwell had the real power, and swept Parliament away. What was left was a military dictatorship, highly unpopular with the vast majority of the nation, but temporarily strong in its military power. Milton raised a paean of prose eulogy to the great dictator—again proclaiming that now was the appointed time; now was the acceptable hour for the nation to begin the reign of righteousness.[6] But Cromwell, for all his skill and strength—his remarkable combination of ruthlessness and moderation—could provide no solution. Milton's notions proved once more irrelevant and illusory. War and taxes and unrest flourished. Cromwell died. The nation floundered into near-anarchy and waited for General Monk to produce what almost everyone now knew was the only available solution: the restoration of the monarchy. Almost everyone: Milton's soul was like a star and dwelt apart. In the very month of the Restoration, May 1660, Milton was still publishing his impassioned plea that the best way of establishing a free republic was by placing central power in the hands of a self-perpetuating grand council of men like Milton—sober, virtuous, republican and ultra-Protestant. There was nothing 'democratic' about Milton; nor realistic either.

But Charles returned: lax, witty, intelligent, lazy, licentious, astute, disinclined to blood. He gave the nation what it needed: twenty-five years of recovery and increasing prosperity, even under the severe challenge of the later years. He gave Milton his life and liberty in the general amnesty, but got no thanks from the bard.

What had Milton done with his life? He had lived in scholarly retirement; had for a few years kept a small school for boys while the Civil War raged; had served a revolutionary assembly and then a military dictator as a mixture of propagandist and minor foreign office official, nowhere at any stage near the levers of decision or able to have any effect whatsoever on policy or the course of events. Successively he had seen his glorious dreams for the religio-political transformation of England collapse into a spreading mess of discontent, first simmering under Cromwell's sword, then seething into tumult as the republic fell apart and men cried out for a return of the old constitution.

Milton was now blind, rejected, living in reduced circumstances, though not really poor. What was the use of it all? What could God mean by thus humiliating and dejecting his chosen one, his champion, his prophet, his trumpet-voice to the people? God is all-wise, all loving; his providence steers all things rightly, and permits evil only to bring forth from it a greater good. Milton clung to this doctrine of a greater good as the central truth. But how hard it was to make sense of God's design in practice! How hard to see any evidence that God could be trusted to govern the world in a rational and responsible way! How hard to find any justification of the ways of God to men—including to Milton.

Milton took up again the project of a great epic. Its formal theme would be the origin of evil in the fall of the angels and the subsequent fall of man, and the overcoming of evil by a greater good. Paradise is lost, but can be regained, even in this life, where evil flourishes as much since Christ as before Christ. Milton preaches salvation through the adoption of an inner disposition, the achievement of an inner peace of mind in spite of tribulation and failure. How can this 'Paradise within thee happier far' be attained? By obedience to God, by humility, by patience, by love. Gone is the political activism. Gone is the confident belief that the sword of sectarian fanaticism can make a Caesarian section in history and bring the new age to birth. If there is to be a millennium within historical time, as Milton still believed, then it will come by God's decision and God's action, not by man's.

Had Milton learnt his lesson completely? Neither in life, nor in the spirit of the poem, is the old stubborn highmindedness wholly subdued. But the drama is there, and the answer given by the poet is a genuine attempt to adopt the prayer: 'Thy will not mine be done'. There is enough knowledge and truth passionately and painfully gained to make a very great poem possible by a poet with truly extraordinary powers. There is also enough that lurks unresolved to make one's judgement ambiguous and variable and hard to fix into a final shape. There are times when one revolts against Milton. But the poem is immeasurably wonderful in various, surprising, and breathtaking ways.

Milton died in 1674, a few months after the visit Dryden paid him. His inner attempt at submission to God's inscrutable will did not alter his unrepentant republicanism and puritanism, which had settled into forms peculiar to himself. He had become a church of one and a political party of one. But emotionally and intellectually he was still located within the field of true believers in the Good Old Cause.

One cannot but wonder what his reaction to the Whig upsurge of 1769-82 would have been. Shaftesbury was then reheating the enthusiasm of the Good Old Cause as part of the motor power of his own different policy. Would Milton have seen the great thundercloud of opposition to the Crown—a thundercloud explosive with elements of republicanism and Puritan revolutionism—as a sign that God was at last showing his hand? Would he have murmured, as the threat of a new Civil War approached:

> Oh how comely it is and how reviving
> To the Spirits of just men long opprest![7]

Or would he have stood fast by his acquired scepticism about the action of politicians and the use of force?—

> Much ostentation vain or fleshly arm,
> And fragile arms, much instrument of war
> Long in preparing, soon to nothing brought,
> Before mine eyes thou hast set; and in my ear
> Vented much policy, and projects deep
> Of enemies, of aids, battles and leagues,
> Plausible to the World, to me worth naught.[8]

One does not know, but may suspect that Milton would have found it difficult to resist the intense excitement of the crisis as Shaftesbury, the great Achitophel, the Archimago of whiggery, fomented and exploited public hysteria over the Popish Plot, set his 'brisk boys' of the London waterfront in motion for demonstration after demonstration against the Government, and raised the hopes of the revolutionary remnants.

Milton would have swallowed the Popish Plot for certain, and might have wrought himself once more into exalted hopes as he saw the Crown under attack. Milton's old vision of a Commonwealth ruled by a permanent élite of virtuous republicans could momentarily have seemed close enough to Shaftesbury's more cynical policy of placing power in the hands of a few immensely wealthy magnates operating behind the façade of Parliament.

III

Dryden, being on the other side, has long received very different treatment from many of his biographers and critics. He has been given no benefit of any doubt; his changes of political and religious position are timeserving and ignoble; he lacks idealism; he is antidemocratic. It is fortunately true, however, that belated justice has recently been done by responsible historians and critics, and that these old prejudicial charges cannot now be respectably maintained. The hostility towards Dryden is not because he was a lesser poet than Milton—as he was by a long way. It is basically because he was fundamentally right. He diagnosed revolutionism as a dangerous social disease. He said that the cry for liberty in the mouths of armed ideological zealots is the signal for disorder and dictatorship. He said reform, yes; revolution, no. He said societies are always imperfect, and politics on any other premises are madness. He said that the only hope people have of peace and happiness and prosperity is founded on law and order: anyone who appoints himself to be above the law, whether king or revolutionary activist or moralistic zealot, is a danger to the liberty and happiness of the community. He said that sound politics are a matter of practical prudent judgement in given situations, not the acting out of a dream-sequence of revolution. He said that toleration of differences of doctrine should be extended to all who are willing to keep the peace; that persecution by established authority is an evil, but so is the attempt by fanatics to force a new belief on an unwilling community. In short, he stated many of the things that most adults know to be true. But strange ideological residues lurk in our culture, our upbringing, our education; and we often resist as low and shabby the liberal conservative's adherence to sober realism.

Dryden's political outlook is very close to that of Shakespeare as evident in the histories. It is both principled and pragmatic. It tries to make the best of an imperfect state of things, but not in a purely opportunist way, because it never loses the sense that there are human norms and constants which are real and sacred because they are God's creation in us. After Dryden it was Edmund Burke who conspicuously reasserted the same appeal to common sense and divine dispensation against the re-emergence of the revolutionary syndrome in a more purely secularized form.

For revolutionism, whatever its pre-history, is a psycho-social disease particularly characteristic of modern Western civilization. We take it for granted that there should be a class of people more or less permanently and professionally devoted to destroying the existing order in the belief that this is the way to bring in a new order, wholly different in its way of working and more or less perfect. Revolutionism has taken various forms over the past few centuries, but in essence it consists of four propositions:

1. A perfect society is possible.
2. The present system is the sole barrier to attaining the perfect society and is therefore essentially evil and must be destroyed, not reformed.
3. The enlightened élite (who define themselves by believing propositions 1 and 2) have a right or mandate to override the majority and impose their will.
4. After the revolution power must be confined to the loyal true believers, while all backward elements are converted or rendered historically inoperative.

The seventeenth-century Puritan form of these propositions clothes them in messianic-millenarian terms:

1. The Kingdom of God is at hand as a political event.
2. The monarchy and established church are the Antichrist which must be destroyed.
3. The Saints (i.e. Puritan zealots) have a mandate from Heaven to overthrow the Government and bring in the new order by force.
4. The new order will be 'the rule of the Saints' in which 'dominion is founded in grace' i.e. power is confined to the Puritan Politburo and its cadres.

It is a matter of taste whether one prefers the clotted but colourful religious terminology of the Puritan version or the grey sociological sludge of later secularized versions. In all cases, as Dostoievsky observed, you start with the demand for total liberation and end with the practice of total despotism. The demand for total liberation justifies the discrediting of all existing authority, the invoking of disorder and violence, the trampling on the wishes and rights of the unenlightened majority. It also justifies the total despotism subsequently imposed, because the reign of perfection will never take shape if ordinary human rights and wishes are allowed to interfere.

Suffused through Dryden's presentation of the issues in *Absalom and Achitophel* and in other writings is one cardinal truth: if you corrode, undermine and destroy legitimate authority, what comes in its place is not freedom but drastic naked power. The idea of legitimate authority is involved in the notion that institutions have a proper function and need an appropriate distribution of rights and duties; it implies a consent which is to a large extent spontaneous and habitual, but not therefore unreasonable; it encloses and qualifies power and minimizes its naked use. Of course legitimate authority is in practice always more or less badly exercised, and often its theoretical justification remains poorly developed and vulnerable to sophistic criticism. It always has something traditional and even 'mystical' about it. It can always seem superstitious and wrong in comparison with an invisible rationalistic perfection. Once destroyed, it is not easily reconstituted.

It is unlikely that a dialogue on this subject ever took place at Bunhill when Dryden visited Milton. Such dialogues are seldom fruitful. The vital dialogue is more often a silent one between books presenting each side—or in a book representing a struggle of tendencies in one poem. There is such a struggle in Milton, complex and evolving, hard to fix in summary form and never really resolved. He would never admit that he was a destroyer of natural and supernatural authority and hierarchy; he drew away from the ranters and fanatics, he saw himself as a rare upholder of rational virtue and true religion in all their simple decency and dignity. And there is something—a good deal—in this; yet not enough: Milton never managed fully to trace the real consequences of his characteristic attitudes.

1974

NOTES

1 For Aubrey's account and another by Jonathan Richardson, see Helen Darbishire (ed.), *The Early Lives of John Milton* (London, 1932), pp. 6-7, 296. Another early reference is *The Monitor* I no. 17 (6-10 April 1713). For discussions see vol. 5, pp. 46-7, of *The Life Records of John Milton*, compiled by J. M. French (5 vols, New Brunswick, N.J., 1949-58); W. R. Parker, *Milton: a Biography* (Oxford, 1968), pp. 634-5; R. D. Havens, 'Dryden's Visit to Milton', *Review of English Studies* I (1925) 348-9; and M. Freedman, 'Dryden's "Memorable Visit" to Milton', *Huntington Library Quarterly* XVIII (1955) 99-108.

2 Recorded by Jonathan Richardson (Darbishire p. 296).

3 *Of Reformation*, in *Complete Prose Works of John Milton*, ed. Don M. Wolfe *et al.* (New Haven, 1953-), vol. 1, p. 616.

4 *Of Reformation*, pp. 616-7.

5 Parker, p. 394.

6 *Defensio Secunda*, in Wolfe *et al.*, vol. 6, pp. 548-686.

7 *Samson Agonistes*, lines 1268-9.

8 *Paradise Regained*, III: 387-93.

J

Wordsworth and Crabbe and the Eighteenth-Century Heritage

IT will be allowed, I hope, that the eighteenth century is particularly well endowed with realistic poetry that digests a large amount of fact: hence the prominence of discursive, didactic and descriptive forms of composition. This appetite for fact admittedly operated within certain conventions. There was an acute sense that matter should be 'to advantage dress'd' in accordance with the norms of elegance and decorum. There was also a liking for generalized statement, prompted by strong need to impose, or seem to impose, cognitive order on recalcitrant particulars. But these conventions, of poetic diction and generalizing treatment, while they assured that poetry should be a product of conspicuous artifice, did not prevent it from being at the same time realistic and factual.

The knowledge digested by this poetry was partly of the natural world, but more of social man and his works. There were limitations: among other things, literary decorum was to a large extent class-conditioned; the life of the lower orders of society was either ignored or dealt with in stylized ways, in condescension or burlesque—there was no way of according it equal dignity or serious import.

Whatever its limitations, the eighteenth-century heritage continued in the nineteenth century to bear witness to the possibility that a poet need not necessarily be a maker of marvellous fantasies or the pneumatic prophet of Utopian or mystical sublimities: he could be an intellectually responsible person in communion with sensible people, able to entertain us and instruct us by showing us things about ourselves and the world we have to live in.

I want to begin by considering how our subject looked from the point of view of one of the most interesting of mid-nineteenth-century minds, Arthur Hugh Clough. He was deeply impressed by the value of the eighteenth-century heritage—which for this purpose must be allowed to include what was accomplished in the Restoration period. He was aware of its limitations, and had to balance it within himself against the romantic tendencies prevailing in his literary world; but the example of the previous period came to seem to him to be of fundamental importance. In a lecture on 'Dryden and His Times', he saw Augustan poetry as participating in the great achievements of the time:

> While Newton was balancing the earth, and Locke weighing the intellect, Dryden was measuring syllables; while Penn and Locke were venturing experiments in government, he was making them in prosody.[1]

By a turn of the wrist this might be a satirical slight upon Dryden, for concerning himself with petty matters while great things were being done. It is to Clough's credit that he sees the perfection of the heroic couplet as no trifle, for it was a main instrument of a great civilization. He says firmly in another lecture that 'the proper manhood of the English nation dates, I believe [,] from the generation which rejected Milton'—meaning, the rejection of ideology and enthusiasm in favour of being 'true to the necessary exigencies and experiences of life'.[2] Though not unaware of the limitations of the eighteenth-century tradition, he praises its empirical grasp:

> . . . there is a cogency in this resting upon only the lowest grounds. The winter-vitality of the moral convictions of Hume is worth more than any summery exuberance of sentiment.[3]

It is less surprising therefore that Clough was notably resistant to the enchantments of Coleridge, Shelley and Keats, and expressed a strong liking for Crabbe when Crabbe's critical fortunes were at a low ebb. Of Crabbe he said that 'there is no one who better represents the general result through the country of the last century'—an interesting phrase.[4] His appreciation of Crabbe is consistent with the kind of dissatisfaction with contemporary poetry he expressed in a review article for the *North American Review* of poems by Alexander Smith and Matthew Arnold, where he asked whether poetry should not deal, 'more than at present it usually does, with general wants, ordinary feelings, the obvious rather than the rare facts of human nature', and looked wistfully at the deserved popularity of the novel:

> The modern novel is preferred to the modern poem, because we do here feel an attempt to include these indispensable latest addenda—these phenomena which, if we forget on Sunday, we must remember on Monday—these positive matters of fact, which people, who are not verse-writers, are obliged to have to do with.[5]

Clough's view of Wordsworth is particularly noteworthy in this regard. In his lecture on Wordsworth he acknowledges Wordsworth to be the chief among modern poets, that is, poets of his own century. He praises his power and originality sincerely, but in rather general and honorific terms; but when he turns to the negative side of his discussion his observations become particular and severely damaging. His chief complaint against Wordsworth is that he allows subjectivity to overwhelm matter of fact:

> . . . instead of looking directly at an object and considering it as a thing in itself, and allowing it to operate upon him as a fact in itself,—he takes the sentiment produced by it in his own mind as the thing; as the important really real fact.—The Real things cease to be real; the world no longer exists; all that exists is the feeling somehow generated in the poet's sensibility.[6]

Wordsworth is a complex, paradoxical, highly original and daring writer who defeats attempts to categorize him. To situate him in this discussion I shall have to examine the great antinomy within his poetic system, the result of which was that he who burst upon the world as the poet of common fact in common language could nevertheless be accused of substituting for the poetry of realism a new subjectivism.

Recent scholarship has stressed how much Wordsworth absorbed and retained from the eighteenth century. But it would be a mistake to use this to obliterate the revolutionary shock that English poetry received on the publication of *Lyrical Ballads*. Hazlitt bears witness to this in a passage in *The Spirit of the Age*:

> It is one of the innovations of the time. It partakes of, and is carried along with, the revolutionary movement of our age: the political changes of the day were the model on which he formed and conducted his poetical experiments. His Muse (it cannot be denied, and without this we cannot explain its character at all) is a levelling one.[7]

Wordsworth apparently proclaimed a new realism, even naturalism. His professed intention as stated in the 1802 Preface was:

> to chuse incidents and situations from common life, and to relate or describe them, throughout, as far as was possible, in a selection of language really used by men . . .

Why could not this programme be seen as a development of the eighteenth-century realist tradition? One reason is that it was carried out in a spirit of 'innovation', in accordance with a populist and primitivist ideology. Wordsworth goes on in the Preface to proclaim a thematic reformation, when he says that he generally chose low and rustic life because—not to put too fine a point on it—uneducated rustics are more genuine people, and better. (On this doctrine, Wordsworth himself could hardly be eligible: being the university-educated son of a middle-class lawyer, he was less fit to be a subject for poetry, and should not have written about himself so much.) He also proclaims a stylistic reformation, and justifies it on similar grounds: the language of uneducated rustics is more genuine, more truthful, and poetically better than that of other classes.

It was in accordance with these populist-primitivist conceptions that readers were asked to welcome the Cumberland Beggar with his bag of scraps; Grandfather Daniel, the village kleptomaniac and his pilfering grandson, aged three; Alice Fell's ragged cloak entangled in the coachwheel; Simon Lee's swollen ankles; Benjamin the Waggoner, with his hangover; and Peter Bell with his ass. These figures were presented as more really real, and the language and sentiment disposed upon them more poetical and true, than what Dryden and Pope could offer on their subjects. Wordsworth purported to be dealing with natural people in a natural language derived from them, in contrast with writers who dealt with artificial people in an artificial language. How justified this contrast is on either side need not detain us.

From the beginning, the reaction to Wordsworth's work was confused and contradictory. For it was obviously *not* just a poetry of common fact in common language; nor did it profess to be merely that. In quoting above from the 1802 Preface, I withheld the two other propositions which make up Wordsworth's attempt at a succinct statement of his intentions. These two counterbalancing clauses make a profound difference:

> . . . and at the same time to throw over them [the common incidents and situations] a certain colouring of imagination, whereby ordinary things should be presented to the mind in an unusual aspect; and, further, and above all, to make these incidents and situations interesting by tracing in them, truly though not ostentatiously, the primary laws of our nature: chiefly, as far as regards the manner in which we associate ideas in a state of excitement.

These two clauses correspond well enough to the two separate tendencies in Wordsworth that pull him away from the poetry of simple fact, but pull him nevertheless in different directions. The facts, he says, will not function poetically unless subdued to the working of subjective forces: feeling, passion, imagination. And even so the facts are not thought to be interesting in themselves; they have to be made interesting by relating them to some philosophical view (here specified as associationism, but Wordsworth's whole attempt at a philosophy is potentially involved). The complete sentence, as now quoted, begs the question whether an ordinary-language poetry about ordinary things can 'at the same time' be subjectively lighted and coloured, and 'further and above all' be the servant of an ideology, interesting chiefly as such. The anatomy I have suggested is between the first two points in Wordsworth's four-point summary—points which seem to offer an improved realism—and the second two points, which place a superior value upon subjectivism on the one hand and philosophical doctrine on the other.

There are certainly poems of Wordsworth, and parts of poems, in which there is a determined emphasis on the common thing in itself, even to that exceedingly small pond in 'The Thorn' which the poet has carefully measured, 'three feet long and two feet wide'. On his fact-observing genre-painting side, Wordsworth has affinities with the engraver Thomas Bewick, whose work he admired. One of the most pleasant but neglected of the poems in the lyrical-ballad style is 'The Two Thieves', which begins with the poet wishing he could exchange his verbal art for the popular graphic realism of Bewick's wood engravings:

> O now that the genius of Bewick were mine!

Wordsworth goes on to give a verbal print, well observed and full of sympathetic good humour, depicting the weak-witted old man and his little grandson, whose combined pilferings are tolerated with amusement by the villagers. The poem was solidly based on a recollection from his Hawkshead school-days.[8]

Hazlitt noted Wordsworth's fondness for Bewick, and connected it with the homely realistic side of his work. He applauded, however, Wordsworth's ability to rise to a more 'ideal' type of painting, exemplified by Poussin, and by Rembrandt. The way he puts it is interesting:

> In art he greatly esteems Bewick's woodcuts and Waterloo's sylvan etchings. But he sometimes takes a higher tone, and gives his mind fair play. We have known him enlarge with a noble intelligence and enthusiasm on Nicolas Poussin's fine landscape-compositions, pointing out the unity of design that pervades them, the superintending mind, the imaginative principle that brings all to bear on the same end . . . His eye also does justice to Rembrandt's fine and masterly effects. In the way in which that artist works something out of nothing, and transforms the stump of a tree, a common figure, into an *ideal* object by the gorgeous light and shade thrown upon it, he perceives an analogy to his own mode of investing the minute details of nature with an atmosphere of sentiment . . .[9]

Hazlitt's language is noticeably Wordsworthian at this point, as he speaks of a transformation of reality by light and shade 'thrown upon' the object from a subjective source.

Because they overlap in their concern for common incidents told in plain words, it is interesting to compare Wordsworth and Crabbe, in respect of each other and in regard to their attitude to the new and old tendencies. Crabbe allowed vestiges of eighteenth-century formality to linger in his diction and syntax, though he progressively reduced his reliance on expressions inconsistent with a plain pedestrian style—possibly under Wordsworth's influence.[10] Wordsworth himself did not wholly abandon inherited formalities of diction and syntax. In his recorded comments Wordsworth acknowledges that Crabbe has made a contribution to literature as a realistic recorder, but resolutely he will not allow that Crabbe is a poet. Writing to Samuel Rogers in 1808 he says:

> I am happy to find that we coincide in opinion about Crabbe's *verses*: for poetry in no sense can they be called . . . After all, if the Picture were true to nature what claim could it have to be called Poetry? . . . The sum of all is, that nineteen out of twenty of Crabbe's Pictures are mere matters of fact; with which the Muses have just about as much to do as they have with a Collection of medical reports, or of Law Cases.[11]

I have excerpted phrases from a detailed discussion, without distorting Wordsworth's intention. Even after Crabbe's major works had appeared, from 1809 onwards, Wordsworth remained adamant that Crabbe, though admirable, was 'unpoetical'; and in the note he dictated to Elizabeth Fenwick concerning 'Lucy Gray' he again shows his abiding notion of what is poetical:

> The way in which the incident was treated, and the spiritualizing of the character, might furnish hints for contrasting the imaginative influences, which I have endeavoured to throw over common life, with Crabbe's matter-of-fact style of handling subjects of the same kind.[12]

'Lucy Gray' is subtitled 'Or, Solitude'. Lucy is 'spiritualized' all right: she is an intangible form, a fleeting presence, with no individuation—just an impression of childhood 'sweetness'. She is hardly more physically there before her death, than she is afterwards, when she has become a phantom. This 'spiritualization' is at the same time a virtual dehumanization; the language reduces her to a part of the natural scene. Like that other Lucy (written of in the same period), Lucy Gray grows like a flower:

> The sweetest thing that ever grew
> Beside a human door!

She is of the company of 'the fawn at play, the hare upon the green', and when she sets off gaily it is as a 'mountain roe' that her feet stir up the powdery snow. As with some other lyrical ballads of Wordsworth, I am left uncertain of the higher meaning intended, at which the subtitle in this case is presumably hinting; but there is no difficulty in accepting that the poet subordinated the realistic possibilities of the material to a 'visionary' treatment. If Crabbe had taken up the story the treatment would have been different. Since I can find no sufficiently comparable story in Crabbe, I shall venture to summarize the Lucy Gray poem Crabbe might have written.

We would certainly have had the situation filled out for us. We would know, for example, what Lucy's mother was doing in town that day. She was attending a 'meeting' of her dissenting sect, to hear a visiting preacher. Her husband, like Crabbe, did not hold with sectarian enthusiasm, and suffered her absence grudgingly, though in general he was fond enough of his wife. He was also fond of his daughter, but unwilling to admit that in her isolation she was becoming shy and rather witless and withdrawn into her own fancies, for want of suitable companions and the mental discipline of school. The man's resentment over his wife's gadding into town to hear the preacher made him unwilling to go and fetch her himself, so he sent Lucy, even though he knew a storm was brewing. It was not exactly callousness, but a failure to let himself estimate the amount of risk. As it happened, the storm came on early, and Lucy could not see her way. Then (as Wordsworth has skilfully implied in his poem) the weather settled again and at night it stopped snowing: if the moon had been up Lucy could have seen her way to safety; but the moon had been up in the daytime and had set by dark, so Lucy missed her footing in the middle of the bridge. The mother had meanwhile reached home safely with the kind help of a neighbour; and the remainder of the poem in Crabbe's version powerfully develops the parents' anguish and self-reproach; with a side-comment, however, on the poor state of paths and bridges in the county.

If I cannot supply the text of Crabbe's version of Lucy, I can bring together for comparison poems by the two poets on the theme, a favourite with each, of the forsaken woman who becomes an eccentric and destitute solitary. Both poets transcend the limitations of eighteenth-century tradition in their ability to give lower-class subjects serious treatment. That is not to say that either poet abandons his sense of his own status and of the position of his humbler characters relatively to that. It is tempting to place Wordsworth's 'Ruth' alongside Crabbe's very powerful 'Ruth' in *Tales of the Hall*; but the comparison is closer if we take the short tale 'Rachel' in *Posthumous Tales*.

Wordsworth's 'Ruth' is one of the poems which leave him vulnerable to the charge made by an anonymous reviewer in 1819, which anticipates Clough's later complaint:

> Wordsworth exhibits it [human life] in a phantasmagoria. He presents to you, not living creatures, but the vivid images of forms which he himself has fashioned, which he moves by his own agency, and tints with his own colours.[13]

Ruth is a solitary neglected child whose father has married again. She is wooed by a youth from the United States. He invites her to share a nomadic existence in his native Georgia, in which they would hunt by day the flying deer, and erect a new temporary shelter each night. Ruth agrees to come with him and be his love on these terms, insisting only that they get married in the village church. They do so; but at the seaport the youth changes his mind and deserts her. We are given to understand that he has had good intentions, but that his moral constitution has been undermined by the climate and beautiful scenery of Georgia, so that the desire for lawless freedom proves stronger in his breast than love for Ruth. The forsaken Ruth becomes an eccentric vagrant, and the poet offers the consolation of a Christian burial.

Ruth has no individual character; she is externally sketched and coloured in a romantic mode. The poet makes an effort to examine the conflicting impulses in the mind of the youth, but to no good effect; for after some stanzas of exotic scene-painting of Georgia, he plunges into the assertion that Nature in its subtropical luxuriance has caused a moral loosening in the youth. Speculation about the influence of climate on temperament or morals would not in itself make Wordsworth more absurd than Coleridge, who found that Christianity exists only in the temperate latitudes 'and degenerates in proportion to the increase of Heat—say from the 40 Deg. of N.L. to the Equator';[14] or than Milton, who inversely thought that intellect tended to seize up in cold regions. Such speculations have been the folly of good minds since Aristotle. What makes Wordsworth's opinion puzzling is that he is the prophet of Nature as stern but kindly nurse. It is evidently a British nurse that he normally has in mind, and he here betrays a feeling that Nature might be reprehensibly lax in other climes. He tries to resolve the confusion by compounding it:

> Yet in his worst pursuits I ween
> That sometimes there did intervene
> Pure hopes of high intent:
> For passions linked to forms so fair
> And stately needs must have their share
> Of noble sentiment.

Magnolias, it seems, are morally laxative, yet at the same time their fair and stately forms should induce high and pure aspirations. This bathetic plunge into cant, when moral analysis was to be supplied, has irremediably blasted the pathos of the poem. Wordsworth's wish to throw a colouring of imagination and romantic feeling over the situation, and to connect it with his doctrine of the influence of nature on man, has in this case damaged the basis of reality on which the poem was to be erected, and has let in absurdity.

Crabbe's 'Rachel' concerns a girl who falls in love with a sailor

named David. There is no defined engagement, and he sails away
and does not return. He has been captured, and his subsequent
experience drives out of his mind the old attachment. She firmly
believes he must be dead, and roams the sea-shore in a deranged
state, fancying she hears the cries of drowning seamen. At last he
does return on a ship. Coming ashore, he is told of Rachel's plight
and goes to see her. When he appears before her in the moonlight
she takes it to be an apparition, and is terrified. He is unable to
calm her, and goes away again. Rachel remains deranged.

One characteristic of Crabbe's telling of the story is that it gathers
in a good deal of observation of individual and social life, even
though it is economically handled. The poet hears the story from a
friend, after they have encountered Rachel on a walk. Her mono-
mania is realistically observed:

> Not pain from pinching cold was in her face,
> But hurrying grief, that knows no resting-place—
> Appearing ever as on business sent,
> The wandering victim of a fix'd intent.

There follows a discussion of whether she would not be better off in
an institution, and reason is given why it seems better to leave her
alone. The story also traverses a period of her life, after she has
first lost her lover, when well-meaning religious neighbours, full of
methodistical zeal, try to console and help her, but succeed only in
disturbing her deeply, and ruining whatever religious consolation
she might have found. The character of David, the sailor, is not developed; but one swift stroke deftly lays bare sufficient truth:

> Her sailor left her, with, perhaps, intent
> To make her his—'tis doubtful what he meant:
> But he was captured, and the life he led
> Drove all such young engagements from his head.

There is no clear blame to be attached; the sailor had hardly defined his intentions to himself, and circumstances then seemed to
dissipate whatever bond of obligation there was. In the light of this,
David's motives on re-appearance are evident without further explanation: concern when he hears about Rachel; a sympathetic approach, with no settled intention; withdrawal from a situation he
cannot cope with. The story ends, as often in Crabbe, with the
weight of unhappiness unrelieved, except for the realistic observation that time and habit have made Rachel more serene. This con-
nects with the observation at the beginning of the poem that she
has enough self-possession to smile in spite of her miserable ob-
session:

> More to engage our friendly thoughts the while,
> She threw upon her miseries a smile,

> That, like the varnish on a picture laid,
> More prominent and bold the figures made.

I have chosen a comparison that was unfavourable to Wordsworth, though many readers then, and perhaps some now, would still prefer the romantic narrative to Crabbe's more realistic treatment. What of Wordsworth at his strongest, in 'Michael' perhaps, or in episodes narrated in *The Prelude*? Many would agree, I think, that the height of Wordsworth's power and originality is displayed in the autobiographical narration of several incidents in Book I of *The Prelude*: the moonlight raid on the woodcock snares set by others; the robbing of the ravens' nest on the windy crag; the theft by night of a rowing boat on the lake. These go as close as possible to fulfilling Wordsworth's fourfold intention of presenting ordinary incidents in ordinary language, yet suffusing them with a peculiar intensity derived from within himself and connecting them with a philosophical idea.

Yet even here the aims are not fully reconciled in an artistic and intellectual whole. The subjective element that Wordsworth supplies is not in this case the cause of trouble, for it is an integral part of the experience presented: in each incident, the nervously excited child feels nature to be animated—a presence makes itself felt; he imagines he hears stealthy steps and breathing after him on the fells; the wind as he hangs on the crag is a voice making 'strange utterance', the clouds move with a more than physical motion, instinct with some mysterious life; the black peak, as he rows the stolen boat out from shore, rises up behind the cliff as if in grim admonition. These are unusual but convincingly presented mental states. It was part of Wordsworth's originality to render them with uncanny precision. We react to the exhilaration and to the thrill of guilty fear and to the sense of a deeper mystery implicit in the experience. They are great poetry of an unheard-of kind. And yet as soon as the poet tries to connect these veridical accounts with his main philosophical theme, the change in mode and quality is disastrous: the voice of poetry and truth is replaced by a parsonical voice intoning cant and indistinct bombast:

> Wisdom and Spirit of the Universe!
> Thou Soul that art the eternity of thought,
> That givest to forms and images a breath
> And everlasting motion . . .

Not ignoring the egotistical sublime of the poet's complacent thanksgiving that Nature's nurture has carefully provided the requisites for:

> The calm existence that is mine when I
> Am worthy of myself!

The transition is intolerable, from the true report of experience to booming mystification in the comment. Wordsworth wanted to suppose that his peculiar mental states were evidence for a theology of nature; we are asked to believe that there is a Wisdom and Spirit of the Universe because he felt something coming after him when he stole the woodcocks. He cannot escape his problem by saying he is merely giving a personal application of a truth known otherwise, for he has no evidence to offer other than his recollection of peculiar states of feeling in times past. Stretched by this demand on credulity, the commonsense reader's mind collapses and gives up.

What emerges from a comparison of Wordsworth and Crabbe is that, while Wordsworth does deal with real and common things in plain language, this is only a partial description of his work: there are intensities and sublimities as well as failures and even absurdities which arise from other elements in his programme, elements that are meant to transcend the merely factual. Crabbe's performance is more constantly realistic in intention and result: indeed it is altogether more coherent and consistent than Wordsworth's. It goes forward from a strong base in eighteenth-century realism, in a straighter way than Wordsworth does; yet, like Wordsworth, in its themes and style it passes beyond the eighteenth-century heritage. One may add that in coming to rely chiefly on narrative, Crabbe largely escaped the problem of much eighteenth-century discursive and descriptive writing—the problem noted by Johnson in his comment on Pope's *Essay on Criticism*, that one thing follows another in no necessary order and the reader's attention may flag for want of propelling interest.

I have not offered a definition of realism but have been content to use the term here in a loose way to point to some recognizable tendencies. I should like to conclude by moving forward from Wordsworth and Crabbe to mention some other poets who in different ways have had a realist inclination. I hesitate to speak of a realist tradition, though some of these poets have received benefits from others: it is rather the diversity I want to emphasize, through which different poets have come by different ways to make very different poems, which nevertheless all stay close to common fact.

Clare is a poet with a different sort of realism. He used little narrative, and a great deal of his descriptive writing is born under the sign of ampersand. Clare's knowledge of nature was much greater than Wordsworth's. (So indeed was Crabbe's, as he demonstrated to Wordsworth when they met and conversed.[15]) Clare assumed that the rendering of local fact in local language provided a genuine and valuable poetry. At times he placed his detailed observation in a nostalgic light, the light of a childhood Eden. But much of his poetry is simply presented as notations of present fact, with an implicit feeling of pleasure and love. However one explains it, there is a hunger of the mind for such a poetry of fact: there is an appetite which Clare's genuine substance, with its authentic verbal flavour, can feed.

Clough, with whose observations I began this discussion, was a poet whose work moved towards realism, most notably in *Amours de Voyage*, which seems to me the best longer Victorian poem. In still another way, the too-much neglected work of William Barnes is rooted deep in ordinary reality.

Poetry has never been contained for long within prescriptions requiring ordinary language and ordinary situations. Keats and Shelley within the Romantic movement were at the beginning of a new development of poetic diction and imaginative poetry which was continued by Tennyson and Swinburne and Rossetti and others. The return to an ordinary-language poetry in the twentieth century has been commonly associated with the modernism of Pound and Eliot, and the poetic currents flowing from them could claim acceptance of a realistic criterion. But there are other original contributions—less cosmopolitan, more regional, more addicted to closely observed immediate fact—made by poets as different as Hardy, Edward Thomas, Frost, Larkin and Betjeman.

I have no intention of setting up a 'great tradition' of realists or of dismissing the Romantics and Symbolists. I do, however, suggest that the modest genuineness of some of this poetry has been too little appreciated. It is not the only kind of poetry, nor the greatest kind. The Romantics aspired to a greater kind, more akin to the traditional forms of high poetry, heroic or religious or idealist—a poetry which uses myth, legend, symbolic fiction, to search the heights and depths of the human condition. Why the work of the Romantics, for all its moments of power and insight, is desperately flawed by unfaithfulness to truth, is a difficult question which needs a different line of enquiry. All I want to say here is that there are moods in which we turn with pleasure to poetry that deals with common actualities. It was a strong tendency within eighteenth-century literature and continues in diverse ways into our own time.

1973

NOTES

1 B. B. Trawick (ed.), *Selected Prose Works of Arthur Hugh Clough* (University of Alabama Press, Alabama 1964), p. 93.

2 Trawick, p. 131.

3 Trawick, p. 138.

4 A. H. Clough, *Prose Remains* (London, 1888), p. 237.

5 Trawick, pp. 144-5.

6 Trawick, p. 121.

7 William Hazlitt, *The Spirit of the Age* (ed. E. D. Mackerness, London, 1969), p. 139. The same parallel with political revolution is conducted with even more malicious vivacity in his caricature of the Lake Poets in *Lectures on the English Poets* (1818).

8 *Wordsworth's Poetical Works* (ed. W. Knight, Edinburgh, 1882-86), ii. 196.

9 Hazlitt, p. 149.

10 Elizabeth Brewster, 'George Crabbe and William Wordsworth', *University of Toronto Quarterly* XLII (1973), 142-55, discusses the point.

11 *Letters of William Wordsworth* (ed. P. Wayne, London, 1954), p. 111.

12 *Wordsworth's Poetical Works*, ii, 84.

13 Unsigned review from the *Edinburgh Monthly Review* in 1819, reprinted in *Crabbe: The Critical Heritage* (ed. A. Pollard, London, 1972), pp. 248-9. The passage occurs in a review of Crabbe's *Tales of the Hall*, in which the reviewer advances his thesis that 'Crabbe is peculiarly the poet of actual life' by mentioning the limitations or faults in this respect of Cowper, Rogers, Byron and Wordsworth. He concludes: 'From all these faults Crabbe is free'.

14 *Unpublished Letters of Samuel Taylor Coleridge* (ed. E. L. Griggs, New Haven, 1933), ii. 392.

15 *Wordsworth's Poetical Works*, viii. 23.

Sex and love in literature

IN the last few years an interesting change has occurred in undergraduate English usage. The earlier love-poetry they are asked to read was governed by certain conventions, generally labelled as those of courtly love. These conventions assign to the man and the woman regular and distinct roles. He is the lover; she is the beloved. *He* is suing, sighing, protesting, adoring, accusing or despairing. *She* is apparently in an exalted position of power and decision: she is the star, the queen, the goddess; she is kind or cruel, granting or refusing favour. This stylized differentiation of roles has a long history: from the eleventh to the seventeenth century love poetry continued to reproduce these standard roles of the lover and the beloved. So deep has been the imprint of this tradition that much of it has lingered on in poetry and social convention even into our own time. The linked terms 'lover' and 'the beloved' have become somewhat old-fashioned and almost purely literary as a pair; but everyone till recently knew that 'lover' is a masculine noun; and that the woman is not the man's lover but his 'beloved'. Yet in the essays or exercises of undergraduates today, 'the beloved' has vanished from their terminology. The word 'lover' applies equally to each.

What this seems to imply is the end of the courtly love tradition—in literature and life. New roles are being sought and found, and connected with these a new rhetoric, a new terminology is coming into being. How far this is good or bad need not be our question at the moment. That 'lover' is becoming a sexually undifferentiated noun may be taken as a hopeful sign that a notion of genuine partnership has replaced the old artificial code which *seemed* to exalt the lady (though it really worked in favour of the gentleman's game). On the other hand, it may be a sign that the necessary biologically-based differentiation of sexual roles within a partnership has become blurred and uncertain, to the loss of both parties. Indeed I think both tendencies are at work. All I want to suggest by this example is that the conventions of literature and life interact. For many centuries people found no difficulty in understanding love-poetry with its conventional stylized roles of lover and beloved. Obviously it corresponded, in some way, to certain features of social life and social ideology. Obviously the literary conventions in turn helped to form and perpetuate certain conventional usages

in society. Educated Western man over centuries has been peculiar
in that he bowed to women, opened doors for women, fetched and
carried for women, gave precedence to women, offered in short many
forms of outward courtesy, deference, respect—whatever the realities
underneath may have been. And it must be admitted that it has not
entirely been a matter of meaningless manners: it has sometimes at
least gone deeper and become a lived ideal of chivalry and reverence.

Literature is insignificant if it does not refer to life. All the great
works offers us a contemplation of the human condition. Minor
works may be more partial and limited but they too offer a view of
part of our experience.

But literature is different from life. It has its own forms, codes,
procedures, measures of success and failure. It creates its own world.
The war at Troy was never much like what happens in the *Iliad,* yet
the *Iliad* somehow has its own truth, because it gives us a view of life
and death and heroism. *King Lear* is an unreal legendary story: yet
somehow it offers us a vision of reality.

The poems of love that constitute a large part of European literature actually present astonishingly little of the day-by-day experience of human beings in love. Yet they have been felt by generations
to be vital and necessary expressions of that experience. There is a
mystery in this that cannot easily be analyzed or explained. I want
to go first to the beginnings of modern Western literature in the
twelfth century to show how one aspect of the love theme was
handled, with long-range results for later literature. And then I want
to switch to the other end: to the radical critique of love which began in nineteenth-century prose fiction and has continued. For this
second purpose I shall use Tolstoy and Solzhenitsyn as examples. For
the twelfth century part I shall be referring to the love-poetry of the
Provençal troubadours and the Old French romances of Chrétien de
Troyes.

The sophisticated love poetry of the troubadours of Provence goes
back to the late eleventh century; it flourished in the twelfth century and continued into the thirteenth. There is a specific kind of
poem which the troubadours called a love-song, *canso d'amor.* The
typical love-situation in these songs is summed up in these four lines
translated from Bernart de Ventadorn:

> Lady, for your love
> I join my hands and worship.
> O sweet body with lively hue,
> You make me suffer great woe.

The worship of the lady, the desire for her white body, and the woe-
ful pain of the lover. And it is always spring! The love of the troubadours of Provence is conventionally labelled by one of the terms

they use: *fin'amors* meaning a refined, lofty, courtly or noble love suitable to high folk and beyond the scope of the vulgar. This *fin'amors* has a number of interesting features. It never occurs within marriage nor as courtship directed towards marriage. The lady is always already married, and the husband is either irrelevant or an odious nuisance. The lover is apparently unmarried; there is no role for his wife, even if she existed; that is, she does not exist in the poem. The man's love is engendered principally by the lady's body: not to any considerable extent by personal qualities or moral or spiritual graces. The lover's aim is the physical enjoyment of the lady's body: his ambitions range from a kiss, to the sight of the lady unclothed, to embracing her naked in bed. The expression of these desires is usually restrained and delicate (at least by our gross standards) but quite clear. It is in order to attain his lady's physical favours that the lover assumes the posture of a devoted supplicant, a willing and uncomplaining servant, always at her command, submitting to all her caprices, and offering unlimited praise and homage. Typically, in the Provençal love-song there is no fruition. The lover remains in the tension of desire and never attains his aim. This seems to be part of the convention of the *canso d'amor*. It should be noted that some other kinds of Provençal poetry—especially the *alba* or dawn-song—do include love's fruition; but the love is still illicit.

Provençal love-songs thus work within a very specialized and narrow set of conventions. Poetry of course thrives within limits and seldom tries to do more than select and abstract from the manifold of real experience. The troubadours showed remarkable skill and invention, and force and passion and subtlety, while working within the convention of passionate adulterous desire, a desire which is almost entirely physical and directed towards a noble lady who is married, a desire whose plan of campaign is unlimited devotion expressed in terms of feudal service, adoration, and worship. There is no note of personal affection or friendship or other ingredients we might have expected.

There are two comments I want to make on this summary of the courtly love expressed by the Provençal troubadours. It is not quite the picture presented by some earlier interpreters. Various schools of interpretation have flourished around these texts, only to wither and die. A great number of things have been read into the texts which they cannot sustain. For example, one school held that the rhetoric of *fin'amors* was a transfer to secular love of religious devotion to the Virgin, so that the refinement of love and the exaltation of women implied by *fin'amors* could be read as having occurred under Christian inspiration and in particular as a result of the rise of the cult of the Virgin. But it is now clear that such evidence as

K

there is flows the other way. Provençal erotic poetry is not a transfer of rhetoric from the cult of the Virgin; it would be truer to say that the rhetoric of the cult of Our Lady, as it developed, was a transfer from secular courtly love poetry. Another school wanted to assert that the love sung by the troubadours was not sensual but platonic or spiritual or mystical. A special version of this was the theory that songs of the troubadours began as a secret language expressing the Catharist heresy which flourished in Provence. None of these interesting ideas has held its ground under the advance of recent scholarship.[1]

The other comment I want to make is that the pattern of sexual love proposed or implied by the troubadours is obviously in conflict with the moral orthodoxy of society and the Church. It is not that the orthodox rules are attacked or defied. They are simply ignored. The poetry is not a critique of marriage or a declaration of free love or libertinism; it takes no account whatsoever of the complex of rights and obligations that marriage properly implies. For it, the sole considerations are the desire that the lady enkindles in the lover and the conduct of his courtship in accordance with conventions held to be 'noble' or 'gentle' in the class sense.

We are separated from troubadour poetry by an alien language, the *langue d'oc* of Provence, and by a very different kind of society. How far should we apply to this kind of poetic love the canons of moral judgement we might apply to sexual relations in real life? Literature frequently provokes this question, and it needs a delicately poised answer. Literature, as we have said, is different from life, yet it has reference to life. It is in some ways a form of play. It extracts themes from life and plays with them, in forms and by procedures that are its own. Take for example the kind of comic fabliau or bawdy story which Chaucer used in the Miller's and Reeve's tales. Or take the bawdy poems of Burns. It is a severe moralist who ignores the fact that these are a kind of play using abstractions from life, and understood to be doing this. I think most of us feel inclined to defend the poetry and fun and vitality of such things against too obsessive a moralism. I don't know, however, that the severe moralist, or wowser, is any worse than his counterpart, the libertine reader who seems also to ignore the difference between the simplified world of bawdy tales and the real complex world. I mean the reader who takes the rules of bawdy stories as applicable to real life. Neither Chaucer nor Burns were so grossly simple-minded. They knew that their literary fun and games were questionable and problematical if brought too closely against the demands of real life.

Well then, how closely should literature be held to be morally accountable? There is no easy answer. Literature is not disconnected from life. It can influence feelings, beliefs and values—and if it can do so for good, it can also do so for evil. To deny this is to reduce literature to triviality. One has to find a point of balance as best one can. Some works invite a more realistic moral response than others. In the case of the troubadour lyrics we have to balance a number of reactions: we may recognize their artistic value and respond to the passionate theme, while acknowledging that the erotic relations are stylized and limited; we may defend these poems from a too obsessive moral censure, while recognizing that they imply a 'life-style' which is morally unacceptable in practice. If twelfth-century poetry seems too far away to be really problematical to us, try the same treatment on modern pop songs, which in a very much lower degree may offer interest and show talent: they are a kind of play; but they are also at times products of the drug-cult or the cult of dropping-out, hanging loose, freeing up, or otherwise disregarding real responsibilities in favour of simple pseudo-solutions. I think we are left with the same difficulty of striking an appropriate balance.

The amoral implications of *fin'amors* as a form of courtly love were bound to provoke reactions. There was bound to be a demand for the salvaging of the attractive idea of romantic love by showing it as possible and even normal within courtship and marriage—and our use of the word 'courtship' is itself a proof of some success in these attempts to bring courtly love inside the pale. C. S. Lewis's finest work of scholarly interpretation, *The Allegory of Love*, traced this process of reclaiming romance for marriage as far as Spenser's rescue operation in *The Faerie Queene*. But oddly enough, Lewis passed lightly over the poet of the twelfth century who first met the challenge, Chrétien de Troyes. More recent criticism has tended to emphasize strongly the importance of this writer of verse romances, who has been called *the* father or *a* father of the modern novel. It seems clear that Chrétien's reaction to the Provençal fashion of amoral courtly love was to ask whether love—as romantic passion— was not possible within marriage. He shaped his verse romances so that most of them carry an affirmative response. His poem *Cligès* especially has been interpreted as deliberately rejecting romantic love outside marriage in favour of combining the roles of lover and husband. The attempt to unite these roles is summed up in the words of the heroine Fénice:

> Who has the heart, let him have the body.

And in his most successful development of this theme, in the romance called *Yvain*, the poet affirms that

> Love which is neither false nor feigned
> Is a precious thing and holy.

It is certainly true, however, that Chrétien did not achieve a literary representation of romantic love within marriage without certain difficulties in handling his materials. I mention these difficulties because they are perhaps a literary equivalent of the difficulties that may arise in real life in accommodating romantic passion within marriage.

For the notion of 'romance' or 'passionate love' as a unique overwhelming experience is a very demanding one. Its relation to other values is always likely to create problems; and this does not cease to be so by incorporating this value into the immensely complex set of needs and responsibilities that constitute marriage. The pattern of worship and adoration, the intense idealization, the idea of a fatal grand ennobling passion, the fevered glamour shot with the light and dark of extreme joy and sorrow, introduce a potentially anarchic element. A good deal of the best prose fiction of the nineteenth and twentieth centuries has been devoted to examining the question of passionate love, whether within marriage or outside it, and it is to two of the greatest masters of the novel that I now turn: to Tolstoy and Solzhenitsyn.

Tolstoy's wrestling with the problems of sexuality, love and marriage deserves to be traced in detail, but I shall mention only one aspect of one book. The book is *Anna Karenina* and it is the affair between Anna and Vronsky that I shall concentrate on.

Anna is a beautiful woman of about twenty-seven. She is married, not unhappily, to a middle-aged official of some consequence, and has a son aged about eight. While the marriage is not unhappy there is a void within it, because her husband is unable to arouse and satisfy her physically or emotionally. Without realizing it, she is ready for passionate abandon. When Vronsky meets her and is seized with a total passion for her, she struggles for a year against the enchantment, but in fact after the first instant the momentum has been irresistible, and she finally gives herself to him. Later she admits the liaison to her husband, and after a crisis she and Vronsky renounce their position and prospects in society and go off to Italy. When they return to Russia the situation deteriorates. They are like Tristan and Isolde in the forest, when the moment comes for them to realize that they have cut themselves off from society. They cannot marry because Karenin has decided against a divorce. She has lost her son and can give Vronsky no legitimate children. He wants to resume his natural role in society, which is still open to him if he will discard her. She cannot resume an equivalent role if she cannot marry him. She desperately tries to hold him by the bond of passion, but she sees it is not enough, and she kills herself in a dreadful sort of despair and, in a sense, vindictiveness.

This is a very crude reminder of the story. I want to make a few particular comments.

In the first place we may observe how little, if at all, the decent
reticence imposed on the novelist by nineteenth-century convention
interferes with Tolstoy's ability to deal with sexual matters. He
manages to convey to us most vividly the sensuous vitality of Anna,
the masculine quality of Vronsky. He manages quite discreetly but
very clearly to convey the emotional and erotic void that makes
Anna vulnerable. He takes only one sentence to narrate her suc-
cumbing to Vronsky, and gives no description of sexual intimacies;
yet we are made fully aware that her overwhelming passion for
Vronsky has the strongest element of sensuous fulfilment, when in
Italy she is able to experience a period of utter happiness, temporarily able to put away the thought of her guilt especially in regard
to her son. And late in the book, when she is talking to her relative
Dolly, she is frank about her need to practise contraception—perhaps
the first mention of the subject in fiction—in order to be able to
keep Vronsky's love as his mistress, since she cannot be wife and
mother.

It is not just that Tolstoy is not impeded by nineteenth-century
restraints. The fact is that if he had taken our twentieth-century
freedoms he would not have improved his novel but might have
gone near to wrecking it. He could have given us a half-acre of detailed descriptions of what Vronsky did to Anna on various occasions and vice versa, in accordance with the formula American publishers now demand. But he could not have integrated such descriptions into his novel: they would have remained alien and irrelevant
and inartistic. Let me quote two true observations by a French
critic, Denis Saurat.[2] He says: 'The story that really holds the attention and passionate interest of most of mankind, male and
female, is the detailed and highly sentimental narrative of what
happens when a man and a woman are in love and there are obstacles, internal and/or external, to the fruition of their love.' This
is true: whatever else the classical novel is and does, it cannot break
away from the love story. Yet the second thing that Denis Saurat
says is equally true: 'The sex story does not make a novel, it mars it'.
This is also true. Descriptions of sexual intimacies are intrusions
and offences against the art of the novel. Why is this so? Not because
sexual intimacies are in themselves indecent, or meaningless, or irrelevant. Not because sexual acts cannot be an expression of personal union—this is what they should be to the partners concerned.
But there is no way in which descriptions of sexual acts can convey
the personal sentiment and commitment of which they can be the
vehicle. The business of the novel is not with sex acts but with personal relations: with sentiments, with motives and problems and
choices; with the way these are conditioned by the characters' life
history, entangled relationships, social conditioning, and so on.

I do not want to pursue this further, except to say bluntly that the cry for freedom to saturate our culture with indecency has very little to do with the maintenance of literary values. It may be urged on other grounds, but surely not as a necessary or desirable condition for literature. The attempt to bring the material which formerly belonged to pornography into serious literature has been a failure. The ludicrous and artistically flawed quality of *Lady Chatterley's Lover* is one of the clearest examples of this. If you want to abandon the public regulation of decency, please do not pretend you are doing literature any favours. You are in fact probably making it harder for artistic integrity to survive.

But I have a second point that interests me more. Anna Karenina and Count Vronsky sacrifice all for their passion for one another; and Tolstoy remorselessly demonstrates that the world is *not* well lost for love.

But is what they feel really love? I do not want to play with words, but to use them to point to the realities. Tolstoy is at pains to show us that Anna and Vronsky as persons have little in common. Vronsky is basically conventional, dissolute, has never known family life or real affection, is honorable only within the limits of a very limited officer-and-gentleman code. Anna does not belong to his set in St Petersburg and would not frequent it except to be with him. Indeed it is obvious that she would not have any interest in him, except for the overwhelming fatal passion that binds her to him. We are not able to inspect Vronsky quite so closely, but the same applies. He recognizes this in a very revealing comment, when she says to him that he must not talk about love and that they are only to be good friends; to which he replies: 'Friends we shall never be, you know that yourself. But whether we shall be the happiest or unhappiest people on earth, that is in your power to decide.'[3]

Passion without friendship? Without real shared interests, personal affection? This is indeed what Tolstoy is presenting. It is a *fatal* passion, a *force* that possesses them: one that makes Anna discard every *personal* obligation. And one of the most telling ways in which this is driven home is that Anna is unable to discuss the problem of her son with Vronsky, and so Vronsky does not understand this vital element in her situation.

It is as if the Provençal troubadour formula (or a version not too far from it) were being put into practice. The lover desires possession; the lady grants possession, because, for her, passionate erotic experience lies outside marriage; all other considerations are ignored or swept aside. And according to Tolstoy reality will not be denied but takes its destructive revenge.

Tolstoy attempts through the other main couple in the book to represent the true values of marriage in the partnership of Levin and Kitty, which is personal and faithful and real, even in its imperfections and troubles. But Levin is rather a special case: he has too much of Tolstoy himself in him to be able to stand for the ordinary man.

If we now turn to two great novels of Solzhenitsyn, *Cancer Ward* and *The First Circle*, we may not think first of the love interest as the salient element. Perhaps it is not. But in both it comes through as particularly important and significant when one examines it.

In *Cancer Ward* the chief character is Oleg Kostoglotov, like Solzhenitsyn himself an ex-soldier and political convict now in exile, who ends up in a cancer ward. He is unmarried and is inevitably drawn to two women in the hospital. The first is a young nurse, Zoya, whose name means life; she is the embodiment of simple vitality. The other is an older woman, a doctor, whose nickname is Vega, the name of a star. It is to her he is most deeply drawn, and she is drawn to him.

When he is due to leave the hospital and return to remote exile both women invite him to take shelter in their room during his wait in the town before he takes the train. The day he spends in the town is like a new beginning for his life: everything is so fresh, so sensuously immediate and alive to him after the cancer ward. It is to Vega, the gentle woman doctor that he intends to go. And he does go, only to find her not home yet. Only then does the realization come to him that he cannot impose himself on her. Or rather he can but he *mustn't*, however much he loves her and needs her. He knows that if he asked her she would probably come with him to share his exile. But he also knows—as she cannot—what that would do to her. Moreover, he knows that the hormone treatment he has been given has affected his sexual capacity; and that his cancer is arrested, not cured. He is no good for her. When he goes to the local N.K.V.D. office he finds that the post-Stalin thaw has begun to take effect, and the possibility of release from exile arises. Perhaps he need not assume that he would be sentencing Vega to exile; perhaps they could be together in this town? The choice of involving Vega or not is his: if he goes to her she will take him in. It is his one apparent chance for some kind of happiness. But he knows it would be at her expense. It could not bring her happiness but only misery; he is still no good for her. He *can* but he *mustn't*; and he obeys that moral imperative and writes a wonderfully honest letter of farewell, and leaves on the train to face the anguish of loneliness and deprivation.

Solzhenitsyn's next novel, *The First Circle*, is set in a special Moscow prison in which scientists are set to work on projects of interest to the State. One of these prisoners is Gleb Nerzhin, another Solzhenitsyn-like character. He is married, and his wife Nadya has waited patiently for him: she had waited during the war, only to get a message that he had been sent to concentration camp for ten years. From this camp he had now been transferred to the special prison in Moscow.

In the prison, one of the officials is a wisp of a girl named Simochka, a lieutenant in the M.G.B. who supervises the work of the prisoners. She is thin and unattractive and rather prim. At twenty-five she has had no boyfriends or even been kissed. She wants to be made love to, and she wants a husband. Alone in the laboratory at night they are drawn together and Nerzhin kisses her. He arranges an assignation with her for the next Monday evening. He has learnt that he is about to be transferred from the special prison, 'the first circle', back to 'the bottomless pit'—the camps. Why shouldn't he take what he can get from her before he goes? Why shouldn't he make love to her as she wants, even though she might be deceived in her hopes of getting him as her husband in the end?

Then unexpectedly during the week-end Nerzhin's wife is allowed to see him. Their interview is very restricted, but they manage to declare to each other their steadfast love. Yet it is not as simple as that. The wife of a political prisoner is in a desperately difficult situation in Soviet society. The easiest way is to get a divorce even if she doesn't mean it to make any difference, and this is what Nadya now hesitantly proposes to Nerzhin. He agrees, though he has a premonition that it will probably mean he will lose her. Having got the divorce, she will probably, without really intending it, get married again. There is a logic of reality that tends to wear down intentions. (Yet later we are shown Nadya resisting the temptation to yield to loneliness and the need for comfort, so we cannot be sure. Indeed we are encouraged to hope that their love will survive.)

Anyway, the visit has brought Nerzhin back into the framework of his real commitments. On the Monday night he explains to Simochka that his wife is the only person he can love. Besides, he is morally bound to his wife because she has given up her youth waiting for him. The poor girl Simochka is crushed. Then she touches the secret chord of Nerzhin's own doubt by saying that his wife will not in the end wait for him. But he says that in any case he will not do anything she could reproach him with; and he goes on to say that it is not because he is especially virtuous, but that his experience in this inhumanly ruthless world has made him in some strange way listen more intently to the voice of conscience, because that is what makes the difference between a man and a beast.

How is such a scene to end? They are in an acoustics laboratory and there is a small wireless set tuned to Moscow. He turns it on and out comes the voice of the popular woman singer of Russian songs, Obukhova. She is singing of love's despair:

> My youth,
> My youth,
> My wasted youth . . .

and again:

> No joy, no comfort do I find,
> I live for him alone . . .

And yet somehow the heart-rending songs, instead of making them feel more wretched, help to calm them. The pain of hopeless longing is expressed. The love song changes nothing, but it too is necessary.

Both these novels of Solzhenitsyn bring the principal male character to the renunciation of what he can have for the asking. Who could blame them in their position if they assuaged their loneliness and need? But they would blame themselves. It is not that they are all that virtuous: indeed they are not without blame already, but something enables them to make the refusal because to be truly human requires it. In *The First Circle* Solzhenitsyn even says of Nerzhin's refusal (and no word of his is written without full intention) that: 'It even seemed as though the decision had not been his own'.[4]

One of the most moving books that has recently come out of Soviet Russia is a memoir by Nadezhda Mandelstam, the wife of the poet Osip Mandelstam who died in a concentration camp in late 1938 or 1939. Mrs Mandelstam comments that to understand some things one 'had to go through a certain schooling'. Few of us have much real idea of that 'certain schooling', which could enable her to make the following comment:

> To think that we could have had an ordinary family life with its bickering, broken hearts and divorce suits! There are people in the world so crazy as not to realize that this is normal human existence of the kind everybody should aim at. What wouldn't we have given for such ordinary heartbreaks![5]

In *Cancer Ward* Solzhenitsyn introduces us to a cleaning woman. She has been in the camps herself and has lost her husband and her daughter in the camps. She is an educated woman and reads in her free time. But she says:

> These literary tragedies are just laughable compared with the ones we live through . . . Children write essays in school about the unhappy, tragic, doomed and I-don't-know-what-else life of Anna Karenina . . . [But] why should I read *Anna Karenina* again? Maybe it's enough— what I've experienced. Where can people read about us? *Us?* Only in a hundred year's time?[6]

Solzhenitsyn has set himself to shorten that hundred years time and has succeeded. The challenge he has thrown out to the literary tragedies of romantic passion is not an idle one. What remains when human beings are stripped down and burned in the furnace of affliction? The answer Solzhenitsyn gives is reassuring. The human constants are still there. Love, tenderness, ecstasy, sensual passion remain possible. Circumstances may give the precarious chance of happiness, or they may cruelly deny it, or destroy it. We have little control over circumstances: little control over the choices we make: and we must make them as persons, as human beings responsible to one another, even if it means renunciation, the defeat of desire, the acceptance of frustration and loss.

Of course it is true that happy love has no history, the novelist can do little with it. Obstacles and troubles are needed. And, in the world that Solzhenitsyn presents, obstacles and troubles are the rule to an abnormal extent, and he must show this. Yet the negative way which his fiction ordains for such characters as I have mentioned is still only a way of affirming the tremendously positive, the indestructible wonder and beauty of human love. It is a long way from *fin'amors*. And also Solzhenitsyn does not see the main problem as the capturing of courtly romance to domesticate it within marriage, as Chrétien de Troyes or Spenser did. He is perhaps nearer to our modern students for whom the man is the lover of woman, and the woman the lover of the man—but, he would insist, only on human terms, as personal commitment. This difficult wisdom has never been given more powerful literary expression.

1972

NOTES

1 I am particularly indebted to Moshé Lazar, *Amour courtois et 'fin' amors' dans la littérature du XIIe siècle* (Paris, 1964).
2 Denis Saurat, 'Novel', in S. H. Steinberg (ed.), *Cassell's Encyclopaedia of Literature* (London, 1953), i. 393, 395.
3 *Anna Karenina* (trans. D. Magarshack, New York, 1961), p. 152.
4 *The First Circle* (trans. M. Guybon, London, 1970), p. 627.
5 Nadezhda Mandelstam, *Hope Against Hope* (trans. Max Hayward, London, 1971), p. 19.
6 *Cancer Ward* (trans. N. Bethell and D. Burg, London, 1968-69), pp. 512-3.

On being an intellectual

'WHY write, if this too easy activity of pushing a pen across paper is not given a certain bull-fighting risk and we do not approach dangerous, agile, and two-horned subjects?' Thus Ortega y Gasset parenthesizes in approaching a 'subtle, delicate and compromising subject' in his book *On Love*.[1] I have long meditated another 'subtle, delicate and compromising subject': the nature and role of the intellectuals—a 'two-horned' topic because of the ambiguity of the concept of the intellectual and because of the dilemmas one can be impaled upon. No one who tries to tell the truth on this subject can expect to pass unscathed; for he is touching a class of persons who combine interior conflicts and self-reproach with an astonishing measure of complacent arrogance and skill in gang-warfare if subjected to criticism—one of the ways in which they resemble a priesthood.

It is frequently remarked that to be an intellectual is something other than being a man of intelligence; intellectuals sometimes are and sometimes are not men of intelligence—they do not necessarily possess a quick shrewd judgement in affairs or a freely-moving unprejudiced mind, they are not always particularly *bright*.

An intellectual is also not the same thing as a professional engaged in one of the brain-trades: many an eminent lawyer or scientist or scholar hardly qualifies as an intellectual nor would wish to be called one; and some intellectuals are not men of a learned profession.

What, then, is the specific character of the intellectual? It is that of a person interested in the more general or philosophical aspects of problems: one who takes seriously the fundamental questions, the basic principles of different world-views. This, in a purely descriptive sense, is what distinguishes the intellectual, whether we use the word in an honourable or a pejorative sense.

In the most honourable sense, the intellectual is he whose delight it is to *know*. He works not just for useful results but so that at the end of his six days' labour he shall reach the Sabbath of the mind in which the truth is contemplated. This is that 'Archimedean point' which Jakob Burckhardt longed for in his *Reflections on History*: to contemplate the truth—in his case, historical truth—not as a partisan, or as enslaved by passions and fears, but in a free and disinterested way. 'Any man', he said, 'with an inkling of what that meant would

145

completely forget fortune and misfortune, and would spend his life in the quest of that wisdom'.[2]

But clearly this tradition of contemplation as the noblest activity of man was already losing its hold in the eighteenth and nineteenth centuries, when 'the intellectuals' first clearly emerged as a specifically modern social phenomenon. The spirit and modes of operation of this modern type cannot be described simply in terms of a vocation to disinterested inquiry.

One of the most interesting examples is the rise of the Russian intelligentsia after the Petrine reforms. By the middle of the nineteenth century it had become a definite caste, which, because of the peculiar Russian conditions, was alienated from the rest of society in an extreme degree. This caste was the bearer of a messianic mission. It took over from the Russian State the notion of public service as man's highest aim; and it took over from the Russian Church the notion of the Christian people as a mystical body whose salvation was the purpose of the whole cosmic drama. But these notions were translated into new terms: public service to 'the people', in defiance of Tsar and God, and their redemption through enlightenment and progress—this was the secular mystique animating the order of intellectuals. Victor Frank has summed this up very justly:

> It is easy to laugh at all this. But with all its faults, with all its political *naiveté*, with all its silliness, the pre-revolutionary Russian intelligentsia was one of the most humane, one of the morally purest heresies of our times. In a one-sided, neurotic sort of way it was the conscience of its nation. Though mostly agnostic or atheistic, it had all the faults and virtues of a militant monastic order . . . When the great trials came, many of its members were to win the martyr's crown.[3]

Under the different social conditions of Western Europe, these messianic tendencies and this quasi-religious devotion to 'the people', although present, never reached such extreme development. The intellectuals were not so drastically alienated from the rest of society: they could frequently gain respect and dignity as professional men, access to the bureaucracy was not denied them, the academies were less hostile, and their political activity was not necessarily conspiratorial. Nevertheless, there is enough in common for the Russian example, through its very exaggerations, to light up features of our Western experience. After all, the Russian development was an imitation of what had happened in Europe.

For the modern intellectuals have everywhere been to some extent an alienated class, 'displaced persons' not at home in the social order. Social and personal insecurity and anxiety seem to play a large part. What they have been chiefly interested in is the idea of social transformation. They are for the most part the children of the Enlightenment, the bearers of the modern ideologies, sectaries of the Religion of Progress, a priesthood of dissent—but the dissent is rooted in a secular dogmatism. Agnostic, sceptical and 'uncommitted' phases mingle with and change over into militant and dogmatic ones. A great number of the Australian university intellectuals who gravitated to Communism did so by an interesting path: positivism had laid waste all possible assumptions and beliefs, leaving a void in which they felt the need, not so much of Marxist philosophy, as of *redemptive action upon society in the name of Progress*. It was this new principle and finality that they sought; but they could not have found it if the Party had not been there with its core of dogma and its coherent purposiveness in the light of that dogma. This was the *prestige* of the Party which bewitched them. Those who did not make this transition floated around as a fellow-traveller, or a philosophical anarchist (as, at a certain stage, I described myself). But what controlled the whole field was the question of a secular gnosis: to that we were all oriented; our free critical activities were really dance-routines to the tunes of ideological pipers. The fact that many of us danced in diverse incoherent snatches instead of performing to the strict choreography of Stalin is not decisive. The eccentrics, the dissenters even from the orthodoxy of dissent, might re-explore Nietzsche, or Stirner, or Sorel, or the anarchism lighted up by the Spanish Civil War (as I did—along with exploring the literary esoterisms of Blake, Mallarmé, Rilke, Stefan George and so on). Never mind, we were all 'enlightened'; we all belonged somehow to the order of illuminati. Even our confessions of not-knowing and uncertainty were somehow superior to the mere ignorance and confusion of those who were not intellectuals.

This brings into view one of the ambiguities which interests me to the point of fascination. 'Liberal intellectuals' present two appearances, both true. They seem to be much given to scepticism and indecisiveness; they have undermined certainty in knowledge, and generated a distrust of the very instrument of knowledge, the intellect; they have relativized all values, denied the rationality of all ends of action; they oppose all conformism and cling to sovereign individualism. Yet they also appear to be dogmatists, arrogant with esoteric certainties, and full of party spirit for causes whose rightness one cannot question without becoming a traitor to humanity and progress.

When Hume philosophized himself into an abyss of scepticism he said to himself that one must nevertheless live as a sensible man of the world. When the modern liberal intellectual has philosophized himself into a void he frequently finds that one must nevertheless cut a figure as a 'progressive': the structure of ideological compul-

sion remains curiously intact as a canon of respectability while
everything else is destroyed. One must act 'as if' its tenets were true,
its aims rational. The mind is a blank sheet; but hold it to the light
and the watermark shows: it is the guild-sign of Progressivism. Hold
it to the fire, and the secret instructions appear, for the invisible
writing has not been expunged.

This type of liberal intellectual has abounded so much in our
time as to have become the standard type one expects to encounter;
it has appropriated the terms 'liberal' and 'intellectual' almost exclusively to itself, so that others are unwilling to claim either label.
Yet the liberalism is questionable when one considers the disquiet-
ing lack of resistance to totalitarianism; and the intellectuality is
also open to serious challenge. It is as if the mind were under a spell,
disconnected from reality and swayed by certain psychological
mechanisms along certain pre-ordained paths, which could easily be
suicidal.

In a society in which tension and anxiety seem to be exacting an
increasing toll in mental illness, even while material welfare and
public education (those supposed cures of all social ills) are also increasing, one would expect the intellectuals, as an exposed group, to
be particularly liable to neurotic reactions. The group attracts to
itself a large number of the personally maladjusted. Elton Mayo remarked on this in relation to students:

> Certain subjects seem to possess a fatal attraction for those unhappy in-
> dividuals—philosophy, literature, sociology, law, economics, and—God
> save us all—government . . . Argument, however rational, that is un-
> relating to a developing point of contact with the external world re-
> mains—however logical—a confusion of indeterminate possibilities. Some
> of these persons—able, unhappy, rebellious—rank as scholars.[4]

The fact is that a great number of intellectuals are engaged in a
predominantly emotional activity, even though it is ideas that are
manipulated in the process. There are several common psychological
mechanisms involved. (How does one know this? Not just by Olym-
pian observation: these are things one knows first in oneself and
recognizes in others.)

Firstly, there is the substitution of fashion-thinking for reality-
thinking. The intellectual too often graduates to acceptance in the
group by donning the current uniform of opinions without having
strictly earned the right to those opinions by a genuine consideration of the problem and the contending views. He knows which are
the O.K. books and the O.K. propositions; and for him to subject
his mind to the impact of unfashionable views requires a degree of
toughness and resolution which most of us develop only slowly, if at

all. The verbal rituals that intellectual groups develop are full of devices for rendering opposing views socially 'impossible'. How many of us who in the thirties discovered we were 'socialists' ever acquired this label by due process of intellectual inquiry? Everyone 'knew' that 'capitalism' was out and 'socialism' in. The sudden bursting of the socialist bubble after the British fiasco and the triumph of liberal economics in Europe merely showed how little realistic inquiry had ever gone into this immense delusion.

Connected with this tyranny of fashion is the compulsively op-positional character of many groups, who are committed, not acci-dentally, but essentially, to saying 'No' and *'ohne mich'* to the con-stitutive propositions of the community. It is not a fact that the dissenting minority always happens to be right. A good deal of the shine has worn off the sex freedom and new education of the 'twen-ties, the popular-fronting and pacificism of the 'thirties, the pro-Stalinism and socialism of the 'forties. The oppositional drive is not a matter of superior wisdom but an emotional *need*. To be against whatever is 'conventional' or 'reactionary' or 'conformist' is a re-assuring guarantee that one is intellectually respectable—which only illustrates the great strength of the pressure to conformism that operates within the minority group.

One of the most potent and obscure mechanisms is the guilt mechanism. One can distinguish between a sensitive but healthy and realistic conscience and a neurotic scrupulosity, or anxiety-guilt not adjusted to reality. The effect of the latter is to paralyse the normal and necessary defence of important values. Because Austra-lian Aborigines suffer legal and social discrimination and sometimes injustice, we shall concentrate wholly on protest and breast-beating on this score and resign our right to oppose Communist slave-labour and genocide. Because of the abuses that occurred under imperial-ism and capitalism we must say there is an equal plague on both houses rendering us unfit to oppose totalitarianism. The Commun-ists regard the manipulation of this guilt-mechanism of the Western intellectuals as the primary weapon in the psychological warfare they direct against this group. The immediate answer of the Com-munists in Australia to the Hungarian scandal was predictable: they launched a full-blast campaign on Aboriginal wrongs in Western Australia. The longer-range programme has been to nullify and bury the Hungarian massacre by concentrating on the guilt and anxiety feelings aroused by colonial problems, race relations in general, and above all nuclear armaments. How successful they have been may be measured by the number of persons who, three years after Hungary, and in the year of Tibet, can be made to confuse peace with the Communist political-warfare term spelt the same way.

At least one other mechanism should be mentioned: perfectionist demands as an excuse for not doing anything worthwhile. False or inappropriate or impossible goals are set up, not as real and attainable objectives, but as a reason for being absent from the good work that can be done. Charitable work, for instance, is bourgeois sentimentality: what is needed is nothing less than a complete reconstitution of society so that charity will be unnecessary, and we must not be diverted from this great aim into actually doing something for someone. H-bomb hysteria frequently exhibits this mechanism. Unilateral disarmament by ourselves is made the exclusive aim, not because there is any chance of this happening, *but precisely because there is no chance*; one is then absolved in a state of superior righteousness from all realistic consideration of the problems.

Common to all these non-rational 'interferences', which convert what is supposed to be an intellectual life into an emotional ritual, is something very disturbing: an impaired reality-sense, and a compulsive drive either to absent oneself from the defence of civilization or actually to attack the essential values involved in that defence. This is the *trahison des clercs*, mid-twentieth century style, and it requires further analysis.

The fact that there are honourable exceptions is no excuse for turning away from the critical problem: why has the record of the liberal intellectuals been so unsatisfactory when there was need of the defence of civilization against totalitarianism?

At least, it is felt, the record is good against Hitler. But is it? Let us not argue now about the strange contradictions of the 'anti-fascism' of the 'thirties, clamouring for disarmament, and showing its democratic *bona fides* by accepting *'la main tendue'* of Communist totalitarianism. Look at the record in Germany itself. Erich Meissner raised the painful question:

> The alarming aspect of our present situation is that the power of resistance and defiance seems to be steadily weakening. There are no indisputable lines of defence . . . The popular instinct is quite right when it concentrates on the question: Why was Hitler insufficiently resisted?
>
> This is, indeed, the crucial problem, but it is in its wider aspects a European problem. Why was there that astounding impotence in the German academic world? Why did the Universities, the centres of learning and culture, collapse and surrender to the invading enemy at the time when unknown parsons, deserted by the Church authorities, began to rally their congregations and put up resistance? The answer is: Humanism, culture, and refinement, all the achievements of modern secularism which were at hand, provided neither courage nor inspiration—the Sword of the Stoics was not in the hands of the intellectual leaders. In the hour of danger it was the much despised Church and not the University where the spirit of man found refuge.[5]

A good deal could be said about the 'liberal' erosion of values which made the breakthrough of Nazism in Germany possible and a judgement on Europe as a whole. But let us turn to the case of Communism, where the liberal intellectuals know that their record is far worse. Why this sorry complicity and connivance between self-proclaimed liberals and the Communist perpetrators of every crime against humanity?

Large parts of the heritage of liberal-progressive Enlightenment are also shared by the Communists. The difference is that the Communists really mean it, are more logical, consequential and determined. They are prepared to use brutal and unscrupulous means from which the liberals shrink, though liberal moral scepticism makes it difficult to justify this shrinking as anything more than squeamishness. Hence the Communists despise the liberals as people who like to play with progressive 'ideals' but are too cowardly to will the means to attain them. But the Communists also realize that this common stock of 'modern' and 'progressive' ideas gives them a vast field in which their propaganda can resonate if skilfully used, and a great deal of conscious and half-conscious fellow-travelling can be encouraged. When Stalin rang the bell, half or more of the Western liberal democratic intellectuals salivated.

What are the strands in the heritage of modern enlightenment which entangled the main body of liberal intellectuals so strangely with the movement that would pitilessly destroy them? What is the ideological source of that tenacity of delusion about Communist reality which even now persists and re-asserts itself, though with subtler rationalizations and precautions?

Liberalism arose as an historical movement, militantly and dogmatically committed to 'humanism', that is, to the view of man as an autonomous being, a sovereign mind and will, not a creature of God. The reverence, devotion, lordship, privileges and power of which Humanity has deprived itself in order to project them upon God must now be recalled to Humanity. This was already present in deism and pantheism: it was stated in the boldest terms in that atheist humanism which Marx regarded as the first principle of Communism. The fundamental word is the serpent's ideology: 'you shall be as gods'. Man shall decide, shall rule, shall reveal, shall determine the categories of good and evil—not God, whether He be dead or alive. Not Christus Pantocrator, who shall divinize men by incorporation with Himself: but Humanitas Pantocrator, who shall divinize all the human units by incorporation in the perfected collectivity on earth.

Hence the decisive option is for secularism. Within this secularist cosmos an enlightened élite will form the vanguard of progress, perfecting man and society by a combination of physical science and in-

L

dustry with the new science invented for the purpose, namely, 'social science', whose application will be 'social engineering'. A rational scheme of society can now be framed by the enlightened élite and organized kindly by democratic processes (liberalism) or with surgical severity (Communism).

In any case, the traditional values and the traditional order of Western civilization have to be liquidated. Man's end lies within this world not in eternity. Man has no created nature with an objective moral law. Man will make and re-make his nature, and assign laws to it at will. Objective morality is replaced by some kind of relativism. We are effectively 'beyond good and evil' as moral absolutes.

Each of the traditional orders constituting European society is marked down for liquidation: the monarchy, the nobility, the clergy, the merchants, the craftsmen, the peasantry. Society will consist of bureaucrats, intellectuals, and proletarian workers.

The orientation is urban-industrial; it favours state control and centralization; 'planning' is preferred to free enterprise. Property, traditionally regarded as a natural right and the basis of civic liberty, is to be voided of the reality of ownership or completely abolished. Egalitarianism, traditionally regarded as destructive of freedom, is the theoretical ideal which is used to undermine the traditional social hierarchy and enlist the support of the masses, even though in the end new privileged élites inevitably emerge. Social utility must prevail: for example, the new education will cease to be intellectually oriented and will be a pragmatist and social-adjustment affair. Women will also be emancipated from their traditional roles and masculinized in the name of feminism. 'Bourgeois' or 'puritanical' ideals of sexual morality and family life are especially under attack as the stronghold of reaction: marriage is a mere tenancy-at-will, terminable if no longer satisfactory or a better bargain can be made. Children should be liberated from parental authority and brought up institutionally by experts. Finally—for we must end somewhere—history is deified as the bringer of progress, success is treated as justification, what is later is better, and man's business is to ride the 'wave of history'.

No wonder so many liberals felt an uneasy admiration for the Communists, and accepted the Communist claim that they were the vanguard of Progress, a continuation by a resolute and militant force of the line of advance liberalism had already pioneered. 'Forward from liberalism' seemed a logical step, and if many did not take it they felt that they were 'soft', and respected the 'steel-hard' cadres of the Party. One has to take into account also the concealed power-worship of many intellectuals; nor, unfortunately, can one ignore the amount of opportunism, calculation of material advantage, and predisposition to the apparently winning side exhibited by individuals.

The high point of this strange but deep-seated collusion is now past. Salutory experience has cast some cold water on these 'advanced ideas'; and the true face of Communism cannot be completely hidden, even from the keen-sighted critical mind of a liberal intellectual.

The Age of Ideology, 1750-1950 (?), may be almost over, though one cannot be too sure. But the delusional framework of that period still lurks behind our disintegrated, hesitant liberalism that would fain settle for peace, comfort, co-existence and neutralism. In parts of the Western world there are signs of a resurgence of a genuine realist intellectuality, determined to break the delusional grip of a pseudo-rational secular gnosis. But if this reviving realism is to be something more dynamic and creative than a stoic conservatism, eaten at the heart by hopelessness and making a stand merely for honour's sake, it must pass beyond the sphere of natural values. The heart of culture is the divine *cultus,* and until this ceases to be thought of as a private and peripheral irrelevance or intrusion, and becomes central, the new springtime of history will be postponed.

We are to an acute degree in the Deuteronomic situation: a choice has been set before us, of life or death, of a blessing or a curse. We may choose which we will and it will be given us.

1959

NOTES

[1] Ortega y Gasset, *On Love* (trans. T. Talbert, London, 1959), p. 127.
[2] Jakob Burckhardt, *Reflections on History* (trans. M. D. H., London, 1943), p. 219.
[3] Victor Frank, 'The Russian Radical Tradition', *Soviet Survey* 29 (July-September 1959), p. 100.
[4] Elton Mayo, *The Social Problems of an Industrial Civilization* (London, 1945), pp. 23-4.
[5] Erich Meissner, *Confusion of Faces* (London, 1946), p. 43.

We are men—what are you?

WHEN the Spanish discoverers first appeared amongst the Caribbean islands, the native Indians took them to be visitants from the world of divine beings. Thus in Cuba, as Columbus reported, the Spaniards were greeted by people bearing gifts and singing for joy, believing that the people and ships came from heaven.[1]

Similar things happened on first contact in the Pacific islands. Captain Cook, for instance, was taken by the Sandwich islanders to be a god returning, and divine honours were paid to him. Swathed in red cloth, perched precariously on a rickety scaffolding some twenty feet high, Cook was addressed as Orono and offerings of pigs were made to him.[2]

In Tasmania, the Aborigines believed in a remote Island of the Dead named Tini Drini, situated in Bass Strait, where the departed lived a spirit-like form of existence. When the English came, England was assumed to be that remote island and the white invaders were the dead returning. Similar conceptions occurred in other parts of Australia.[3]

For Melanesia, the picture has been put together for us by that fine and sympathetic observer Codrington in his book *The Melanesians* (1891):

> There are still natives in these islands who remember when a white man was first seen, and what he was taken to be. In the Banks' Islands, for example, the natives believed the world to consist of their own group, with the Torres Islands, the three or four northern New Hebrides, and perhaps Tikopia, round which the ocean spread till it was shut in by the foundations of the sky. The first vessels they remember to have seen were whalers, which they did not believe to come from any country in the world; they were indeed quite sure that they did not, but must have been made out at sea, because they knew that no men in the world had such vessels. In the same way they were sure that the voyagers were not men; if they were they would be black. What were they then? They were ghosts, and being ghosts, of necessity those of men who had lived in the world. When Mr Patteson first landed at Mota, the Mission party having been seen in the previous year at Vanua Lava, there was a division of opinion among the natives; some said that the brothers of Qat had returned, certain supernatural beings of whom stories are told; others maintained that they were ghosts. Mr Patteson retired from the heat and crowd into an empty house, the owner of which had lately died; this settled the question, he was the ghost of the late householder, and

knew his home. A very short acquaintance with white visitors shews that they are not ghosts, but certainly does not shew that they are men; the conjecture then is that they are beings of another order, spirits or demons, powerful no doubt, but mischievous. A ghost would be received in a peaceful and respectful manner as European visitors have always in the first instance been received; a being not a living man or ghost has wonderful things with him to see and to procure, but he probably brings disease and disaster. To the question why the Santa Cruz people shot at Bishop Patteson's party in 1864, when, as far as can be known, they had not as yet any injuries from white men to avenge, the natives have replied that their elder men said that these strange beings would bring nothing but harm, and that it was well to drive them away; and as to shooting at them, they were not men, and the arrows could not do them much harm.[4]

The coastal peoples of New Guinea retain, in some cases at least, the memory of what their fathers thought when the white men first appeared. I have myself heard accounts from the people around Madang of the reaction to the appearance of the Russian scientist Miklouho-Maclay. They thought he might be Kilibob, the deity who founded their culture. And by a native of Kopar, at the mouth of the Sepik, I was given an instance of the alternative type of judgement: the white men had been taken to be evil spirits.

The men who have conducted exploratory patrols into the Central Highlands, which were penetrated only in the 1930s, also came across this strange mode of interpretation. Thus J. L. Taylor records in his report on the exploration of the Purari headwaters:

> In some villages I visited in this area we were regarded as people who had returned from the dead, some of the party being actually recognized as ones who had died in recent years. Scenes of great emotion and enthusiasm were witnessed as we passed through the villages, laughing or crying people rushing to caress or kiss or even touch the members of my party. The recognized ones were asked to stay and take their old places in the community.[5]

This of course involved native police and carriers; but it was the presence of the white men that set off the misunderstanding.

Certainly it did not take long for the people to realize that the Europeans were in fact living human beings. But even so an aura of the uncanny lingered about them. Where did they come from? Why had they no women? Look, too, at the strange forms of wealth and the supernormal powers they had somehow acquired. And too often their actions inspired fear and distrust. The German observer Richard Parkinson in his book *Dreissig Jahre in der Südsee* (Stuttgart, 1926) remarks that in all his years in the Bismarck Archipelago he found no substantiated case of a white man having been eaten when killed by cannibalistic natives. He believed that the usual

reason given by natives, when asked, that the white man's flesh did
not taste good, was an evasion, and thought that the real reason
was that given by an old chief of the Shortland Islands: *Spirit belong
all white man no good!* In general, the natives believed that by
eating the slain, one incorporated in oneself something of his
strength. In the case of the white man they may have feared to allow
the white man's spirit to gain an influence over them.

It is not to be thought that these original encounters were between
mythomanic savages and clear-eyed Europeans devoid of illusions.
Certainly some of the early navigators were realistic enough to see
that the savages were just ordinary men and women with the normal
spread of vices and virtues, reason and stupidity, though formed in
a different culture. Quiros and Cook could not understand
everything they saw, and might misinterpret some things, but they
did see straight through to the essential humanity of the primitives,
and did not systematically misinterpret by applying some false pre-
conception. But from the beginning there were others who did systematically misinterpret; and these ideological distortions split in
two opposite directions.

Either the native was the Noble Savage, inhabitant of a primitive
paradise uncorrupted by civilization; or he was a subhuman creature whose uncivilized state was due to a brutish inferiority of
nature.

The first idea was taken up more enthusiastically by those back
home. Thus it was the court humanist Peter Martyr who gave wide
currency to the Golden Age version of the life of the Caribbean Indians, in writing up the discoveries of Columbus. Translated by
Richard Eden into English, his idealization became an ingredient
in Shakespeare's *The Tempest*.[6] This strain of myth-making had its
greatest fortune in the eighteenth century when Diderot and other
ideologues in Paris acclaimed Bougainville's discovery of the New
Cythera, namely, Tahiti. They fabricated a vision of the paradise
of Natural Man, having a good start from the enthusiastic accounts
of Rousseauistically-inclined members of the expedition, such as
Philibert de Commerson, who told of the delights of innocent sexuality and wrote: 'I can state that it is the only corner of the earth
where live men without vices, without prejudices, without wants,
without dissensions'.[7] The reservations of the realistic Bougainville
were swept aside.

On the other hand, the notion of the natural brutishness and inferiority of the dark savage had more success amongst settlers on the
spot, who had to grapple with the inadequacies of the native when
faced with European demands, or who wanted a justification for en-
slaving or exterminating or otherwise mistreating the inhabitants.
The Spanish settlers in the New World found it convenient to

believe that the Indians were without souls and therefore without personal rights, until rebuked by the Bull of Paul III which affirmed the contrary and forbade the enslavement of the Indians.

The Christian belief in the spiritual equality and brotherhood of men as *persons*, and the scientific understanding of primitive forms of social and mental life, were slow in breaking through the twin distortions which idealized or debased the savage. Missionaries and scientists themselves fell victim to the prevailing prejudices. Thus the pseudo-theological idea that the black races were subject to the curse laid on Ham's posterity—that they should be hewers of wood and drawers of water forever—an idea born in rabbinical circles and taken over by Dutch Calvinists, also had quite a success amongst Catholic missionaries in Africa in the nineteenth century. And as late as the nineteen-thirties among scientists we find the entomologist Evelyn Cheesman writing as follows of the Papuans amongst whom she had travelled:

I have given offence to missionaries by using such a word, but far the best attitude to take towards natives is to look upon them all as a superior kind of animal. We are just as responsible for their well-being, and they are just as deserving of kindness and justice at our hands. We can find them every bit as interesting and study them quite as well . . .[8]

Here also is one of the leaders of thought in France in the twentieth century, Julien Benda:

The humanitarianism which holds in honour the abstract quality of what is human, is the only one which allows us to love *all* men. Obviously, as soon as we look at men in the concrete, we inevitably find that this quality is distributed in different quantities, and we have to say with Renan: 'In reality one is *more or less* a man, *more or less* the son of God . . . I see no reason why a Papuan should be immortal'.[9]

Had Renan or Benda spoken with the French missionaries who, at the time they were writing, were working amongst the same Papuans, their superficial levity might have been curbed.

So great, then, was the initial 'distance' between the men who encountered one another in different parts of the world in the last few centuries that the first conquest of knowledge had to be an acceptance of the most elementary fact: that they shared a common humanity. Not gods or demons or ghosts on one side; not specimens of Adamic innocence or mere anthropoids on the other: simply men on both sides. Primitive peoples often apply to themselves as a designation the word in their language which means 'men'. Thus when asked by the explorer the name of their tribe, their reply is: 'We are *men*'. But, as we have seen, their reply frequently has another implication. It means also: '*We* are men—what are you?' This for both sides has been the first question in anthropology.

Such a simple conquest of knowledge is even now by no means complete, either in theory or in practice.

In practice the human relations that exist in colour-stratified societies, where discrimination is practised on grounds of skin colour, indicate a partial failure of *effective* realization of our common humanity. The black man may not be subject to the curse of Ham; but does he feel any the less under a curse if the very skin he was born with is a permanent disqualification and badge of inferiority?

In theory, things are not satisfactory either. It is not the discredited race theories which we need bother with. The problem lies rather in a defect in our philosophical anthropology—that is, in the general theory of what constitutes the human person, as distinct from the particular inquiries pursued in empirical anthropology. Certain assumptions often present among social scientists tend, far more than they wish to admit, to deprive human oneness of its full meaning. I refer to the 'positivist' or 'scientistic' approach.

The lurking philosophical assumption is that the only kind of knowledge which is truly knowledge is that which can be physically verified by sense-observation. This usually goes hand in hand with the methodological assumption that the social sciences must take the methods of the physical sciences as their model. So we get attempts at creating a 'social physics', at imaging society as a kind of geometry, at dismissing everything from view that cannot be quantified or given statistical form. One result is the elimination in principle of what is specifically human: namely, the intellectuality of man, his free will, and his responsibility towards an objective order of moral truths.

In this view there is no such thing as a common humanity. There is no 'human nature', only the immense variety of observable human behaviours. One kind of behaviour has to do with the assertion, implicitly or explicitly, of principles governing social life, of metaphysical beliefs, of what we queasily and slipperily like to call 'values'. But these assertions are all trans-empirical in their content: there is no way of establishing their truth or falsity by purely empirical observation: and so, on a positivist view, the only thing verifiable about them is that they *are* put forward; and the only problem is to *relate* them to the particular social circumstances which are their sufficient cause. For since they have no objective character as possible knowledge, they must be explained wholly as products of the social situation in which they occur.

So we come easily to a position of cultural and moral relativism. Principles, beliefs and values have no possible truth-content; they are validated only in the sense that they are the demands or conventions that arise in a particular society. But this means that there

is no community of mankind with access (however fallible or imperfect) to objective principles of order which can be intellectually
recognized and which are valid for all. If we praise or condemn
what is done in another society we are merely imposing our socially-
determined approvals and disapprovals on a society that happens to
have a different set of approvals and disapprovals. There is no common ethical measure between cultures: each constitutes a closed
world.

This is not, let it be noted, the tradition in which our Common
Law was formed. The basis of that tradition is the belief in a
'natural moral law', pre-existing and superior to the diverse enact-
ments and conventions of men. When applied to the assertion of
governmental authority over peoples of an alien culture this leads
(*a*) to the assertion that there are some basic human rights and principles of conduct which are binding for all social systems and all
governments, and (*b*) to an effort to distinguish between what is
merely different and legitimately tolerable in the usages of other
peoples and what is intolerable because contrary to natural law. It is
this approach which is given expression, for instance, in the legisla-
tion of Australian New Guinea, where the *Laws Repeal and Adopt-
ing Ordinance* states:

> The tribal institutions, customs and usages of the aboriginal natives of
> the Territory shall not be subject to this Ordinance and shall, subject
> to the provisions of the Ordinances of the Territory from time to time
> in force, *be permitted to continue in existence in so far as the same are
> not repugnant to the general principles of humanity.*

The full consequences of the positivist and relativist approach,
with its tendency to break up the reality of human oneness, frequently trouble those who adhere to it. They often fall into an
honourable inconsistency rather than accept the logic of their position, speaking and acting *as if* there were after all cognizable moral
truths of universal application founded in human nature as such.
But others seek to maintain their relativism doggedly against all
comers.

The cost of maintaining this position is to substitute for the
human person in his fullness a psychophysical simulacrum, meth-
odically deprived of rational dignity. When the primitive accosts
such theorists he might well say: '*We* are men—what are *you*?' And
the theorists might well say: 'We have no human nature in common
with you, though we have important observable biological similarities and similar basic needs in respect of food, sex, breathing,
micturition etc. . . . We regard ourselves as socially-determined
phenomena and do not pretend to any rational principles of order
and conduct; for, as our great teacher Bertrand Russell says, man

can exhibit a certain cleverness in choosing means to an end, but
ends themselves are not susceptible of rational judgement, being
determined by passion and prejudice. We intend by superior power
and scientific means to dominate and change your lives, but we
claim no rational justification for interfering with you.'

This is, so far, mainly a difficulty in the theoretical domain. But
one wonders if it will not accumulate practical effects, as theoretical
positions tend to do. Meanwhile signs continually appear that
among social scientists there is some realization of the uncomfortable dilemmas into which positivism thrusts its adherents. Thus an
American scholar, William L. Kolb, has remarked that a good deal
of current thinking takes a direction inimical to social freedom.
'Sociologists', he notes, 'have believed for some time that in order for
a society to exist the members of that society must share a system of
values'. Furthermore, it seems that it is necessary for at least most
men in that society to believe that these values are objectively *true*,
if society is to be satisfactorily maintained. But if the real truth is
that none of such values can claim to be 'true', the sociologist is
placed in an intolerable dilemma: 'To give all men access to this
truth would be to destroy society, for men cannot know to be false
what they must believe to be true'. The practical result would seem
to be that most men should be denied access to this dangerous truth
about the nature of their values. The final illumination must be
confined to the initiate. Kolb goes on to indicate a way out of the
dilemma:

> But perhaps the positivist can forsake his positivism. There is nothing in
> science that compels one to assert the subjective character of values . . .
> When the sociologist restores his belief in the objectivity of values while,
> at the same time, remaining humble about their final content, he rejoins
> the human race in its eternal quest.[10]

Whether we are going to see any mass movement towards re-
joining the human race amongst social scientists tainted with positivism remains to be seen. It is rather more likely that when the
sons of the Melanesian primitives shortly arrive at our universities
they will be told by their teachers that only the choice of means
can be rational, the choice of ends and principles being necessarily
irrational. Let us hope they do not learn this lesson too thoroughly.
Nihilism does not invariably take polite academic forms.

1960

NOTES

1 See S. E. Morison, *Admiral of the Ocean Sea: a Life of Christopher Columbus* (2 vols, Boston, 1942), II, 121-2, and *The Journal of Christopher Columbus*, trans. C. Jane (New York, 1960), p. 54.
2 J. C. Beaglehole (ed.), *The Journals of Captain Cook on his Voyages of Discovery*, vol. 3 (Cambridge, 1967), pp. 505-6.
3 E. A. Worms, 'Tasmanian Mythological Terms', *Anthropos* LV (1960), 1-16.
4 R. H. Codrington, *The Melanesians* (Oxford, 1891), pp. 11-12.
5 Unpublished report in the library of the Australian School of Pacific Administration, Sydney.
6 Richard Eden, *The Decades of the Newe Worlde* (1555) and *The History of Travayle in the West and East Indies* (1577).
7 Denis Diderot, *Supplément au voyage de Bougainville* (Geneva, 1955), p. 82.
8 Evelyn Cheesman, *The Two Roads of Papua* (London, 1935), p. 222.
9 Julien Benda, *The Treason of the Intellectuals* (trans. R. Aldington, New York, 1969), p. 8.
10 William L. Kolb, 'Values, Positivism and the Functional Theory of Religion', *Social Forces* XXXI (1953), 305-11.

My New Guinea

I

IT was near sunset on an afternoon early in 1944. Our canoe was laden with large hands of ripe yellow bananas, with pawpaws and betelnuts and a rooster, and American carbines and grenades. We were paddling slowly on the smooth green water of Patusi Bay. I had joined a patrol led by Lieutenant H. L. Robinson of ANGAU, the purpose of which was to mop up surviving groups of Japanese hiding in villages on the south coast of Manus. The war in these parts had dwindled from MacArthur's massive assault-strokes to this improvised guerrilla operation on a petty scale. Apart from a few native policemen, our troops were villagers who had volunteered for the occasion and had been equipped with whatever arms were available, including Japanese weapons.

We passed at leisure the tiny Peri islands: little coral platforms, and rich green dobs of rock and vegetation that looked as if they had fallen carelessly from the Creator's hand as it withdrew from forming the main island. In the distance the big volcano lightly smoked. The Peri islands are the scene of Margaret Mead's well-known anthropological study, *Growing Up in New Guinea* (1930). When she returned twenty-five years later, in 1953, to make a study of the new generation (recorded in her book *New Lives for Old*, 1956) she found that the people had quitted these islands and moved to another site, for a reason I shall mention later.

My companion on that patrol, Lt Robinson, was a pre-war resident of New Guinea who had been caught by the Japanese when they invaded New Britain in 1942. He was in a party of prisoners being marched single-file along a winding track through tall grass; at an S-bend he slipped out of sight, lay hidden, and escaped. (The rest of the prisoners were later massacred at Tol plantation.) He wandered with his hands tied behind his back, fevered and starving and pretty well out of his mind, until finally picked up by a rescue party. Now he was a military government officer with a record of laconic courage in forward areas. (After the war he stayed in New Guinea as a labour recruiter but was murdered by natives in one of the more remote villages of New Britain.)

Robinson knew a good deal about violence and fear and courage and death. I knew nothing. Next morning was to be my initiation when we surprised a group of Japanese near the mouth of the Wari river. Meanwhile as we glided past the houses standing on piles over the water our crew exchanged low-voiced courteous greetings with the old folk sitting there. It struck me that they, too, knew by daily experience about death—and birth—in a way that I in my twenty-six years had not begun to learn.

We screen birth away from domestic experience. We keep death out of sight so efficiently that it is quite possible for people to grow to mature age without having seen a dead human body. We even remove the killing of animals for food so far from urban conscious-ness that it is an emotional shock for gentle-minded people to wit-ness the killing of a fowl or a sheep. And as for knowledge of sex—we seem to have achieved the maximum of erotic signals and display with the minimum of real understanding of sexuality.

But this was a world in which the facts of life and death were known; a world where the inexorable organic rhythms were insis-tent. I have picked my way for years, with many turnings and stum-blings, across the field of speculation that opens out from this point of realization; and I trust I have learnt to avoid the pitfalls of senti-mentalizing the primitive. Nevertheless this point is valid: there is a difference in psychic tone between a society in which the elementary realities of life and death are matters of common experience, and one like ours in which so much is screened off, and dealt with in a specialized way, so that there is always the danger that when it does enter into the experience of the ordinary individual it does so with an effect of unbalancing shock and disarray.

At any rate, the first corpses I had ever seen at close quarters were those of the Japanese whom we attacked by surprise next morning. They died from bullets or grenade-fragments, or in many cases they lay with their chests blown out by the grenade which they had held against themselves in a soldier's suicide. The flies, appearing as the sun rose, crept into the pale pink shells of their gaping mouths.

But such incidents were extra-curricular for me, and it was not long before I returned to the business which had taken me to New Guinea at that time and which held me bound thereafter to New Guinea's concerns for seventeen years: the study of what in wartime we called its 'civil affairs'. It was as a performing flea in A. A. Con-lon's remarkable circus, the Australian Army Directorate of Re-search and Civil Affairs, that I encountered the challenge of a voca-tion I had not expected, and have never regretted, in spite of diffi-culties.

It is strange, though, how things come round. When I was fifteen I read *The Golden Bough*—borrowing volume after volume from that true *alma mater* of mine, the City of Sydney Lending Library. After wandering dazed and excited through Sir James Frazer's ethnological labyrinth, in which, incidentally, my disturbed religious faith finally died, I thought I should like to become an anthropologist, and pursue research amongst the primitives. Later I veered away, and wanted above all to be a literary scholar, simply because all I wanted to do was to read literature, and especially poetry. It seemed to me to be an excellent idea to be paid to read poetry, and it still does. But as it turned out, it was the world of the primitives that got first claim on me; and when, immediately after the war, the opportunity came of a choice between literature and government as academic roads, I felt bound to continue sharing in the enterprise of building the Australian School of Pacific Administration, for the labourers available in the field at that time were indeed few, and the whole enterprise uncertain, but important.

II

I have mentioned the Peri islands, where Margaret Mead studied an island culture still in a primitive state. When she left the first time, the people were preparing to change their way of life by accepting the Christianity of the Catholic Mission.

Much had happened by the time she returned twenty-five years later.

The people of Manus, as elsewhere in New Guinea, were very conscious of the fact that the Australians, having been chased out of the islands by the more powerful Japanese, were re-installed only by the power and favour of the United States. Nor was it only American power that impressed them: still more it was American wealth and generosity. It struck many of the people that if they had to be ruled by someone, it would be better to go to the biggest firm in the business. Why put up with the Americans' poor cousins, the Australians, if they could get really big material progress by hitching on to the United States? In August 1946 there was still a U.S. naval base in Manus. The leaders of many of the Manus communities requested an interview with the commander, at which they said that they wanted the United States to take them over, because their previous rulers—first the Germans, then the Australians—while using them as labourers had done nothing for them and given them no schooling. They pointed out that it was the Americans who had re-conquered the islands, while the Australians had fled in 1942.

There was a to-do in Port Moresby when the embarrassed U.S. commander reported this matter. A very senior official, the late Mr Robert Melrose, who had been District Officer in Manus after the First World War, went up to talk to the people. They gave him a bad hearing, and spoke of the failure of the government to do anything for them in the past. He said, 'It's a new government now'. A spokesman said, 'But we notice you're still in it'. He promised schools and progress. A spokesman stood up and said, 'You told my father the same thing twenty-five years ago'.

Well, the Americans left Manus in due course. But the minds of the people remained disturbed, seeking a road of progress and feeling that all visible roads were blocked. Their frustrated longings and resentment turned them against the Catholic Mission too. To the Melanesian, a religion is above all a technology: it is the knowledge of how to bring the community into the correct relation, by rites and spells, with the divinities and spirit-beings and cosmic forces that can make or mar man's this-worldly wealth and well-being. Christianity, as the religion of the white man, had been accepted by the people as the road of progress. But it had not worked for them. If the Catholic missionaries had the 'secret of the wealth' they were keeping it shut away from the people: the talk of the Mission was not 'straight'. The true way must be sought elsewhere.

Now a wave of Cargo Cult swept over the Manus people. Cargo Cult is a recurring phenomenon in Melanesia: it has a structure analogous with the millenarian cults of disturbed and frustrated elements of society in mediaeval Europe. The Cargo is the white man's wealth. God, or the spirit-ancestors, will send the Cargo to the people, in ships or planes. In preparation for the event, the cult prophet or leader often orders that all the old forms of property must be thrown away into the sea. What the Peri people threw away at this time, along with their personal belongings, was the religion of the missionaries.

The wave of Cargo Cult subsided, but the breach with the Mission was not healed. Among the people a New Way was now proclaimed, by a new magnetic leader, named Paliau, a former policeman who had been a civil affairs officer for the Japanese in Rabaul and had now returned home. Paliau combined religious revelation with a secular programme. Everything was to be made modern; the past was to be abandoned. It was then that the people of Peri, under the influence of Paliau's movement, left their tiny islands and built a new village elsewhere.

When Margaret Mead left these people the second time, the people were again preparing with tense excitement to embrace a new life. The Administration was attempting to canalize and legitimize the modernist movement of Paliau by creating a system of elected local government, into which these energies could safely flow. The people of Peri were waiting to be included in a Local Government Council which would give the New Way an approved institutional form. Great expectations, conceived always in an apocalyptic mode, with magical shortcuts in the absence of real knowledge of causes . . . and the results always, in the nature of things, so slow, so

meagre. And the everyday routine of the white man's type of institution so exacting, so drab, in its actual working.

Everywhere in Papua and New Guinea in those post-war years
one encountered the signs of restless frustrated seeking for change
and material progress. The Cargo itself—the white man's wealth—
was a symbol. It was not merely a question of desire for material
goods. These things were the outward signs of status and prestige.
The deepest desire of the Melanesian was to recover his status in a
world where once he was on top of creation, but, since the coming
of the white man, he had suddenly found himself at the bottom
of every scale of values—social, economic, cultural. Many, and sometimes very frank and bitter, were the expressions of this feeling of
frustration I heard in those years. But the most revealing text is one
recorded by a friend of mine, J. H. Wootten, in converse with a
leader of a cult movement in an inland village in Manus:

> If the Germans had taught us, we would now be the same as you. If the
> Japanese had taught us we would now be brothers.[1] If the English had
> taught us we would now have one fashion. But no, you hide your know-
> ledge. You have no feeling for us. We are your dogs, your pigs. We work
> for you, we are your pick, your shovel, your car, your engine, your cow.
> You do not want us to understand. One generation grows up, works and
> dies. Another comes, works and follows it to the grave. Another, another
> and another. But when will the whiteman disclose to us one of his ideas?
> . . . Some of our men have been to school with the mission. We were look-
> ing for a road and thought we had found it. But the road was not
> straight. They did not show us the straight road that would lead us on to
> your knowledge, your ideas, your language . . . Our minds, brother, are
> like a worm under the earth, trying to find a way to the surface. We go
> on and on and on, and we are just about to come up when the white-
> man says, 'no', and blocks the way. We go back. We make another
> tunnel. Again we work on and on. Again we are just about to find a
> way out when the whiteman says, 'No, no good you have understanding',
> and blocks the way . . . If the whiteman would only open his hand, we
> would be brothers. But he keeps it tightly shut. He has locked all his
> knowledge in a box, and where are we to find the key? We are but dogs
> and pigs . . .'[2]

What could one say to this? It was not in relation to Manus, but
to an area to which I gave much attention in Papua, that I wrote in
one of my notebooks: 'Right through this district, one has only to
sit down and give them time to make up their minds to talk and
they will fasten to one's shoulders the whole weary load of their ambitions and frustrations'. It was in this area of Papua, the Kairuku
sub-district, that I arranged in 1949 to stay for a few days in a particular village, Bereina. I did not know what I had set in motion.
Great things were expected of this event. They were convinced that

I, a teacher from Australia, was the answer to their problem . . . if only I could be induced to stay with them and teach and guide them.

My reception was therefore on a lavish scale: a fowl and heaped vegetables were presented; a dance (or *sing-sing*) was organized for the evening; the Village Constable knelt down to unlace my boots. Mika, the village's prime mover in modern affairs, chairman of a so-called Co-operative Society, had vacated his own house, and provided me with the best Papuan cook I ever found. These attentions were acutely embarrassing. One could make return on the spot for gifts and hospitality, but one could not produce the great results which they were hoping for. All I could do was promise to speak on their behalf to the Administration, and tell people in Australia of their needs.

They danced that night as they had not danced for years. The old men began remembering songs and dances that had been almost forgotten. These are people who have a flair for display, in bird-of-paradise plumes and parrot feathers and bright flowers, with brilliant painting of the body and face, and gleaming white shell and bone ornaments, and oiled copper skin, the whole gorgeous show swaying and chanting in lines to the rhythm of the hand-drum, while the women, with their coloured grass skirts aflow, and their breasts gleaming in the firelight, clap hands and sway in chorus. Mika, as a modern business man, took no part in these backward festivities, but was pleased if they had the right effect on me. Another progressive person, a bitter neurotic educated woman, married to an uneducated man, said to me: 'Papua is the worst place in the world, I think. The people are too slow, their brains are no good, they are too much in the dance, they sleep instead of work. They are too much inside their own customs; you cannot do anything with them. I say to them: You lie down and sleep: you want something, but think that money has hands and feet to walk up the road to you'.

The *sing-sing* went on all night. When I fell asleep it had so penetrated and pulsed through me that it continued in my dreams to be the intoxicating medium in which I existed physically and mentally. The last of the dancers did not halt until midday the next day.

I did try to arrange certain kinds of help for Mika and his 'Co-operative'. But what could one really do? The Administration's resources were strained out in all directions and could not stretch to continuous contact with Bereina, which was a village of poor prospects and no significance. I visited the village two years later. There was a Co-operative officer at Kairuku who was trying to help. But Mika's affairs were sinking into a mess and he was becoming

M

discouraged. It was not for another three years that I returned, walking down this time from the mountains at the back and coming in unannounced. The village was in a depressingly demoralized state. Mika's venture had finally collapsed and several hundred pounds worth of stock was unaccounted for. I thought back to the welcome and the feast, and their earnest pleas for me to stay with them and show them how to progress. I wasn't very happy with the taste of these things in the mouth, but it is a taste one has to get used to in New Guinea.

III

> Chère Nouvelle-Guinée, quelle école de détachement et de sainteté, si l'on voulait! Tout, la terre et les gens—même ceux que l'on élève et veut aimer—vous tiennent à distance et se dérobent tellement! J'en ai parfois le vif et douloureux sentiment . . . Oui, de quoi faire de la grande sainteté, à la rude école du détachement et du travail uniquement pour Dieu.

No two persons were better qualified to speak of New Guinea, with its harshness and unyieldingness, as 'a school of detachment and of sanctity', than the writer of the letter from which this passage is quoted, and the person to whom it was written.

The writer was Alain de Boismenu, whom I knew only in his old age when he lived in deep retirement in the field of his missionary labours in Papua.[3] Part of that field was the area I have just been speaking of. Alain de Boismenu was once described by his friend Paul Claudel as 'the bishop with heart of a lion'.[4] Indeed he had the quality of lion and eagle, but also the sweetness and gentleness which sometimes flowers in such men, especially in old age. I would nominate him as the person in my experience who most completely exemplified 'greatness'—an inspiring force of mind and will, large views, courage, intense affections and complete self-abnegation, cheerfulness, candour, a noble simplicity utterly devoid of pretension. And behind these qualities something more, as all his associates knew: a rare sanctity and unerring spiritual discernment. Very characteristic was the reply he once gave to the question: 'By what sign can sanctity be recognized?' His answer was: 'By naturalness'.[5]

The same qualities were present in the person to whom he wrote the letter from which I quoted: Marie-Thérèse Noblet, a Frenchwoman who was the first superior of an order of Papuan sisters. I never met her, for she died in 1930, yet she has had a deep influence on my life, in ways that I need not attempt to trace here, and perhaps could not fully do so if I tried.

It is indeed strange how things come round. If it was in the midst of Sir James Frazer's speculations on the primitive that my early religious faith succumbed, it was in the midst of the actually primitive that it stirred and woke at last to a fuller and more assured life. Now, to be a believing Christian means to accept as fact what the gospels say not only of the action of divine power (as in miracles) but also of the action of created spiritual beings—angels and demons. I think that to a modern unbeliever the notion of angelic activity and demonic activity in the cosmos seems much more absurdly remote from the possibility of sober acceptance than the notion of divine activity. And I also think that if one subjected the faith of a modern believer to a sort of depth-analysis to determine which parts were real to the mind and imagination and will, and which were unreal, one would find that the action of angels, but especially of fallen angels, demons, was somewhat uneasily assented to, poorly developed, and mainly pushed out of sight. (This, of course, has nothing to do with the truth or falsity of the belief, which is not to be decided by prevailing climates of opinion or one's state of imaginative habituation.) I raise this question here because the life of Marie-Thérèse Noblet presents both believer and unbeliever with a startling and disconcerting challenge. It was the locus not only of apparent divine action but also, apparently, of violent and outrageous demonic action.

It was only after her death that the hidden facts, hitherto known only to her spiritual director, Archbishop de Boismenu, and a very few others, were made public, and the 'case' has been the subject of considerable controversy in Europe.[6] My own acceptance of the authenticity of Marie-Thérèse's mystical way rests very largely on my confidence in the chief witness, Alain de Boismenu: not a weak-minded, credulous or inexperienced observer, but a man of ripe experience, keen and shrewd judgement, and flawless probity.

It is not my wish to draw the possibly unwilling, perhaps smiling or irritated, reader further into the realm of the preternatural. Indeed I would repeat the warning that the inquirer is likely to find the facts, as asserted, disconcerting and not at all in conformity with a sober Anglo-Saxon good taste. I mention them here because they cannot be excluded from the picture of New Guinea I am trying to present—the image that is in my memory, with the colours and lighting and relief given by my feelings and recollections. Part of the reality and grandeur of New Guinea is that it has been a 'school of sanctity' for some—and I could willingly name others, living and dead, besides the two I have mentioned. The paths of New Guinea can be hard, exhausting, and at times dangerous. Even the magnificence of scene, in lowland rain-forests or on mountain-heights, may quickly become a weight and oppression as the spirit tires. For those who have truly undertaken the *dur métier*, as Boismenu repeatedly

called it, the 'hard trade' of evangelism, the roads can be a veritable
via crucis: let no one make light of it. The gaiety, charm, practical good sense, and endurance which I found so conspicuously
among these French missionaries, are more often than not acquired
and perfected at the price of pain and desolation. That is the law
of the spiritual kingdom. One of the masters in that kingdom was
the old prelate who lived in almost eremitical retirement amongst
the citrus trees in the green valley of Kubuna. Amongst sayings
of his which I vividly remember, there are some words he wrote
long ago—words which I have often repeated to myself, and sometimes to others, in some recent troubles quite different from those
that Boismenu had in mind:

> In the apostolate one must be neither an optimist nor a pessimist. Opti-
> mism has its dangers, its errors, yet it is at times the spring of fine initia-
> tives and serious work. Pessimism, on the other hand is the source of
> nothing whatever, it paralyses all impulse, deadens every generous feel-
> ing; it is usually a screen for laziness, and always the sign of a certain
> wilfulness of character; it is the canker of zeal . . . Between the two is
> *confidence in God*.[7]

IV

What kind of New Guinea are we making? Admittedly in the
long run it will be what the native people themselves can make of
it. But we must bear a great deal of responsibility, while the initia-
tive still remains with us.

Ever since 1944, when I first went there, I have felt that New
Guinea would be a test of our quality as a nation: that something
worthwhile could be created there; and on the other hand that
failure could come through lack of foresight, understanding, sympathy, and clear principles of action. Perhaps this is an excessively
nationalist way of viewing the matter, but I can't help that now.

The question, what kind of New Guinea? has a decidedly political
aspect today and an urgency, which hardly anyone would have admitted possible fifteen—or ten—or even five years ago. My own concern, though today it is dominated by the political problem (discussion of which I initiated in the early fifties, in a rather unreceptive
atmosphere) has passed through three stages, of which the 'political'
is the last. The other two I would name, in retrospect, the 'reformist', and the 'social'.

If I have given the impression earlier that the original emotional
tie between myself and New Guinea was merely sympathy with the
native people, I take the opportunity of correcting it. It was as
much, if not more, a feeling for my fellow-Australians in the field
staff of the Native Affairs Department. I admired the work that some

of them—men like Jim Taylor and Ivan Champion and Keith Mc-Carthy—had done in uncontrolled areas. I admired the courage and steadfastness which many men had shown when everything seemed to crumble under the Japanese advance in 1942, and the work done in forward areas throughout the war. There was an element of hero-worship in my sentiments, such as the timid and sedentary are prone to feel.

I also felt involved in the enterprise which largely arose from A. A. Conlon's Directorate of Research and Civil Affairs and which came out in public as the 'Ward policy' of reform and development in Papua and New Guinea. Though there were anguished cries of 'socialism' and worse, the policy amounted to no more than a belated attempt to catch up with the policies in colonial adminis-tration accepted by British Conservatives. We never did fully catch up: partly because of the inherent difficulties of the territory, and partly because of administrative inertia. But at any rate this was the reformist enterprise to which I felt committed. The Australian School of Pacific Administration was the academic part of the pro-gramme, and on two occasions I chose to remain with it, during its precarious formative period, rather than accept invitations to teach at the London School of Economics, and transfer my interests to British South-East Asian territories.

It was as I sank deeper into the study of the problems thrown up by our initial reformist programme that I entered the second stage of my concern, in which I could see exemplified in the small field of New Guinea the great drama of the disintegration of traditional cultures, and the groping for the means of creating a new social order in the modern world. It became for me a period of intellec-tual crisis, because every question about the nature of man and so-ciety was opened up. I was concerned with the question by what means, with what constitutive propositions, through what creative forces, under what disciplines, a civilization could come into being and be maintained in being. How were the New Guinea people going to step out of a decayed primitive culture, and embrace and make their own, in knowledge and habit, in inward acceptance and institutional result, those things that seem to be essential: for example, the acceptance of the notion of the human 'person' with its structure of intellect and free will and moral responsibility, its in-trinsic and inalienable dignity and obligations and rights, its need to find the freedom of self-fulfilment through order and love? (If anyone thinks that this notion of the 'person', with all it implies, is something that comes automatically and universally, and does not have to be learned, and learned by heart, he has not understood his own civilization.) How, moreover, was the new social life to flower colourfully into figurations of meaningful beauty through art and rite and celebration that generate energy and bring communion and joy? What wisdom would build this house, and furnish and decorate it, and maintain it?

Certainly, I decided, it was not our sterile secularism with its will to *desecrate*, literally, all departments of life; nor our disintegrated liberalism with its inability to rationally affirm or practically defend its own values; nor our mixture of shiftless hedonism with abstract and unreal U.N.-type clichés. These things were the late luxury products or parasitical features of a Western civilization which had been founded and formed and maintained by far other commitments and disciplines, enthusiasms and sacrifices. Not to realize the gravity of the problem thus opened up seemed to me to be intellectually dishonourable and morally irresponsible. The shapeless cannot give shape, nor the formless form, nor the unbelieving belief, nor the disordered order, nor the meaningless meaning, nor the irresolute resolution.

There are some troubled words written by Elspeth Huxley in 1948, in regard to Africa, that have not lost their force:

> We have ignored the heart, indeed our outlook seems to grow ever more materialistic, and the modern thesis to be that literacy, hygiene and acquaintance with trade unions and co-operatives will of themselves transform Africans, newly freed from ignorance and superstition, into good citizens of a progressive state . . . We who kill the slave-raid, the juju, the leopard cult, the human sacrifice and even, so often, the dance of the warriors, seem only to have the school band and the information room, the latrine-drive and the tax exemption form to offer in return. Ours seems at times a drab and half-apologetic empire that we only half-believe in ourselves. Life today in the villages lacks colour and drama, the people are in danger of starvation of the soul.[8]

Very often I have been invaded by a feeling of the *sterility* of our contact with New Guinea. So much courage and admirable work shown in the pacification of the country, so much good work put into basic administration, so much effort expended on social and economic improvement, and yet nothing seems to take deep root, and nothing flowers.

And then sometimes I wonder whether the explanation is not really much simpler than I had thought. The great enterprise of European colonialism, which now turns out to have been fairly short-lived for most of the world, bred rejection in the hearts of its subjects, in spite of so much of incomparable value that it brought. Why? Perhaps the simple answer is: the white woman. While European men went out to Asia and Africa and the Pacific without wife and family, they entered into a different sort of relationship, socially and sexually, with the people. When the white wife came out all was inevitably different. It is not the woman's fault if her urge to create and defend a home, and bring up children by the standards of her own community, made her wish to draw a circle of exclusion round her domain. People indulge in a lot of shoddy moral indignation about the 'settler mentality'. Let them face in practice the decisions involved, and then talk. (One is reminded of university teachers in New York, who keep their children away from the Negro- and Puerto-Rican-filled public schools, sending them to private schools, and who then lecture and write articles on the need for forcible immediate integration in the South.) No, the white woman is perhaps the real ruin of empires. If New Guinea had become a mulatto society it would be a slatternly, but more colourful and easy-going society, with the minor vices of concubinage and sloth, rather than the major respectable vices of cold-heartedness and hypocrisy.

Anyway, the course is set now. The seeds have been sown and the reaping is not far hence. I have not wanted in these rather personal notations to say very much about the political problem as it now confronts us. Ten years ago I was of the view that we should make the effort to bind New Guinea permanently to Australia, so that the people would advance to self-government under the same constitutional roof as ourselves. The drift of events, and the arguments advanced by John Kerr, have convinced me that the only practical policy is to encourage the New Guinea people to set up political house on their own—preferably, as Kerr has suggested, in a general Melanesian Federation or Union.[9]

The big question now is the correct estimate of the tempo at which political events will move, and what should be done in view of that tempo. There has been talk of us needing thirty years to create the conditions for self-government. This, I fear, is foolish talk both ways. Thirty years would not be nearly enough for genuine preparation in a non-lunatic world. On the other hand, in the actual, lunatic, world we have not got thirty years. This means we have got to think and act, deeply, quickly, and coherently. New Guinea is still a test of our quality as a people.

There the great island lies with its archaic bird-reptile shape. The smoking mountains speak low thunder, the earth shakes lightly, the sun glares down on the impenetrable dark-green mantle of forest with its baroque folds, the cloud-shadows pass over the green, a white cockatoo rises off the tree-tops like a torn scrap of paper, like an unread message . . .

1961

NOTES

1 These Japanese were not the war-time occupying force but the Japanese who developed the first plantations in Manus under the German regime. By 'the English' are meant the pre-war Australian settlers and officials.
2 J. H. Wootten, unpublished manuscript quoted by permission of the author.
3 Alain de Boismenu, letter to Mother Marie-Thérèse Noblet, quoted in A. Dupeyrat and F. de la Noë, *Sainteté au Naturel: Alain de Boismenu* (Paris, 1958), p. 100.
4 Paul Claudel, quoted by Maria Winowska, *Malgré toi, Satan!: Vie de Marie-Thérèse Noblet* (Paris, 1955), p. 154.
5 Dupeyrat and de la Noë, p. 40.
6 A controversy was conducted in *Etudes Carmélitaines* in 1938 and 1939; the medical and psychological problems are well analysed in P. Giscard, *Mystique ou hystérie?: à propos de Marie-Thérèse Noblet* (Paris, 1952).
7 Pastoral Letter, 24 February 1908.
8 Elspeth Huxley, *African Dilemmas* (London, 1948), pp. 20-1.
9 John Kerr, *The Political Future of New Guinea* (Sydney, 1959).

Journey into Egypt

IN the year of Napoleon's Russian campaign, when the forces of Revolution and Reaction were in arms and the consciousness of Europe was stirred to its depths, Joseph von Eichendorff, then a young man of twenty-four, finished his novel *Ahnung und Gegenwart* (Premonition and Actuality). A Christian nobleman of singular greatness and simplicity of heart and marvellous lyric powers, the friend of Schlegel, Brentano, Görres, Arnim and Novalis, he stood amidst the most powerful and esoteric currents of Romanticism, but knew how to eliminate from what touched him everything feverish and poisonous, and expressed what remained with undying freshness and charm. Without philosophical pretensions, he understood very well what was going on, and at the close of his novel, in describing the parting of the two brothers Friedrich and Rudolf, he symbolized briefly the inner crisis of European literature.

Friedrich has concluded that in the Babylonish confusion of modern times only the recovery of religious truth and genuine piety can restore to the common life law, freedom, honour, and poetry; and he has therefore decided to devote himself to God in the cloister. His brother Rudolf, a disturbed and moody child of the age, is also deserting the common life, not in hope and charitable concern like Friedrich, but in restless despair. 'I beg you', says Friedrich, 'Don't sink down so dreadfully into yourself. You will find no consolation there'. Rudolf answers: 'Within myself it is like a fathomless abyss, all silent and still'. Friedrich expresses the wish that his brother's potential greatness of spirit might be freed from what frustrates it. Can he not turn to religion, since he has admitted that 'no scientific philosophy contented me, for I never found in it either God or myself'? But Rudolf answers darkly: 'You mean well, but that is how things are with me: I cannot believe. And so, since Heaven will have none of me, I intend to devote myself to magic. I am going to Egypt, the land of ancient wonders'.

The modern period of poetry—from the French Revolution onwards—has indeed been, in its most typical developments, a journey into Egypt, land of Hermes Trismegistus, taken by men who were seeking a new reality, a new power, a new function and role. They were, as Erich Heller puts it, 'disinherited minds', deprived by 'scientific philosophy' of the themes and inspiration and social role formerly available to the poets of Christendom, yet unable to find what they needed in the new world of ideas and action which was issuing from the Enlightenment.[1] Between a rejected Christianity and a repulsive secularized Modernity which was anti-poetic in mood and tendency, they sought a third road—and found the track of the ancient mysteries of occultism or gnosticism. In the most advanced cases, they did not merely attach themselves to this underground tradition as a source of themes and images: they used it to make a new doctrine in which the poetical imagination itself was a preternatural power, a power of prophecy, theosis, and *transformation of reality*. The role claimed by orthodox Christianity for God and religion, by the secular ideologues for 'scientific philosophy' and political revolution, and by the occultist masters for gnosis and initiation, was claimed by them for poetry itself. While they could convince themselves of this Magian task, they were no longer displaced persons of the wars of the Enlightenment: though despised and rejected by the ignorant world, they were in imagination the secret masters of reality. Romanticism and Symbolism were thus based on an esoteric doctrine, the Magian Heresy, as it might be called. Even though the full illuminati were few, the general crowd of poets picked up the influence in an exoteric way, drawn along in external imitation, using the jargon of 'creative' writing and poetic 'magic', or vaguely claiming for poetic imagination a special power of intuiting 'truth' and a quasi-religious character. Even Matthew Arnold wrote: 'Most of what passes with us for religion and philosophy will be replaced by poetry', though he did not imply by this that poetry must become preternaturalized in order to fulfil this task. The last exoteric degradations of the idea flicker in pronouncements on poetry by such twentieth-century critics as I. A. Richards, who says that 'it can save us', and Middleton Murry who says that it offers us 'visible salvation'. How far these vague echoes seem from the full esoterism of Mallarmé, for instance! Jacques Schérer's researches into his manuscripts have revealed that from 1866 onwards for several years Mallarmé lived in the grandiose delusion that he was destined to perform the literary equivalent of the 'Great Work' of the alchemists.[2] His Philosophers' Stone was to be 'The Book' which he would write (and publish for immense profits). The famous Tuesday gatherings were meant to become the esoteric chapel of a new Literary Religion, in which all the godlike powers hitherto claimed by religion and occultism would be appropriated by man, and in which Mallarmé would be the Supreme Pontiff.

II

Before I venture further in describing the varieties of this Magian ambition it is important to understand more fully the process of estrangement that produced it, and the peculiar desperation which made these poets fight their own inexorcizable scepticism in order to preserve the dream.

The arresting thing is that the secularist progressivism of the En-lightenment which repelled the poets was itself an essentially gnos-tic movement, a reproduction in naturalistic terms of the ancient cosmic illuminism which had been the most formidable rival of Christian orthodoxy. Underneath an apparent scientific scepti-cism there was the pressure of gnostic myth which continuously generated the ideologies and 'political religions' of modern times. Eric Voegelin has acutely analyzed the neo-gnostic character of Modernity in his book *The New Science of Politics*. The two faces of Freemasonry might be taken as a significant witness: for while in one aspect it claimed to be the inheritor of a pre-Christian gnosis, in another it was a vehicle for militant secularism. Others besides Voegelin have recognized the masked religious-magical character of Modernity. Mircéa Eliade, for instance, examines the crypto-religious character of many features of the life of unreligious modern man, mentioning Marxism and the historicist philosophies; the initiatic patterns of war, sport 'trials', and psycho-analysis; the degenerated paradisal mystique of nudity-cults and free-love; the profaned 'myths' underlying the cinema and crime fiction; and so on.[3]

The poets were initially quite ready to celebrate the onset of Modernity and find their themes and social role as spokesmen for the new age. Who could be against intellectual progress, against liberty, equality and fraternity, against the abolition of oppression and obscurantism? The new discoveries of science filled most of them with enthusiasm. The outbreak of the French Revolution found most of the poets on its side. But something manifestly went wrong. As the religious and metaphysical residues drained away and Modernity became increasingly naturalistic and secularized, and as industrial and commercial society became more blatantly utilitarian and materialist, bewilderment and anguish seized the poets. Not science, but 'scientific philosophy', seemed to wither poetry at its root by emptying the world of the values and associa-tions on which the poetic imagination feeds:

> Do not all charms fly
> At the mere touch of cold philosophy?

lamented Keats. The wisdom of the new world seemed a cold prison-house which deprived the poet of his function and dismissed his imaginings as dreams unrelated to reality:

> What benefit canst thou do, or all thy tribe,
> To the great world? Thou art a dreaming thing,
> A fever of thyself . . .

the Priestess says to Keats in 'The Fall of Hyperion'. Keats essays an answer by distinguishing between idle fantasy and a poetry embodying a superior wisdom:

> sure not all
> Those melodies sung into the World's ear
> Are useless; sure a poet is a sage;
> A humanist, physician to all men.[4]

But what is this 'wisdom' of the poetic visionary, and how can it be reconciled with the ideologies of Progress?

The problem therefore was not simply a clash between poetry and 'scientific' scepticism. There was no lack of grandiose visions, rationalistic millenniums and positivist Utopias. Progress in fact had its own mythology. But the poets found that the new myths were barren of poetic nutriment. As the nineteenth century wore on this became more painfully obvious. The secular mythologies of Democracy, Socialism, Imperialism and so on were celebrated by a sub-standard verse rhetoric whose beginnings are already seen in some of Shelley's poetical declamations; but somehow genuine poetry refused the task. In measure as the disillusion set in, the poets turned back, partly towards what they could appropriate of Christianity, but mainly towards a more archaic form of cosmic mysticism. The reason for their retreat was that the radical secularization of gnosis undertaken by the Enlightenment made a difference that was crucial for poetry. It meant the loss of overtones, of symbolic resonance, of those transcendental dimensions of experience in which wisdom and mystery are felt to lie. Marxism, for instance, might itself recognize its kinship with the revolutionary millenarianism of the mediaeval heresies, but the coming of the Classless Society is a barren thing to the imagination in comparison with the apocalyptic splendours of millenarian enthusiasm. The pretensions of social scientism may be hardly less superstitious than those of alchemy and magic, but how poor they are in symbolic suggestion to man's psyche! Modern historicism may be as arrogant in its attempts at a gnosis of history, but it is a grey earthbound thing compared with Joachim of Flora's prophecies or the Hindu cosmic cycles. Modern 'charismatic' rulers like Hitler or Stalin have hardly the cosmic grandeur of the Divine Kings of archaic States. All is flattened down to one naturalistic level, and the sense of correspondences linking ascending levels of being in a magical-religious cosmos disappears. The Logos has become merely the ideologue's lecture-room drone, the radio voice of the Fuehrer, the clamour of the Press and the roar of the masses in industrial cities. The Sanctum Regnum has become at best the Welfare State, at worst the totalitarian nightmare.

So it was that poetry became increasingly hostile to secular pro-gressivism. Lacking external support it turned in upon itself and tried to produce from its substance the validation it required. It proclaimed a doctrine of art-for-art's sake or pure poetry, which was first of all a refusal of any commitments to the prevailing de-mands of modern civilization. But more than that, it sought to be the principle of its own mysticism, to divinize itself: poetic im-agination was itself to be the Logos; poetic 'rêverie' was in Mal-larmé's terms to become '*le Rêve*', the true gnosis, the Absolute be-come Word. The poets went to Egypt to become Magi.

III

One of the first consequences of this Romantic perversion of poetry was the stress laid on 'inspiration' as a privileged intuition. William Blake, right at the beginning of the modern period, ad-vanced the claims of the inspired poet to their fullest extent. Poetic inspiration was for him the same as the prophetic inspiration of revealed religions. He is consistent in this over a wide span of time. In *A Vision of the Last Judgment* he says that Poetry, Painting and Music are 'the three Powers in Man of conversing with Paradise, which the flood did not Sweep away'. In *The Marriage of Heaven and Hell* he has Ezekiel say: 'we of Israel taught that the Poetic Genius (as you now call it) was the first principle, and all others merely derivative . . .' And one of the principles he enunciates in *All Religions are One* is: 'The Religions of all Nations are derived from each Nation's different reception of the Poetic Genius, which is everywhere call'd the Spirit of Prophecy'. Blake noted that 1757, the year of his birth, had been prophesied by Swedenborg to be the beginning of a new order, and he very modestly concluded that the prophecy was verified in him as the most advanced bearer of revela-tion.[5] His is the voice of the Bard in *Milton* who sings:

Mark well my words: they are of your eternal salvation

About the same time in Germany Hölderlin, standing between the tensions of the Enlightenment, of Christianity, and the Orphic call of Ancient Greece, conceived the poet to be the vessel of divine in-spiration; he wrote as a leader of the mysteries. It is symptomatic of the ambiguous and uncertain dogmatic basis of such performances that Nietzsche in his famous passage on inspiration in *Ecce Homo* could take over the same attitude in speaking of the superlative merit of his *Also Sprach Zarathustra:* 'If one had the smallest ves-tige of superstition in one, it would hardly be possible completely to set aside the idea that one is the mere incarnation, mouthpiece, or medium of an almighty power'. This act of inspiration, he said, was 'the *highest* deed'. Zarathustra is beyond the range of even the greatest poets: 'by the side of Zarathustra, Dante is no more than a believer, and not one who first *creates* the truth—that is to say not a world-ruling spirit, a fate . . .' The poets of the Veda were priests, dependent on a pre-existing doctrine, and therefore not in the same class as the great originator Nietzsche-Zarathustra, who creates the objects of his own literary rhapsody.

Here we meet in their full pretension two other marked features of Romanticism which became vulgarized in literary jargon: the claim of the inspired one to *creation* and hence *originality*. Shut out from orthodox tradition and rejecting the actual world around them, the poets had to stand alone: they must bring into being a world of ideas as the object of their contemplation by an act of imaginative energy; they must be originators.[6] How much higher and more exciting such a task can seem than that of poets like Dante who were content to act in dependence upon an existing body of beliefs and images which were not their own and which they acknowledged to be far above them! So today everyone has to be a 'creative' writer and have care for his 'originality'—even if it is in reality no more than mannerism and subjective fantasy.

It is with this new demand for 'creation' that the idea of poetry as a magical operation enters in. The poetic word becomes a spell or incantation which brings into being the marvels it speaks of. Of course the analogy between poetic 'magic' and magic proper (like the analogy between poetic 'inspiration' and the afflatus of the inspired prophet) is an old commonplace: what is new is the attempt to turn the *analogy* into an *identity*. Novalis was perhaps the earliest of the moderns to advance the proposition seriously with his 'magical idealism'. Out of Hegel and Fichte he produced a doctrine which set up the poetic imagination as the World-Spirit; and out of occultist readings he saw the re-creation of reality as a magical task to be performed by the poet who is also, *ipso facto*, the supreme philosopher. 'Poetry is the true absolutely Real. This is the kernel of my philosophy: the more poetical, the truer . . . Poetry is an act of creation . . . The magician is a poet: the prophet is to the magician as the man of taste is to the poet . . . The poetical philosopher is *en état de Créateur absolu*.' What is needed is a transformation of the cosmos, and the means of this is magical power which transforms existing reality into something imagined and interiorly experienced. 'It is easy to see why in the end everything becomes poetry: does not the world in the end become feeling?'[7] This last theme is also that taken up a century later by Rilke, who remains very close to Novalis in all his main themes. The transformation of reality by the 'heartwork' of poetic imagination is the theme of the

Duino Elegies and of the *Sonnets to Orpheus*. In the ninth elegy he says:

> Earth, is it not this you want: an invisible
> Resurrection in us?—Is not this your dream,
> To be one day invisible?—Earth! Invisible!
> What task do you press on us, if not transformation?

Seen thus, the transforming operation consists essentially of converting outer reality into a new world of imagination that arises inwardly in consciousness, a higher and more perfect world. In Rilke's *Elegies* the Angels stand for the higher consciousness which alone can complete this task: in the *Sonnets* it is Orpheus who is the master of transformation. Rilke preserves the main theme of Novalis without pressing the magical jargon. In both cases the result is a bold statement of another characteristic of Romanticism: its intense subjectivism: 'Inwards goes the secret way; within us or nowhere lies eternity with its worlds . . .' says Novalis.[8]

Along the paths we have so far indicated—paths which are apparently different but which readily cross and combine in the shifting and unsystematic thought of the poets concerned—one thing is constant: poetry must not be content to be mere 'literature' (a word of abuse amongst the French Symbolists). Whether magical or prophetic, it must attain to a preternatural power of revelation or transformation. Whether as hierophant or shaman or master-mage or godlike thaumaturge, the poet is the true initiator of that new order, that Third Realm of the Spirit, which neither orthodox Christianity or the progressivist ideologues of materialistic enlightenment could bring about. Christendom, said Novalis in *Die Christenheit oder Europa*, must be re-established, but it will be a new Magian Christendom 'which will take to its bosom all the souls that thirst for the supernatural, and which will reconcile the old world with the new'.

Certainly there was no lack of applicants for the post of cosmic renewer. The case of Rimbaud, who aspired by the alchemy of the word to become master and transformer of reality (*'il a peut-être des secrets pour changer la vie?'*) is too well known to need further comment.[9] Mallarmé, as we have already mentioned, had no less megalomaniac a programme.

It is not surprising that both these would-be masters confessed defeat. Baudelaire, who understood the Magian dream but was not carried away by it into its remoter absurdities because of the persistence of Christian residues in his complex mind, could have warned both enthusiasts of the dangers of mental self-destruction inherent in the quest. Silence, sterility, abandonment of the dream, were one revenge taken by nature on the *hubris* of the poet. Another

common symptom of the inevitable contrast between transcendental pretensions and real life is the peculiar 'irony' cultivated by
many of the German Romantics and developed by Laforgue and
others as a sort of safety-valve. It is peculiar precisely because its
background is not normal human pride and illusion but the private
ambition to climb into the seats of the gods.

IV

With the exception of Nietzsche, the representatives of the Magian heresy so far mentioned were, or tried desperately to be, believers in the Absolute and in supra-terrestrial orders of being.
Whether or not they retained the conception of a transcendental
God or, more typically, had a purely cosmic or pantheist system,
they were foes of the scientistic naturalism which the nineteenth
century identified with Science. Despite their claim to originality
they were in fact drawing heavily on a pre-existing tradition: the
counter-current of occultism, gnosticism and theosophy which
runs from pre-Christian times underneath orthodox Christianity.
From Blake to Yeats the 'originality' of hermetic modern poetry has
been limited to two factors operating upon the common stock of
cabbalistic and theosophical ideas. The first is the degree to which
the poet edits and accommodates his occult orthodoxy by conces-
sions to secularist and sceptical ideas. The second is the degree to
which the poet uses private associations and uncommon reading
sources to build up a system that looks at first sight highly original
because the symbols are new and peculiar to the poet. This has
given us the fatiguing experience of a series of rather opaque private universes which each poet-image spins out of his subjectivity. If
we complain, we are scolded by earnest commentators for not being
able to interpret all the idiosyncratic features by reference to a
primordial Tradition which we can freely grasp if we spend our
waking lives reading Neoplatonist and Gnostic remains, Indian and
Chinese wisdom books, alchemical treatises, the Cabbala, Jacob
Boehme, Paracelsus, Eliphas Lévi, and so on down to René Guénon
and the latest gurus. If we say we have other things to do with our
minds we are clearly not 'serious' and will never be initiates.

With most of these poets, however, belief in the systems they developed was at best precarious: it was a frenzied act of the will taking off from a ground of naturalistic Enlightenment which they desperately wished to escape, if only because they knew that no poetical
flowers would grow in it. Towards the end of the Romantic-Symbolist hey-day, in the twilight of increasing disillusion and confusion
stretching into our own day, a last sophistication appeared: renunciation of the Absolute and an attempt to work out the essential
themes in purely naturalistic terms. Nietzsche led the way: and

Rilke was largely concerned with elaborating an ersatz-spirituality within the limits of naturalism. Valéry finished off the French Symbolist tradition by the same manoeuvre. Behind the refined scepticism of his writings lies the dream of Rimbaud's esoterist masters: the ambition to reach the 'central point' at which consciousness becomes all-powerful and the 'Great Work' can be accomplished by the master of reality. Valéry sought this in terms of the complete self-consciousness of the individual ego. He deserted poetry in order to reach this 'central point' of self-consciousness, from which writing poetry or doing anything else would be merely the gratuitous exercise, in a particular direction, of a universal mastery. When he returned to poetry he affected to despise it as a mere pastime (again the scorn for mere 'literature') but his baffled Magian ambition is reflected in his demand that poetry should be the crystalline product of a wholly conscious intellectual will; and his preoccupation with the Absolute is seen in his deliberate inversion of themes, so that Nothingness is put in the place of Being: the classical temple of his poems is devoted to a nihilist rite.

The Surrealist excursion was also an exasperated attempt to fulfil the Magian dream within the framework of sceptical naturalism. Starting, as André Breton says, from 'the death of God' and abandoning all metaphysical conceptions of the traditional kind, Surrealism nevertheless reproduces all the old themes. In *What is Surrealism?* Breton defines the task as 'the transmutation of those two seemingly contradictory states, dream and reality, into a sort of absolute reality, or surreality'. The scorn for mere literature becomes a war of destruction: 'the hordes of words which were literally unleashed and to which Dada and surrealism deliberately opened their doors . . . will penetrate the idiotic little towns of that literature which is still taught . . . and they will capture a fine number of turrets.' Surreality is in fact the 'Great Work' once more, the Mallarméan 'Dream', the appropriation of the oneiric powers hidden in past religions. 'This surreality', Breton quotes Aragon as saying, 'is the common horizon of religions, magics, poetry, intoxications . . .'[10] The drive towards inwardness and subjectivity which Novalis pioneered here reaches its last stage, the plunge into sheer 'subconscious' irrationality and induced mental pathology. From this night-realm the transformation of daylight reality is to proceed. One can hardly go further. Surrealism is the final stultification; the Romantic Revolution has devoured its own children. 'I ended by treating the disorder of my mind as sacred', Rimbaud bitterly confessed in *Une Saison en Enfer*. The history of illuminism was fabled long ago in the Genesis story in which the Serpent deceived man into eating of the Tree of Gnosis—'your eyes will be opened, and you yourselves will be like gods . . .' But the knowledge that it brought was of

N

shame and alienation. '*Dure nuit! le sang sèche fume sur ma face, et je n'ai rien derrière moi, que cet horrible arbrisseau* . . .'[11] St Augustine in the *Confessions* records all that Rimbaud had painfully to rediscover about those who succumb to the gnostic lure:

> Many endeavouring to return unto Thee, and of themselves unable, have . . . fallen into the desire of curious visions, and been accounted worthy to be deluded. For they, being high minded, sought Thee by the pride of learning, swelling out, rather than smiting upon, their breasts, and so by the agreement of their heart drew unto themselves the 'princes of the air', the fellow-conspirators of their pride, by whom, through magical influences, they were deceived . . .'[12]

In a study which follows a somewhat similar path to mine, Wladimir Weidlé remarked:

> When the real world threatens to collapse, what importance can one attach to the collapse of imaginary worlds? Compared with the torments inflicted on living human creatures what are the pangs of creation or the deprivations of the fictive faculty? But in fact the answer to these questions is not as simple as one might at first be inclined to think, for the power to create is the noblest of man's abilities, and whatever impedes its activity may connect with deeper causes, causes more worthy of attention than all the other woes that befall us.[13]

There are times when it seems unworthy to be worrying about the style of the fiddling while the city is burning. But *panic* reaction, that is, obliteratingly total dismay, is not helpful. Everything has its right to consideration in its own order if humanity is to keep *humanitas*. The plight of poetry is not trivial. Caring about it will not reduce malnutrition or political murder or the other gross evils of our time. Ceasing to care about poetry and failing to see it as part of the life of the spirit will not put us in a better frame of mind either.

The Magian poets did not, and could not, fulfil their ambition: the literary equivalent of the Philosophers' Stone eluded their experiments. Poetry is a natural, not a preternatural or supernatural thing: it is not, except in an analogical sense, 'inspired' or 'creative' or 'magical'. The beauty, mystery and power of poetic speech are no more, but no less, than the beauty, mystery and power of man's natural being—not of angelic or divine being. Certainly, poetry, like other things on the natural plane, bears an analogy with the supernatural, and it can dimly mirror the true mysteries; but it is not itself a sacrament or rite or initiation.

If the Romantic-Symbolist movement did not do what it set out to do, what did it really produce? The general characteristics of 'modern' poetry have been studied by Hugo Friedrich in *Die Struk-*

tur der Modernen Lyrik (1956) with penetrating insight, and Frank Kermode in *The Romantic Image* (1957) has acutely examined one central feature. My comments can conveniently start from these sources.

The doctrine of the autonomous super-real imagination meant in practice an increasingly unrestrained subjectivity. The older canons of perfection were replaced by their opposites: poetry became deliberately a-logical, obscure, chaotic, heterogeneous, abnormal, fragmentary, incoherent, arbitrary. There was a search for a deeper, more expressive musicality, but at the same time the cultivation of extreme intensity, dissonance, violent shock. The characteristics sought are those of dream life rather than of waking consciousness. Intellectual power (which was considerable in the greater poets) was directed not towards an harmonious fullness of objective expression but towards the more cunning development of means to estrange poetry from classical normality and order. The statement of these negative categories in which the poets worked reads like a reproach, and ultimately one is entitled to judge their productions by the norms of *poesis perennis* which they rejected, but one cannot ignore the *fascination* (the word in its strictest meaning is the highest compliment these poets could seek) of the work and the degree to which it speaks home to the soul of modern man.

The suppression of objective order, of the logical connections of discourse, of the 'prosaic' element of description, explanation, assertion and narration which might bring the poet into collision with reason and experience, led straight to a special cult of the poetic image or symbol. This was conceived as a vehicle of an imaginative truth which was *sui generis* and otherwise inexpressible. It was a kind of superword operating in a non-logical sphere of superior intuition. A poem should be as much as possible composed of images, forming as it were a total self-subsistent image independent of ordinary reality, purified of discursive matter or paraphrasable meaning. A poem was an *icon*, making the ineffable visible, or a magical *sign* of which the poet was the operator.

Kermode criticizes adversely the consequences of this cult of the image. He resents the way that a poem like *Paradise Lost* has been undervalued because of the prejudice against the discursive mode. Nevertheless he does not seem to face the problem in its fundamental difficulty. The crisis of modernity came through the discrediting of the older themes of poetic discourse which were, immediately with Milton, mediately with more secular poets, rooted in religious tradition. Kermode accepts the prevailing outlook of naturalism, and seems to assume that a new discursive poetry can flourish without the sort of tradition which once supported it. But this is just what the Romantics and Symbolists knew could not happen: we are not going to get anything like a *Paradise Lost* or a *Paradise Regained* in the mental climate of Comte or Marx or Bertrand Russell or John Dewey. It is because Kermode does not face this difficulty that he is anxious to prove that the dissociation of reason and imagination, of which the modern movement complains, is an historical myth invented by the poets. On the contrary, this dissociation is a fact, without which the Romantic-Symbolist agony loses its meaning and dignity. It is not to be argued away merely because a long, complex and gradual crisis in history is variously analysed and variously dated by different people.

Surprisingly, after analysing very well the special use of the non-logical image, Kermode finally suggests that it could after all be retained in discursive poetry if its nineteenth-century occultist basis were replaced by 'modern language-theory' (oh blessed word Mesopotamia!). But neither the semanticists nor the linguistic philosophers, nor Cassirer and Langer, nor even the syncretist symbolics of Jung, will restore savour to the salt of poetry when it is denatured by naturalism.

One danger for contemporary poetry is that the literary procedures of the Romantic-Symbolist movement will be carried on unintelligently without the functional justification they had in the work of the esoterist masters who at least knew what they were trying to do. The cult of the image merely as a literary vogue, the pursuit of intensity, shock, ambiguity, perversity and ellipsis of expression as an acquired habit, or a sentimental reaction to the stress of modern experience, have not much to recommend them.

Another danger inherent in the whole movement is the debasement of the language of spirituality which it inevitably causes. A symbolic language originally developed from the doctrines and liturgy and mysticism of a transcendental religion is being exploited and degraded by re-interpretation in a purely subjective sense. These equivocal manoeuvres begin with the gnostic use made by Blake of Christian forms of expression, and with the Spiritual Songs of Novalis, some of which have found their way into the hymn-books though they are magico-theosophical in intention. God, Christ, the Spirit, the Blessed Virgin, the Mystical Body, grace, salvation, damnation, the sacraments, are treated as mystic masks and hermetic keys at the disposal of the individual poet. 'Taoism *sans* Tao', the psychologizing and subjectivizing of metaphysical realities, tends to destroy the sense of proportion and inflate the ego. Rilke writes his *Book of Hours* ostensibly as a breviary of devotion to God; but Rilke's God is, variably, sex, the unconscious, or the Orphic essence of poetic inspiration.

In the *Duino Elegies* the Angels are symbols of a higher mode of human consciousness, like Orpheus in the *Sonnets*. 'By making the mistake', Rilke wrote to his Polish translator Witold Hulewicz, 'of applying Catholic conceptions of death, of the hereafter, of eternity, to the *Elegies* and *Sonnets*, one is withdrawing oneself completely from their point of departure, and preparing for oneself a more and more fundamental misunderstanding. The "Angel" of the *Elegies* has nothing to do with the angel of the Christian heaven'.[14] One recognizes here the lofty tone and portentous severity of the mystagogue defending his higher truths from confusion with Christian puerilities.

The parasitic character of all gnosticism as an arrogant human fantasy attaching itself to religious doctrine and rite, and feeding destructively on it, is here exemplified. The pearls of such poetry are too often paste imitations of authentic spirituality; its mysteries are parodies of the *magnalia Dei*. And wherever this occurs the whole operation threatens to become vulgar and ridiculous just when it seeks to be most impressive and refined. Projections of the poet's ego fill the universe. The subtle pride and hermetic exclusiveness of such writing is partly a defence raised against the intrusion of commonsense and laughter. A caustically just reviewer (it turns out to be Erich Heller) in *The Times Literary Supplement* underlined the danger which threatens such poetry by remarking how it emerges in the intolerable pretentiousness of Rilke's letters:

> Rilke was not only the maker of exquisite poetry; he was also the inventor of an infectiously bedevilling pose: the pose of presenting the utmost of intellectual and psychological complexity in the traditional costume of *sancta simplicitas*, and the most audacious excesses of spiritual pride in the guise of devout humility . . . The most common symptoms of a total immersion in Rilkean spirituality are an irresistible desire to describe the indescribable (indeed, first to reduce to an indescribable state what normally *can* be described), and secondly the loss of a sense of the comic.[15]

The question is whether the infection has not gone deep into Rilke's poetry as well, for all its achievement.

Slowly and painfully it seems that some poets have been seeking a return to the highroad of *poesis perennis*. There is much to be observed from this point of view in such diverse figures as Claudel, Hofmannsthal, Hopkins, Eliot, Pound, though in many respects they remain creatures of their time and have not provided models for a new tradition. Certainly it is not a question of abandoning anything that is permanently valuable in Romanticism and Symbolism: we need a new poetic Moses who, having overcome the magicians of Egypt, will lead us, laden with the spoils of the Egyptians, to the Promised Land. Certainly, too, one must face how hard it is to restore normality in the arts in a civilization that is still so unfavourable. Without allowing oneself to sink into the defeatist mood of the historical determinists, one must recognize the difficulties that abound in a time when to seek to be normal is itself a kind of abnormality.

But there lies the only road. The Romantic-Symbolist movement in its unredeemed form has risen to dazzling and seductive performances, but all the time there has gone on a perversion and subtle debasement of traditional meanings and symbols, and only sterility and bewilderment lie ahead in that direction. Let me conclude, as I began, with Eichendorff's *Ahnung und Gegenwart*. In Chapter 13, he takes his hero to a literary entertainment where the divinity of the poet's art is already the accepted commonplace of literary fashion. One enthusiast casts loving glances at something during his declamation: it is his own image in a mirror. A poetess renders an allegorical tale in which the princess is understood by one critic to be 'The Virgin Mary as Universal Love'. Friedrich protests: have we got away from sophistic attacks on religion only to start 'poeticizing and volatilizing its holy truths? He warns that those who treat the true mysteries as agreeable matter at the disposal of the poet's arbitrary fantasy will end by leaving the heavens waste and bare. 'The greatest sin of our present-day poetry is . . . its empty, wilful, self-destructive intoxication with images.' With these unwelcome truths he spoils the party.

1974

NOTES

1 Erich Heller, *The Disinherited Mind* (London, 1959).
2 Jacques Schérer, *Le 'Livre' de Mallarmé* (Paris, 1957).
3 Mircéa Eliade, *Das Heilige und das Profane* (Hamburg, 1957), pp. 119-26.
4 Keats, 'Lamia' II: 229-30, 'The Fall of Hyperion' I: 167-9, 187-90.
5 In *The Marriage of Heaven and Hell*, begun in 1790, Blake wrote: 'As a new heaven is begun, and it is now thirty-three years since its advent . . .' This includes a reference to the thirty-three years of Christ's earthly messianic mission.
6 Brennan's succinct statement of this desperate search for creative powers is:
    What do I know? myself alone,
    a gulf of uncreated night,
    wherein no star may e'er be shown
    save I create it in my might.
                (*Poems 1913*, no. 42)
7 Novalis, *Fragmente*, 11, 16, 25, 76, 454.
8 Novalis, *Blütenstaub*, 16.
9 Rimbaud, *Une Saison en Enfer* ('Perhaps he has secrets for *transforming life*?').
10 André Breton, *What is Surrealism?* (trans. D. Gascoyne, London, 1936), pp. 75-6.
11 Rimbaud, *Une Saison en Enfer* ('Hard-spent night! the dried blood smokes on my face, and I've nothing behind me but this horrible stunted tree!') .

12 St Augustine, *Confessions* (trans. E. Pusey, London, 1907), p. 247.
13 Wladimir Weidlé, *Les Abeilles d'Aristée* (Paris, 1954), p. 289.
14 Quoted in Rainer Maria Rilke, *Duino Elegies* (trans. J. B. Leishman and Stephen Spender, London, 1939), p. 101.
15 *Times Literary Supplement*, 11 July 1952, p. 456.

The Moabit Sonnets of Albrecht Haushofer

ALBRECHT Haushofer was not a great poet. But there is one group of his poems which has intrinsic merit and a special interest because of the circumstances in which it was written. It is a set of sonnets called the *Moabiter Sonette* written in the last year of the Second World War, while Haushofer was in gaol for his opposition to the Nazi regime. These sonnets attain their full significance only when viewed in the context of the Nazi period.

There is a mysterious background to Hitler and the principal Nazi leaders, an esoteric Nazism that has never been fully explored and elucidated. They had strange crazy beliefs. They were cunning, and they used science and technology; yet they were fundamentally committed to irrationalism. They believed in magic, in astrology, in strange prophecies and myths. They saw themselves as ushering in a new cosmic order. In league with cosmic powers, they were dedicated to changing life on earth, bringing into being a new creation and a race of higher men. Hitler was an evil Messiah, a satanic mystic, a man of dreams and trances. Many people who knew him have commented on the strange force that seemed at times to possess this otherwise commonplace and vulgar man. Hermann Rauschning, for example, compared Hitler to a 'medium' possessed by 'genuinely daemonic powers'.[1]

One man who exercised a special influence over Hitler was Karl Haushofer, a professor of political geography in the University of Munich, who became Hitler's acknowledged theoretician in the dubious science of geopolitics. Haushofer could never become a fully accredited Nazi because he had a Jewish wife. It is with his son Albrecht Haushofer that we are concerned.

Albrecht was, like his father, an academic: he became professor of political geography in the University of Berlin. From initial acceptance of Hitler, Albrecht tortuously arrived at a deep and humanistically principled opposition to his regime. When Hitler's war began he foresaw that Germany's initial victories would in the end draw the great world powers into the struggle and bring about her crushing defeat. He joined the 'Kreisau circle' of Graf von Moltke which played an important part in the internal resistance. In his book *The German Opposition to Hitler* Hans Rothfels speaks of Haushofer's *Moabit Sonnets* as belonging to 'the most impressive moral and religious documents of the German Resistance movement'.[2]

Several times between 1941 and 1943 an attempt to eliminate Hitler was planned and success seemed assured. But each time it was frustrated by unforeseeable chance. After Stalingrad, Haushofer began to feel that the chance of saving the German people had been lost. He was not directly involved in the last and best known of the plots against Hitler, the July Plot of 1944, though some of his associates were. But he was rounded up with others and put in the Moabit gaol in Berlin. His brother Heinz was also put in the same gaol, though he had never had any part in Albrecht's activities. Alone in a cell, and wearing chains, Albrecht Haushofer composed the eighty sonnets which he named the *Moabiter Sonette*. He wrote them out in an exercise book.

In the very last night of the Nazi regime, on 23 April 1945, when Berlin was falling to the Allied armies, Albrecht and thirteen other prisoners were taken out of their cells and told they were being set free. They walked through the gateway of the prison, while the gunfire of the victorious Allies could be heard very close at hand. Then they were overtaken by an S.S. squad and all were executed. Albrecht was 42 years of age.

Not long after, Heinz was freed, and as he walked out he found his brother's dead body, with his hand still clutching the exercise book with the *Moabit Sonnets* in it. They were published in 1946.[3]

I have translated a number of these sonnets as best I can, using as much freedom as seemed necessary to make them effective as poems in English. The first in the series is called 'In Fetters'; it speaks of the solidarity the poet feels with the suffering of his fellow-prisoners whom he cannot see.

IN FETTERS

For him who nightly sleeps here in distress
The walls are full of life, though they seem bare.
Destiny and guilt weave in the air
Grey webs that fill the vaulted emptiness.

From all the suffering that these walls confine
Through iron grilles and masonry there steals
A living breath, a tremor, that reveals
The misery of other souls than mine.

I'm not the first to feel these fetters bite;
Not the first victim here upon whose grief
The will of one man feeds its appetite.

Waking and sleeping resemble one another.
Listening intently, through the walls I trace
The trembling hands of many an unseen brother.

The second sonnet forms a pair with this first one. Now it is the dead, passing out of the world into the darkness, with whom he feels he has invisible communion.

NOCTURNAL INTIMATIONS

Still other tidings flow in from the night
Through almost unknown layers of my being:
A wave of sounds and faces upwards fleeing
Conveys a last sense of the dead in flight.

It's just a feeling, not to be translated:
The dead call out to us in their own way,
With starry sounds. But still at break of day
One thing at least remains that can be stated,

One certainty:— Just as of all the matter
That was created when the world began
Not even the smallest speck can be destroyed.

So little can one breath of soul be lost.
But where it goes to when it leaves the body,
That is the question, as I face the void.

Haushofer was a deeply spiritual man, but not a convinced Christian or a believer in any particular religion. From his travels through the world and his wide reading he know a good deal about various religions, and some of the sonnets show him yearning wistfully for some faith that could stay him in his distress. In the following sonnet, for instance, he speaks of Tibetan mysticism, based on the doctrine that the small illusory self must realize its identity with the great Universal Self, and that those who reach this height of illumination acquire spiritual power which they can exert upon others for their good.

TIBETAN SECRET

In that land, where bright winter-storms blow round
The highest rooftops of this world of ours,
Hid in the shelter of monastic towers
Adepts of esoteric arts are found.

The wisest of the wise in those stone hives
Pursue the discipline that we neglect.
Exempt from time and space they can direct
A ray of soul upon far distant lives.

What symphonies and fugues are to the deaf,
What red and green are to the colour-blind,
Such are these arts to slaves of here and now.

As the soul's wonder, once a shy belief,
Rises to highest power, the little 'I'
Becomes transformed into the mighty 'Thou'.

But Haushofer was no initiate of such a mystical doctrine. What
he faced was darkness and the threat of annihilating death. He
tells us that he has often contemplated suicide. The reason he gives
at the end of one sonnet for not committing suicide is typical of
the man: the feeling that suicide is like deserting one's post.

ON THE THRESHOLD

The means of exit from this dire existence,
With eye and hand, in thought, I've tried them all.
One violent shock—and through the prison wall
My soul would pass at once without resistance.

Even before the sentry here could mark
What's happening and undo the iron door,
One violent shock—and then my soul would soar
Out to the light—far out into the dark.

What restrains others—wishes, hopes, beliefs—
These are extinct in me: life seems a play
Of idle shadows without sense or aim.

Whether it's God or Devil that torments us,
What holds me from the brink is still the same:
It's simply not allowed to slip away.

One of the tenderest and most touching of the sonnets that deal
with this prison-life is one in which he amuses himself by watching
a pair of courting sparrows.

SPARROWS

Sometimes I have visitors. The grating
That holds me captive offers others rest.
A pair of sparrows come to be my guest,
A sparrow lady and her cavalier.

They love with bickering and tenderness,
They bill, and have so much to tell each other.
And if a rival sparrow came to woo,
Oh what a frightful struggle would ensue!

How very strange it feels to stand so close
In fetters, and observe untrammelled life.
I watch them—do those black bright eyes watch me?

Their glance is outward. A chirrup, a flirt of wings—
The rustled ironwork's empty. I'm alone.
How gladly would I with the sparrows flee!

In his solitude his thoughts roam the world that he has known. He makes his 'stations' or devout meditations on the things his spirit values deeply: music, painting, books, the architecture of great cities.

Haushofer was a good pianist, and music is an important part of the artistic heritage to which he turns in thought. He remembers his piano lessons as a child, and his music mistress, and the Beethoven sonatas he played:

BEETHOVEN

At sixteen I was scolded at home, because
Instead of practising the Opus 2
And getting all those pounding triplets right,
I dared the great One Hundred and Eleven.

But my old teacher, a mistress of her art,
She let me play it; then she nodded, saying:
'You know, it was a deaf man who wrote that.
You'll come to understand it later on.'

And she fell silent. 'When your heart's been broken,
And goes on beating, and must go on and on.'
She looked at me with large eyes brimmed with kindness;

Then sitting down she played the whole sonata.
In these days it comes often in my thoughts,
That time my long-dead teacher sat and played.

As he sits in gaol he thinks of the brave men who attempted the July plot, many of whom were imprisoned in the Moabit gaol and executed there—in a particularly brutal fashion by being hung on meathooks. (A film was made for Hitler to view.) In the poem called 'Companions' Haushofer recites some of their names, and extols their virtues—with a certain pride, for he was a fellow-traveller on the same perilous road:

COMPANIONS

Today as into torpid dreams I sank,
I saw the whole crowd pass across the scene:
Saw Yorck and Moltke, Schulenburg, Schwerin,
Hassel and Popitz, Helferich and Planck—

Not one but of his duty was aware,
Not one but was to interest a stranger;
In glory and in power, in deathly danger,
They took the people's life into their care.

Look at them well: they are worth contemplating:
They all had intellect and rank and name;
On the same errand to those cells they came,

And for them all the hangman's noose was waiting.
At times rule passes to a madman's gang,
And then the best heads are the ones they hang.

And now he thinks of his father, as one who had supported the
Nazi dream of power, and he recalls Virgil's famous line about
stirring up the powers of hell if the powers of heaven will not
do what is wanted.[4] The sonnet is named 'Acheron', after one of
the rivers of the classical underworld.

ACHERON

If on the gods above there's no reliance
Then in the depths must Acheron be stirred.
So runs a poet's memorable word:
My father often said it in defiance.

His eye was blinded by the dream of might.
But I have known the misery and shame:
Destruction, famine, slaughter, wounds and flame,
The shuddering horror of a devil's night.

Farewell to everything that life holds dear
Deliberately and often I have said—
To country, love, and work, to wine and bread.

Now, overreached by darkness, I am here;
And Acheron is close and life is far,
A weary eye looks vainly for a star.

There is a later sonnet about his father which is a very remarkable one. It ascribes to Karl Haushofer a quite decisive role in
initiating the Hitler regime.

MY FATHER

There is an oriental tale I've read,
Full of deep import, as such stories are:
The Evil One sits crouched in a sealed jar
Sunk by God's hand down on the dark sea-bed.

Once in a thousand years destiny
Grants the decision to a fisherman:
Will he release the captive, as he can,
Or throw his find straight back into the sea?

That fatal choice was given to my father.
There was a moment when he could decide
To keep the Demon in captivity,

Or let him loose. My father broke the seal.
He didn't notice that dark breath go free;
He let it out to wander far and wide.

The question is, whether Albrecht Haushofer is resorting to a kind of rhetorical exaggeration when he says that there was a moment when his father could have decided whether to unleash Hitler or not. Perhaps the poet is in deadly earnest. About the time of the formation of the Nazi Party, Hitler was introduced to Haushofer by Rudolf Hess, who had been Haushofer's assistant in the University of Munich. Hess is alleged to have said in prison after the war that Karl Haushofer was the Secret Master directing Hitler's mediumistic mind. Whether or not he was a decisive influence on Hitler—the proposition is doubtful—it is quite possible that Albrecht believed that his father played this role at a certain time.

Very different in tone is the poem which Albrecht addressed with tender and anguished love to his mother. He evokes for us the Bavarian alpine country of his home.

MOTHER

I see you standing in the candle's glow
Framed in a doorway's heavy arch of stone.
You feel the mountain coolness moving down.
It's chilly, Mother . . . but you do not go.

You watch me hurry off to that unsure
Remainder that my fate holds in its keeping;
You smile with such a smile as is pure weeping,
And feel the pain for which there is no cure.

I see you standing in your lovelight's glow,
And on your forehead as your white hair lifts
A cold breath from enormous darkness drifts.

You watch me vanish, then your head sinks low.
The candle's beads are still thrown far and wide—
It's chilly, Mother . . . Mother—go inside.

On 14 March 1946, Karl Haushofer, the father, killed his wife Martha and committed suicide.

The other member of the family who is mentioned in the poems is Albrecht's brother Heinz who was also in prison.

MY BROTHER

My brother's in this gaol, a prisoner too,
With neither part nor sympathy in my crime:
Yet he must patiently wait out his time,
Till they have done with me what they will do.

My brother hasn't travelled round the earth,
Has never known the hazards of the sea:
The season's crop was his anxiety,
And children, as swift years brought them to birth.

He'll see—I hope—his native place once more,
His parents, and his shrewd courageous wife,
His brown fields, and the skies of alpine blue.

May the young elders bloom for him anew—
The soil's his love; its faithful care his life:
May it reward him, and his children too.

Among the poems of tender personal feeling there is a sonnet that refers to one whom he had loved in youth, who had died young, and was buried at Engadine in eastern Switzerland. Many times in the past the poet might have wished that the beloved face would come to him in dreams, but now after so long it has happened.

SEEN IN DREAMS

So long in dreams you have avoided me,
You who died early. Yet today you came,
So young, so wonderfully close—the same
As that first time we parted hopefully.

How bright the stars blazed then in the night sky,
How full of hope the world: how long ago.
How grievous what your few years would bestow,
How far it drove me forth in misery.

Now in my sleep you test me. It's all past;
No pain or sorrow rises any more.
You nod and whisper. Are you well at last?

And I lie still. My heart beats on serene.
What's left is only thanks—the thanks I send
Up to your mountain grave at Engadine.

One of the notable public events of Hitler's time was the Olympic Games held in Berlin in 1936. I have translated two sonnets in which Haushofer reflects upon this occasion. The first evokes brilliantly the dazzling illuminations, the crowd, and the parade of young German athletes as they march past, not knowing what purpose their ruler has in mind for them.

OLYMPIC FESTIVAL

It was the last of their spectaculars.
Their arrogance rejoiced in such displays.
The sky was hollowed out by searchlight rays
Whose dazzling brilliance blotted out the stars.

Freed from their everyday of motley care,
The crowd gaped at the young folk on parade,
And marvelling saw the Grecian torch-flame fade
To nothing in that cupola of glare.

I was not taken in by all the glamour.
I knew what those trained energies were for:
To serve the monstrous purposes of war.

I knew the mask, I knew the face beneath:
A nation's youth, marching with happy breath,
Already, rank on rank, consigned to death.

In the other sonnet, Haushofer remembers sitting at dinner with two Englishmen. One was a friend of his, Sir Robert Vansittart, of the Foreign Office—a man notably opposed to any policy of appeasement of Hitler. The other Englishman is not named, except that we are told he was a lord. This English lord cynically compared the crowd watching the Games to the crowds of ancient Rome:

ARENA

That last night of the Games we three sat late
Myself, Vansittart, and a visitor,
An English lord. Outside, the fireworks blazed.
Reflections danced and sparkled in the wine.

'I have been wondering', said our visitor,
'What is still lacking in this festival,
And now I have it; to intoxicate
The masses you need the wild beasts and the blood.'

He smiled maliciously. Old knowledge showed
So clearly in his well-cut features, it was
A Caesar speaking: 'All the rest's a sham.

'Now they wave flags for victory; soon they'll bellow
'For blood: that's when they're genuine.' Vansittart
Said nothing. Nor did I. Our guest was right.

Many of the poems are historical meditations on the nature of
power. One of the most telling of these refers to an event in the so-
called Albigensian crusade in the early thirteenth century. The
Papacy wanted the Catharist heresy rooted out of southern France,
and enlisted the aid of the French king. An army under the re-
doubtable Simon de Montfort carried the policy out with dreadful
thoroughness. This poem presents to us a dialogue between a Roman Cardinal clothed in purple, and Simon de Montfort clad in
armour. It is the man of war who is basically humane, the man of
God who is the ruthless fanatic.

TRUST IN GOD

It was the Albigensian crusade.
The papal wrath, enacted by a king,
Was extirpating heresy in Provence.
A city was marked down for massacre.

Simon de Montfort, who had breached the wall,
Stood brooding as he watched the butchery;
'Legate—aren't there believers here as well?'
So spoke the iron-clad to the purple-robed.

'If it's your wish, I'll issue an instruction
To spare the innocent.' The Cardinal
Raised a restraining hand. 'In every place

God knows his own. Just go on with the killing.'
He frowned, and added: 'What you lack, my son,
Is in its deepest sense real trust in God.'

There is one poem which perhaps more than any other shows the
scrupulous sense of moral responsibility which was the motive force
of Haushofer's public life. With severe self-judgement, he blames
himself for not having spoken out sooner and more clearly. The
record shows that even in 1940, in the midst of Hitler's greatest
triumphs, he gave a public lecture in which he said that all the
great powers would inevitably be drawn into the war—and would
be drawn in against Germany. In his university lectures, which were
monitored by the Gestapo, he resorted to historical analogies as a
way of speaking indirectly about the current situation. For his
initiated students his meaning was evident. Few risked as much as
he did. But in retrospect he felt he should have done more.

o

GUILT

Of what their courts call guilt I take small heed.
To have done nothing for the aftertime
Of my own people would have been a crime:
That would have been delinquency indeed.

Yet I am guilty—otherwise than they think.
I should have seen my duty earlier.
Called evil evil with much less demur:
I let my judgement falter at the brink.

That is the charge I make in my own heart.
I paltered with the truth for far too long,
Hid from myself and others what was wrong.

I knew where this must end, right from the start;
I uttered warnings—but not loud and clear:
That is the real guilt that I must bear.

One of Haushofer's heroes was a great Roman of the later Roman
Empire, Boethius. Boethius was not only an eminent statesman: he
was also a dedicated scholar and a philosopher. The emperor Theo-
doric imprisoned him on the charge of conspiring against him in
order to restore the republic, and later executed him. His famous
book of moral wisdom, *The Consolations of Philosophy*, was written
in prison—while, outside, the Roman Empire was collapsing. Haushofer felt an affinity between his fate and that of the ancient
scholar-philosopher and political prisoner. He reflects that the
sufferings of Boethius availed nothing at the time—his world fell
apart just the same. Yet his example lived on to inspire others, and
the book he wrote influenced men for centuries:

His death could not avert catastrophe—
The virtue of the ancient world was gone—
His death could but shed lustre on its close.

But later his example has consoled
And helped so many whom like destiny
Has forced to travel down the selfsame road.

I do not claim for Haushofer very high rank as a poet. But I
hope that even in translation his sonnets come out as moving and
significant. It is firm and clear writing, disciplined, as his life was
disciplined, by adherence to the values which he felt were essential to civilization, by the acceptance of a share of responsibility for
the way things would turn out in his own time for his own people,
by his anguish and love, and refusal to take the easy way out, even

when things seemed hopeless, because 'it's simply not allowed to slip away'.

1972

NOTES

1 Hermann Rauschning, *Hitler Speaks* (London, 1939), pp. 252-3.
2 Hans Rothfels, *The German Opposition to Hitler* (London, 1961), p. 128.
3 Albrecht Haushofer, *Moabiter Sonette* (Berlin, 1946).
4 *Æneid*, VII: 312, *Flectere si nequeo superos, Acheronta movebo* ('If I cannot bend the gods, I will move the powers of hell').

The poetry of Georg Trakl

THE Austrian poet Georg Trakl is still not a big name in twentieth-century literature; and considering that he died at the age of twenty-seven one might not expect that his achievement would be of the first magnitude. Contrary to legend, it is exceptional for poets to create masterpieces while still young. But Trakl is one of the exceptions. In the last two years of his life he found his authentic voice, his real subject, his special mode of expression. Thus his valuable work consists of 109 poems completed between about 1912 and 1914. Some of these are in my opinion perhaps the finest poetry written in our century, with none of that taint of the factitious or the mountebank that clings to the work of some greater names.

I differ from most of Trakl's admirers and critics in one important respect. My preference is not for his very last poems, but for the ones immediately before them: for the first half of his mature period more than for the second. There is a paperback volume of translations of Trakl done by four very capable English poets and scholars.[1] Except for two late poems for which I have offered my own version, there is no overlap between the poems I am presenting here and those which they present. What they have done is to translate the later half of Trakl's mature work: they have given us the free-verse 'Expressionist' Trakl, as he chiefly appears in literary histories and critical discussions. I am more convinced by the *penultimate* part of his mature output: some fifty poems which are well-formed lyrics of extraordinary, intense, inward and mysterious beauty, unease, disgust, and suffering dread. The most one must concede is that traces of the stage properties of early twentieth-century literary decadence linger here and there.

I first came across Trakl in anthologies of modern German poetry. He made no impression on me until I read a lyric called 'Winter Evening', which I was moved to translate. This was in 1958. The translation went well except that in trying to keep the metrical form and rhyme scheme I produced a last line which makes explicit what the text leaves implicit. Even so I think my version is close enough to give some sense of the original:

WINTER NIGHTFALL
Snow falls on the darkening boughs,
Evening bell rings through the shade;

For many guests the table's laid,
Well-appointed in the house.

Travellers come from field and fold
By dark pathways to the gate;
The Tree of Grace has blossomed late,
Turning earth's cool sap to gold.

Hard with pain the stony sill;
Indoors on the table shine
With pure brightness bread and wine;
Enter, wanderer, take your fill.

This poem seems very simple. It is very musical and shapely. It has
a set of clear visual and auditory images: the vesper bell, the snow,
the table laid, the tree still wearing its autumn gold. It is a poem
which to a marvellous degree has the best qualities of German song-
lyric. But it is also exceptionally subtle and complex. It shows us a
house ready at evening as a refuge for travellers as they come on
their different paths. Then the table laid with bread and wine
makes the house like a church. But then we become aware that
this house is also finally a grave, whose threshold of stony pain the
wayfarer must cross; and the waiting meal is not on this side of
death but on the other. There is a controlled ambiguity, a range
of multiple meaning kept afloat by the simple words and images,
and this is typical of Trakl.

My next encounter with Trakl was a couple of years later when I
was in Vienna and bought what was then the standard volume of
his poems.[2] The first thing that this did for me was to show me how
very difficult Trakl's work is for the unprepared reader. German
readers have found it difficult—enchanting and yet baffling. I could
make little of it at first; indeed it was not till nearly ten years later,
in 1970 in a period of convalescence, that with the aid of a com-
mentator I began to learn Trakl's difficult personal language and
realize his achievement.[3]

The next poem I translated will also show the sort of thing that
attracted me strongly. It is again a shapely lyric. Again the scene and
situation are clearly set before us: the farmer's wife is expecting the
birth of a baby; the farmer is at work in the harvest, and comes
in sunburnt, 'brown as a Moor', at the end of the day. The poem
is called 'Woman's Blessing'.[4]

WOMAN'S BLESSING

You move among your womenfolk,
Smiling often, but oppressed,
For the anxious days have come,
The poppy fades white at the fence.

Like your body swollen-ripe
The grapes are golden on the slope.
The pond reflects the sky's far height,
And a scythe clatters in the field.

Evening dew rolls in the bushes,
Autumn-red the leaves flow down.
Brown as a Moor the farmer greets
His wife with a rough tender love.

The dominant note in this poem is a sense of human fullness, the goodness of natural processes, and of human love. This is one of the ground-tones of Trakl's work, and I wanted to establish it first, just because, though it is important for understanding him, it is not the dominant mood and theme of most of his work. On the contrary, in much of it natural rightness is threatened or replaced by evil and corruption. I think the best way of approaching this tension between good and evil is to tell something of Trakl's own tormented life.

He was born in Salzburg in 1887. Salzburg is Mozart's city, the city of an old aristocratic and Catholic culture, full of the monuments of its prince-bishops. The Trakls were a long-established Protestant family in this predominantly Catholic city. Georg's father was a prosperous ironmonger, a good-natured kindly man. His mother was strangely remote from her six children, far more interested in her collection of antique furniture, glass and porcelain, in which she was a real connoisseur. From puberty onwards something deeply pathological emerged in Trakl's personality. He was constitutionally very strong and healthy, but there was a manic-depressive tendency and by the age of eighteen he had already begun the copious intake of drugs which continued through the rest of his life: ether, opium, cocaine and other drugs as well as alcohol. The large quantities of intoxicants he consumed had remarkably little apparent effect on his strong constitution and his behaviour. It was as if he had a painful excess of consciousness which he vainly tried to blot out.

Having failed at school he became a pharmacist's assistant (which made access to drugs easy) and it was as a pharmacist that he did his military training. He could not settle in any job. His external life would have been more wretched if he had not been helped by discerning and admiring friends. His chief benefactor was an editor and publisher in Innsbruck, named Ficker, who gave him friendship, hospitality and help. It is interesting that it was by Ficker's suggestion that the philosopher Wittgenstein made a grant of money to support Trakl.[5]

Within Trakl's family there was one relationship which was of special importance for his destiny. His sister Gretl, four years younger than he, resembled him closely in appearance and temperament. They entered into a passionate incestuous love which was the most important emotional experience of Trakl's life. Although the truth cannot be known, the probability is strong that the connection was physical. Gretl was a talented pianist—the sound of her playing is heard in several poems. In 1910 she went to Berlin to study under the famous Dohnanyi. In 1912, to Georg's distress, she married a much older man, a bookseller named Langen. She outlived her brother, but after his death she went to pieces and in 1917 committed suicide by shooting herself.

In Trakl's poetry the sister is a recurring presence, openly or in disguise. She is an ambiguous presence, for his relation with her was ambivalent. She is his soul's companion, but also the source of evil and guilt. In the later poetry, though in fact she was still alive, she is often represented as having passed already into the other world beyond death; at times it is as a Beatrice-figure that she beckons to him. Indeed, as we shall see, in his very last poem, 'Grodek', she appears in this role.

When war broke out in 1914 Trakl was drafted as a pharmacist with the rank of lieutenant in the Austrian army on the eastern front. After a battle at a place in Galicia called Grodek, he found himself in charge of a shed full of about one hundred seriously wounded men, without help or medical supplies. For two days and nights he listened, helpless, to the groans and cries, heard men pleading with him to put them out of their torment. One, wounded in the bladder, blew his brains out in front of Trakl. For relief he went outside for a walk, only to see in the autumn trees the bodies of local Ruthenians whom the Austrians had hanged on suspicion of being spies or pro-Russian. All the nightmares of Trakl's obsessed and tormented inner world seemed to have taken on objective existence. During the subsequent retreat, Trakl suddenly said he could stand it no longer and tried to shoot himself, but was prevented. In his increasingly psychotic state, he then became convinced that he would be charged on this account as having shown cowardice in the face of the enemy.

Shortly afterwards he was recalled to a base hospital at Cracow. He thought it was for further service, but in fact it was for psychiatric observation. He was put in a basement room more like a prison-cell than a hospital room. The other occupant was a Czech officer suffering from delirium tremens. A fortnight later Trakl died of a self-administered overdose of cocaine which he had somehow acquired and kept hidden.

One of the most powerful of the poems in his ultimate style is the one he showed his friend Ficker when Ficker visited him in the

garrison hospital just before the end. The scene is the battlefield
named in the title, with the sound of the guns, the cries of the
wounded and dying, the day ending in a red sunset like the
gathered blood of the slain. Night falls, the moonlight and stars
appear over the battlefield; in the darkness the poet's sister appears to welcome the souls of the heroes who died in battle. The
poem is in a rather free form metrically and grammatically.

GRODEK

At evening deadly weapons resound
Through the autumn woods, the golden plains,
And the blue lakes, over which rolls
A darker sun; night embraces
Dying warriors, the wild complaint
Of their broken mouths.
Yet quietly there gathers in the pasture-ground
Red cloud, in which dwells an angry god,
Red blood gathers, lunar coolness.
All roads lead into black corruption.
Under golden twigs of the night and stars
The sister's shade sways through the silent thicket,
To greet the ghosts of the heroes, bleeding heads,
And softly in the reeds the dark flutes of autumn sound.
O prouder grief! you altars of bronze,
The hot flame of the spirit today is fed by a mightier pain,
The grandsons unborn.

The poem at first seems to offer no hope or consolation. It is a fearsome apocalypse in which man seems doomed to succumb in ultimate darkness and despair. But, however terrible, it is not a nihilis-
tic vision. There is a background of quiet and peace, of cool
moonlight, of the starry night, of the gentle fluting wind among the
reeds. The dead are heroes, not abandoned carrion, and they are
given a hero's welcome in the other world. And though there is the
anguish of their death, and the waste of future life (the unborn
grandsons) yet the anguish serves to make the flame of the spirit
burn strongly, burning like the flame on an altar.

When Trakl is called an Expressionist poet it is to poems like
this that the label is applied. The form is free verse. Images and
symbols have become a kind of semi-abstract language, not tied to
realistic description, freely using fantasy, and designed to express
inner feelings. In this poem we can still recognize a particular situation: it is Grodek, a battlefield, at nightfall. More typically Expressionist is the other war poem called 'Lament'. Again it is an apocalyptic lament over man's fate, but the seascape in the poem is a
purely fantastic one. The symbolic script has become detached from

any particular place and situation. The sister is again present, seemingly watching over the disaster from another realm:

LAMENT

Sleep and death, the dusky eagles
Sweep round and round this head all night:
The icy wave of eternity
Would swallow up man's golden image.
Against dreadful reefs
His purple body shatters.
And the dark voice laments
Over the sea.
Sister of stormy sadness
See a small distressed boat sinking
Under stars,
Under the silent visage of night.

As I mentioned earlier, it is not really this later, free-form Expressionist poetry that attracts me most in Trakl's work. It is the poems completed in the earlier half of his brief period of mature composition that seem to me to achieve a marvellous balance. These poems are beautifully shaped lyrics that mingle sound and colour in a way I cannot hope to render in translation. They are set in a recognizable place and construct a recognizable situation out of a relatively small number of elements. The place in many of the poems is Salzburg, the city and the surrounding countryside. It is usually autumn, but sometimes other seasons appear. There is often a solitary figure moving through the landscape, walking, listening, seeing. Sometimes the poet refers to himself as 'eye', but more often he avoids saying 'I' and leaves this solitary figure as 'the solitary' or 'a stranger' or 'the silent one'. Nothing much happens. But the scene, apparently so simple, becomes charged with meaning. It is a landscape of the soul, of the divided soul in torment and longing. An example is the poem named 'Decay', an earlier poem reworked and perfected.

DECAY

At evening as the bells are ringing peace
I follow from afar the flight of birds;
Strung out in flocks, like files of pious pilgrims,
They vanish into autumn-clear distance.

Wandering where the Garden gathers twilight
I yearn after their brighter destinies
And feel the hour-hand almost cease to move . . .
Thus over clouds I follow those far journeys.

Then a breath makes me shudder with decay.
A blackbird sings lament in the bare tree.
A red-leafed vine sways on the rusty trellis.

And like pale children in a dance of death
Round about dark fountain-rims, that crumble,
Blue asters bow and shiver in the wind.

This is not an autumn of fulfilment and contentment. The spirit
cannot rest or be consoled in its surroundings, because it is a
landscape of decay. But in this landscape there is also the sound of
the vesper bells, and the sight of the cranes or other migrating birds
like pilgrims on the way to a far distant land, a holy land. The
watcher's spirit is drawn to make the transition with the birds from
this existence to those 'brighter destinies', from here to the beyond.
So rapt in yearning is he that time almost stands still, the hour-hand
almost ceases to move.

What we find in this poem is repeated in the dynamics of many
other poems. There are images representing this existence: and
usually they are not affirmations of natural goodness: what prevails
is decay, and evil. But there are also images which represent a
heaven beyond: like the blue sky, the migrating birds. And there
is the idea of a transition, a passing over from here to the other
realm—the idea, but not necessarily an actual release. Take, for example, the poem called 'Music in the Mirabell Garden'. It is the
same garden as mentioned in the previous poem, an eighteenth-
century public garden in Salzburg, with grey baroque statues (such
as the statue of the faun which this poem will mention).[6] It is evening again, and autumn. Sober anonymous citizens walk through on
their way home. As dusk falls, lovers glide into the shadows,
watched by the faun with dead eyes out of the world of the past—
what a complex of suggestions that contains! Then the poet walks
back to his family home in the old city. He does not use the pro-
noun 'I'; it is a stranger that has gone into the parental house. A
dog rushes to greet him. His sister is playing the piano in another
part of the house.

MUSIC IN THE MIRABELL GARDEN

A fountain sings. The clouds stand
So white, so soft, in the clear blue.
Discreetly silent people pass
As it grows late in the old garden.

Ancestral marble has gone grey.
A birdflight wavers into space.
A faun looks with dead eyes after
Shadows that glide into the dark.

Leaves fall red from the old tree
And circle through the open window.
Firelight glowing in the spacious room
Paints the wall with anguished spectres.

A pallid stranger entered. A dog
Bounds through decrepit passageways.
The maid puts out a lamp. Listen:
The sounds of a sonata by night.

At the beginning of this poem there was the song of the fountain;
the pure white clouds in the blue sky of heaven; again a flock of
birds is going out into the far distance. But the poet is trapped in
this existence, where he is a stranger. He goes into the decaying old
house; autumn leaves blow in through the open window; the fire-
light makes ghosts perform a sinister dance on the walls; a light is
put out. And then ambiguously, without comment, we are left in
the dark, with the sounds of the piano, as the sister plays.

One of the most beautiful lyrics is called 'Transfigured Autumn'.
Here the note of sinister decay is absent for once. Autumn is the
perfection of the year, the time of harvest and vintage. The farmer
can say 'It is good', almost like God pronouncing it is good after his
creation. Yet the goodness of this natural world here and now cannot hold the spirit. It prepares to pass over, to pass beyond—and the
transition this time is expressed by the idea of drifting down the
river, letting the images of the day go past and dwindle.

TRANSFIGURED AUTUMN

Powerfully thus the year ends
With golden wine and garden fruits.
The woods around are wondrously silent,
And are the solitary one's companions.

And there the farmer says: 'It is good'.
Ring soft and long, you evening bells,
Right to the end give a joyful mood.
A travelling flock of birds cries greeting.

It is love's mild season. In the boat
Down the blue river, beautifully
Image after image dwindles—
It vanishes into rest and silence.

The next poem takes us back into the city of Salzburg. It evokes
the old churches and the monuments of an old social order in the
coats-of-arms and in the barracks and the Mirabell Garden where
the military band plays. We see the young boys dreaming of the future, and the young girls shyly awaiting their future to reveal it-

self. The watcher stands at the flower-decorated window-sill, apart
from life.

BEAUTIFUL CITY

Old public squares in sunny silence.
Enveloped deep in blue and gold
Gentle nuns hurry, dream-like,
Under the beech-trees' sultry silence.

From the lit brown of churches
Death's pure images gaze forth,
Coloured coats-of-arms of princes.
Crowns shimmer in the churches.

Horses rear up from the fountain.
Flower-stems threaten claw-like from trees.
Boys, bewildered with dreams, play
Quietly at evening by the fountain.

Girls stand shyly in the doorways,
Looking out into coloured life.
Their moist lips tremble as
They wait there in the doorways.

Bells flutter with tremulous sounds;
March-beat rings out, and call of guards.
Strangers listen on the stairways.
High in the blue are organ-sounds.

Shrill instruments strike up a tune.
Laughter of fine ladies trills
Through the leaf-frame of the garden.
Young mothers softly sing a tune.

A scent steals in at flowery windows,
Mingling incense, tar, and lilac.
Weary eyelids flicker silver
Through the flowers at the windows.

In the poem called 'In a Deserted Room', the 'composition of
place' is very precise. We are in the parental house. An organ is
heard from a church nearby. Outside are the lights and movement
and noises of life—and a prospect of the far distance, the beyond.
Inside there is something sinister and mad about the dance of
shadows on the yellowing wallpaper or hangings. There are enigmatic presences in the house. And his mother's antique furniture
and glassware grow dim in the dusk. The watcher, still the solitary
and alienated one, bows his head in submission to a destiny which
we cannot fully decipher.

IN A DESERTED ROOM

Windows, brightly-coloured flowerbeds,
An organ plays into the room.
Shadows on the wall-paper
Dance dementedly round and round.

Ablaze with light the bushes sway,
And midges in a swarm vibrate.
Out in the field scythes are mowing
And an old stream of water sings.

Whose breath comes caressing me?
Swallows make rapid errant strokes.
There the golden woodland flows
Out quietly into boundlessness.

Flames flicker in the flowerbeds.
Giddying the round-dance goes
Crazily on the yellowing paper.
Someone looks in at the door.

Sweet smell of incense and of pears.
Glassware and cabinets grow dim.
Slowly the fevered forehead bows
Under the white stars in submission.

Trakl's poems work within a restricted range of recurring themes, images, key-words. But they are very varied and subtle and 'polysemous' and 'multivalent' within that range. Hence the wide disagreements among interpreters about his real position and intentions.

Because there is so much that is fearful and horrible and distraught in the poems, it is important to establish that their foundation is a vision of innocence, of peace and happiness, of goodness and rightness, and of intimacy with God. Among the most untranslateable of his poems is one which I have nevertheless dared to translate because it establishes this primal vision.

We are in the neighbourhood of Salzburg, in a room looking out into a garden. There is a convent church nearby: girls go into the grounds with the statue of the Virgin encircled by roses. A beggar kneels entranced in prayer by a stone cross. The divine presence seems everywhere: the breeze blowing from the blue sky is like God's breath; a voice—bird or man?—singing as evening comes, is like an angel, singing the children to sleep. The original has an intoxicating lyrical quality with its intermingling of colour and movement and sound and light.

SPIRITUAL SONG

A fluttering flower-bed paints
Exquisite embroideries, signs.
Into the room that views the garden,
God's azure breath is blowing,
Gladly blowing.
A cross surmounts the tangle of vine.

Hear the happy village-noises.
A gardener scythes along the wall.
An organ playing softly
Mixes sound with golden light,
Sound and light.
Love blesses bread and wine.

And girls too go inside.
The cock crows at the last one in.
A decaying trellis gently gives,
Where in rosaries of roses,
Wreath and row,
Mary stands still, white and fine.

A beggar there at the old stone
Seems to have died sunk in prayer.
Softly a shepherd leaves the hill.
And in the hedge an angel sings,
In the hedge nearby:
He sings the children into sleep.

The next poem is in shocking contrast. It is a vision of a degraded world. The scene is not Salzburg this time, but Innsbruck, the other main setting for Trakl's poetry. It is an industrial suburb in the autumn when the warm enervating wind called the Föhn is blowing. Factory sirens howl, there is a confused movement of life, the slaughter-house empties into the river; and as nearly always the poet is there as watcher, estranged, alien.

SUBURB IN THE FÖHN

Late afternoon. The place is waste and brown.
A mouldy smell pervades the atmosphere.
A train thunders over the arched bridge—
Sparrows flutter above bush and fence.

Crouching hovels, paths struggling everywhere,
In the parks a confusion and commotion,
A howling noise rises above muffled movement.
A red dress floats among a crowd of children.

Enamoured rats squeal on the rubbish-tip.
Women carrying baskets full of entrails,
A nauseating troop, full of filth and mange,
Emerge towards me out of the dusk.

A drain suddenly spews greasy blood
From the slaughterhouse into the still river.
Sultry winds brighten the meagre bushes,
And the red stain slowly spreads in the water.

A whispering that drowns in turbid sleep.
Forms waver up out of the canals,
Perhaps a remembrance of an earlier life,
Rising and sinking on the warm winds.

Out of clouds shimmering avenues emerge,
Complete with fine carriages, gallant horsemen.
The one sees a ship run aground against cliffs,
And often there are rose-coloured mosques.

In the last stanza the poet's fantasy seeks something beyond the immediate scene. In the afternoon sky he sees the broad beams of the sun ray out from a cloud, and he imagines these as highways full of a more graceful kind of life; and he also sees other exotic images in the clouds such as mosques. Trakl borrowed these effects from Rimbaud, and I am not sure that they really give the right ending to the poem; but the main vision of everyday degradation is impressively disgusting and unmistakably original.

It is not only urban scenes that Trakl uses to build up the terrible tensions of his value-charged world. There are countryside visions too, and I want to present several of these.

One is a short poem called 'In Winter', which might be called non-committal. There is snow and silence, distant sounds, a faint gleam of light from the village. There is a sense of menace: jackdaws fly round, hunters come down from the forest-slope, a hunted creature bleeds to death and ravens dabble their beaks in the blood. There is a sense also of expectancy, but the poem closes enigmatically: is it the poet himself, this nameless and solitary one, whose footfall is heard in the emptiness?

IN WINTER

The field is shining white and cold.
The sky is lonely and enormous.
Jackdaws circle above the pond
And hunters descend from the forest.

A silence dwells in dark treetops.
A gleam of fire steals out of the huts.
At times a distant sledge tinkles,
And slowly rises the grey moon.

A creature bleeds to death on the border,
And ravens dabble their beaks in blood-filled gutters.
The reeds quiver yellow and erect.
Frost, smoke, in the empty grove a footstep.

A companion piece is 'The Ravens', in which the presence of evil—of lustful greed and cruelty and death—is represented by the carrion birds.

THE RAVENS

Over the dark corner at midday
The ravens hasten with harsh cry.
Their shadow glides past the listening hind,
And often one sees them morosely resting.

O how they disturb the brown stillness
In which the field stands entranced
Like a woman heavy with premonition,
And often one can hear them quarrelling

About some carrion that somewhere they scent;
And suddenly they fly off north
And dwindle like a funeral procession
Into airs that tremble with sensual delight.

In other poems flocks of birds are like pious pilgrims departing: but here the ravens are like a funeral procession. Yet the poem is not just a presentation of evil. As in most of Trakl's poems there is a counterpointing of positive signs. Here it is the listening hind, the gentle wild creature; and also especially the brown fallow-field awaiting the new spring, the new birth, 'like a woman heavy with premonition'.

This interplay of positive and negative in a value-changed landscape is very evident in two other poems. One is 'Melancholy of the Evening'. The setting is outside Innsbruck. Again there is a shy creature of the forest, a trembling hind. We follow a stream down the slope and come out on the dark indistinct plain. The poem ends with the sense of expectancy: birds migrating at night, a symbol of the transition to the beyond, to a spiritual home; and the breeze in the reeds is like a stir of the spirit.

MELANCHOLY OF THE EVENING

The forest that spreads out extinct—
And shadows fringe it round, like hedges.
The trembling creature comes out of hiding,
While a stream glides very quietly

Through brakes of fern and past old stones,
And flashes silver from leafy windings.
Soon it is heard in black gorges—
And maybe stars are out already.

There seems no bulk on the dark plain—
Scattered villages, marsh and pond,
And something deceptively like a fire.
A cold gleam flits across the roads.

In the sky one senses movement,
An army of wild birds wandering
Towards those other, brighter, regions.
The stir in the reeds rises and sinks.

The other poem is a little longer and more complex. It is in three parts and I will interpose a comment before each part. It is called 'Glad Spring'; but the gladness of spring, its hope of new life, is kept in tension with more negative signs. Much is indistinct and ambiguous in the early season. The collision of positive and negative sensations is rather vividly expressed in the last line of the first part, where the toads creep among the young leeks in the vegetable plot.

GLAD SPRING

Part 1
The dry reeds of last year still line
The brook that crosses the yellow fallow field.
Sounds glide through the greyness wondrously.
An odour of warm dung is wafted by.

Willow-catkins toss gently in the wind,
A soldier dreamily sings his song of sadness.
A stirring in the meadow fades listlessly,
A child stands in the contours tender and mild.

The birch-trees there, the black thicket of thorn,
Dissolving shapes flee in the smoke.
Bright green flourishes, while other green decays,
And toads creep among the sprouting leeks.

P

The second part relates the new life in nature to the goodness of love in human beings. Not high romantic love, but something more basic and everyday which the anonymous poet-observer feels in the vigorous washerwoman working at the stream and in the workingman coming home to his wife in his hut—probably the wife is the washerwoman. The poet's declaration of love for the washerwoman is quite selfless and impersonal—he is rejoicing in the natural rightness of what she is—but it sets the translator a real task in getting the tone right. The other thing to be noticed especially is the way the sound of the church-bells drops gently down into the joyfulness of the new spring.

GLAD SPRING

Part 2
You sturdy washerwoman, I love you true.
The stream still bears the sky's golden load.
A small fish flashes by and fades;
A waxen face glides off through alder-trees.

Soft lingering bell-sounds sink down into gardens,
A small bird is trilling as if gone crazy.
The tender corn softly swells enraptured,
And diligent bees still gather earnestly.

Come love now to the weary workingman!
Into his hut a ray of clear light falls.
The forest streams harsh and pale through the twilight
And buds flicker gaily now and then.

In the third part the dynamics of positive and negative in the poem are intensified. Sickness and fever contradict health, but the primary emphasis is on the goodness of natural growth and love. Yet it is summed up in a paradox: 'So *painfully* good and true is all that lives'.

GLAD SPRING

Part 3
And yet how sickly all this becoming seems!
A breath of fever circles round a hamlet;
Yet a mild spirit beckons out of branches
And opens the heart wide and timorous.

Overspill of blossom softly runs away.
What is unborn takes care of its own peace.
The lovers in their love flower to their stars,
And sweeter flows their breathing through the night.

So painfully good and true is all that lives;
And quietly an old stone touches you:
'Verily I am with you all the days'.
O mouth! that quivers through the willow-trees.

The old stone that quietly touches us is evidently a cross or a statue
of Christ: Perhaps it bears as an inscription the words of God
which the poet utters 'Truly I will be with you always'. It is a gospel
message from beyond, but it is present here and now. This, like the
earlier image of the bell-sounds dropping down into the gardens,
gives a third, a vertical, dimension to the poem. The counterpoint
of positive and negative within the spring landscape is transcended
by God's word from above. But we must notice also how the figure
of the poet reacts. His is the waxen (bloodless and lifeless) face that
glides off through alder-trees in Part 2, and his is the anguished
mouth that quivers through the willow-trees in the last line, as if
shrinking back in anguish from encounter with God's promise.

Religious implications emerge frequently from Trakl's poems,
and it is time to be somewhat more explicit about this, so far as one
can. Trakl, as I have mentioned, was of an old Protestant family
in the predominantly Catholic city of Salzburg. His mother's strange
remoteness from her children brought Georg into closer communion with an Alsatian governess named Marie Boring, who became a mother-substitute. She introduced him to a wide range of
modern French literature, and also influenced him through her own
fervent and rather bigoted Catholic piety, which she conscientiously
and improperly tried to impress on the children in her charge. The
result for Trakl was an unspecific perhaps ambiguous but deep and
persistent Christian outlook, with a Catholic coloration due to his
Salzburg surroundings and the influence of his governess. A sombre,
nearly despairing, personal religion seems to have remained with
him in spite of the excesses and aberrations of his disturbed personal life. One of the most striking of the rather scanty records of
him is an account by the Swiss writer Hans Limbach of meeting
Trakl in Innsbruck.[7] This was around the New Year of 1914, in the
last year therefore of Trakl's life. Trakl in conversation declared
himself a believing Christian, and said he meant by that a belief in
Christ as uniquely God's son, and as Saviour. His deeply pessimistic
view of man's condition appeared when he made a remark that mankind had never before sunk so deep as it had now sunk *after* the
resurrection of Christ. 'It *couldn't* sink so deep before', he added.
His conception apparently was that both the utmost heights and the
utmost depths had been opened up by the action of Christ upon
human destiny. Man could rise further but could fall further as well.
The tendency of Trakl's mind was to see his world, and himself, as
involved in that uttermost fall.[8]

In Trakl's world, the rightness and goodness of natural love, which we have seen him affirm, is more frequently replaced by an almost Manichean vision of the flesh and its desires as evil. Sensuality has the sign of damnation over it. Life has become impure and bestial. There are two characteristic visions of evil based on farm-house scenes. Neither of these poems has been easy to translate, and there are strangenesses and obscurities in them, which do not, however, impede the main effect.

The first is called 'The Farmhands'. When it starts, it might look as if this is to be a simple healthy rural scene: the harvest-workers, men and women, eating their midday meal at the farm-house before going back to their toil. But a sultry and increasingly brutish atmosphere develops in the poem. The girls secretly respond to the lustful glances of the men; their blood hammers at them. The sensuality is expended in the demonic energy with which the reapers advance on the crop with their sickles moving in unison.

THE FARMHANDS

In front of the window, a strident green and red,
In the smoke-blackened lower room
The farmhands, men and girls, are at their meal;
And they pour the wine and they break the bread.

In the deep noonday silence falls.
Now and then a scanty word.
The fields vibrate with uniform glare,
And the sky is leaden and wide.

The fire flutters freakishly in the hearth
And a swarm of flies hums. The girls
Listen bashfully and mute. The blood
Hammers at them in their temples.

And when an animal smell breathes into the room
Glances meet full of greedy lust.
A farmhand says grace in a flat murmur,
And a cock crows under the door.

Then back in the field. A shudder seizes
Them often in the furious storm of harvest.
And then in a ghostly rhythm, in and out,
The ringing scythes keep time.

The other poem is 'The Farm-girl'. It is unusual in Trakl's work because it is in the tradition of a narrative ballad. The girl has been made pregnant by a farmhand who has deserted her. We see him later in the poem jeering at her while he goes on with his blacksmithing. She dies untended in childbirth and her pale ghost haunts the village.

THE FARM-GIRL

1.

At a wellside in the twilight
She often stands as if bewitched
Drawing water in the twilight.
Buckets travel up and down.

In the beech-trees jackdaws flutter
And she stands there like a shadow.
And her yellow hair flutters,
Rats squeal in the empty yard.

Under the coaxing of decay
She lets her inflamed lids droop.
Withered grasses in decay
Bow themselves down at her feet.

2.

Quietly she works in her room.
Long since the yard lies desolate.
In the elder-tree outside the room
Plaintively a blackbird flutes.

Her silvery image in the mirror
Looks out at her like a stranger.
It turns wan in the twilight mirror:
She shudders at its purity.

Dreamily a farmhand sings in darkness.
She goes rigid, shaken with pain.
Redness drips down through the darkness.
The southwind knocks violently at the gate.

3.

At night over the bare paddock
She flutters about in fever-dreams.
The wind whines morosely in the paddock
And the moon listens from the trees.

Soon the stars around go pale.
And exhausted by her trouble
Her tired cheeks go waxen-pale.
A rotten smell breathes from the ground.

Reeds rustle drearily in the pond.
She hunches up against the cold.
A distant cock crows. Over the pond
Morning showers fall hard and grey.

4.

In the smithy sounds the hammer
And she slips quietly past the doorway.
Glowing red he swings the hammer
And she seems as if dead.

As in a dream, she's struck by laughter;
And she reels into the smithy,
Timidly crouched before his laughter,
Hard and brutal like his hammer.

The shed is filled with blazing sparks.
With helpless gestures of her hands
She tries to fend off the wild sparks,
And pitches on the floor in stupor.

5.

.   Slenderly stretched out on the bed
She wakes up full of sweet unease,
And sees the dirty unkempt bed
Covered over with golden light,

Sees mignonettes there at the window,
And the bright blue of the sky.
And the wind brings to the window
The distant tinkle of a bell.

Shadows glide across the pillow.
Slowly the midday hour is rung.
She breathes heavily in her pillow
And her mouth is like a wound.

6.

At evening hover blood-soaked cloths,
Clouds above the silent forests
That are covered with black cloths.
Sparrows are noisy in the fields.

She lies quite white in the darkness.
A cooing of doves sounds under the eaves.
Like carrion in bush and darkness
Flies are buzzing round her mouth.

Dreamlike resounds in the brown hamlet
The noise of fiddles and of dancing.
Her face floats through the hamlet,
Her hair drifts in the leafless branches.

In Trakl's world, colours take on meanings. The colours of life tend to become tainted and suffused with evil suggestions: for example red, the red of blood, the red of the red blouses of girls, has often a negative value. So too has yellow. The good colours are those of heaven: the blue and gold of the sky and the sun are named as God's colours. But also white, the cold glitter of stars, or the white of bloodless flesh or ghosts, often implies a purity superior to the colours of life. This colour-language is not inflexibly fixed, but one can see it at work in such a poem as 'In The Red Foliage Full Of Guitars'. It is a scene by the river, late afternoon, the washer-woman still working, but in the courtyard of the inn there is singing and lovemaking. But the sensuality is tainted and a cheat.

IN THE RED FOLIAGE FULL OF GUITARS

In the red foliage full of guitars
Girls' yellow hair moves to and fro
By the fence, where sunflowers stand.
Through clouds travels a golden cart.

In the quiet of brown shadows, the old
Fall mute and idiotically embrace.
The orphans are sweetly singing vespers.
Humming flies hover in yellow fumes.

At the brook the women are still working.
Their hung-out washing swells on the breeze.
The little one that I have always liked
Comes once more through the grey twilight.

From the tepid sky sparrows pitch down
Into green holes full of putrescence.
A smell of bread and harsh spices cheats
The hungry one with false anticipation.

The images of a natural hunger aroused but not satisfied, and of sparrows feeding their appetite on putrid matter, are meant to spread a suggestion back through the poem. There is a later poem which develops this further. Again there are the red blouses of the girls, the smell of bread, the yellow sunflowers, the strumming of guitars, and also the clatter-clang of money. But this second poem is called 'The Accursed Ones', and the scene shifts to where a prostitute receives the boy whose sensuality has been aroused. He experiences a death of the spirit in her embrace.

Out of this tormenting conflict between good and evil in the soul there spring violent storms. One of the earlier poems objectifies such a storm of the spirit by a brilliant description of an evening thunderstorm. The 'fire-rider' which is mentioned in it is a lightning bolt. The sick in the hospital are mental patients.

EVENING THUNDERSTORM

O the red evening hours! At the open
Window the vine glistens and sways,
Writhing confusedly into the blue.
Dreadful phantoms nest therein.

Dust dances in the stench of gutters.
Gusts of wind rattle the panes.
Lightning-strokes drive glaring clouds,
A team of thundering wild horses.

Loudly the pond-mirror shatters.
Seagulls cry round the window-frames.
A fire-rider springs from the hill
And crashes in flames against a pine.

The sick are screaming in the hospital.
Night's blueish plumage whirs.
All at once the glittering rain
Roars down in torrents on the roofs.

I have shown how in various poems there emerges an alternative to damnation: a vision of innocence, a hope of transcendence, a passing over from life to a higher state. The symbols that render this are various, the autumn-clear distance into which migrating birds fly, the sound of bells, the blue and gold of the clear sky, the breeze in the garden, the stars in the sky. The tension is never really resolved. Let me present one last poem which is typical of Trakl: it uses his personal language; it keeps us in this world, suspended between death and life, this time with hope predominating. It is in autumn, as usual. The patients in the hospital are out in the sun. The bells are ringing. The birds, too, tell their gospel news from far away, life is good, and even the hospital rooms where death enters are today wide open and full of sunshine.

IN AUTUMN

The sunflowers are bright along the fence.
Sick people are sitting out in the sunshine.
In the field the women at their toil,
Into which falls the ringing of cloister-bells.

The birds tell you news from far away,
Into which falls the ringing of cloister-bells.
Softly a fiddle sounds from the village.
Today the tawny wine is being pressed.

People there appear joyful and mild.
Today the tawny wine is being pressed.
The rooms where death comes are open wide
And brightly painted with the sunshine.

1973

NOTES

1 *Selected Poems: George Trakl*, ed. Christopher Middleton, trans. by him and Robert Grenier, Michael Hamburger and David Luke (London, 1968).
2 Georg Trakl, *Dichtungen* (Salzburg, 1938) .
3 Eduard Lachmann, *Kreuz und Abend* (Salzburg, 1954). Some of Lachmann's interpretations are contested by other commentators—there is much disagreement among them—but his book is very helpful as an initial guide. A useful review of Trakl studies is by Christa Sass, *Georg Trakl* (Stuttgart, 1974).
4 The text given here is an amendment of the version in my *Collected Poems 1936-1970* (Sydney, 1971), p. 220.
5 Wittgenstein had come into his father's fortune and wished to spend some of it in a worthy cause. At Ficker's suggestion he made grants to Rilke and Trakl. He did not know Trakl's work at the time, and on reading it said: 'I don't understand it, but its tone pleases me. It is the tone of someone truly gifted with genius'. See Otto Basil, *Trakl* (Hamburg, 1965).
6 I could not find this statue in the Mirabell when I visited Salzburg in 1973, in the appropriate seasons of spring and autumn.
7 Hans Limbach, 'Begegnung mit Georg Trakl', *Erinnerung an Georg Trakl* (3rd edn, Salzburg, 1966), pp. 117-26.
8 It must be added that the above tentative sketch of Trakl's religious attitude is not only very much simplified but also radically contested by some commentators.

Index

Index